THE UNIVERSAL GĪTĀ

THE UNIVERSAL GĪTĀ

Western Images of the *Bhagavad Gītā*
a bicentenary survey

Eric J. Sharpe

OPEN COURT PUBLISHING COMPANY
LA SALLE, ILLINOIS 61301

OPEN COURT and the above logo are registered in
the U.S. Patent and Trademark Office

Published by arrangement with Gerald Duckworth & Co. Ltd., London

© 1985 by Eric J. Sharpe

Library of Congress Cataloging in Publication Data

Sharpe, Eric J., 1933–
   The universal Gītā

   Bibliography: p.
   Includes index.
   1. Bhagavadgītā—Appreciation.   2. Bhagavadgītā—
Study.   I. Title.
BL1138.67.S53   1985   294.5′924   85–5062
ISBN 0-8126-9001-X

Printed and bound in the United Kingdom

Contents

Chapter Four: Theories of Origin

Part Two: 1885–1985

Chapter Five: Renaissance, Radicalism and Theosophy

Chapter Six: Gandhi's Gita

Chapter Seven: Rudolf Otto, J.W. Hauer and T.S. Eliot

Chapter Eight: The Gita and the Counter-Culture

Contents

Chapter Nine: Ethical Monotheism and Social Caste

THE

BHĂGVĂT-GEĒTĀ,

OR

DIALOGUES

OF

KRĚĚSHNĂ AND *ĂRJŎŎN;*

IN EIGHTEEN LECTURES;

WITH

NOTES.

—————

TRANSLATED FROM THE ORIGINAL, IN THE *Sănſkrĕĕt*, OR ANCIENT
LANGUAGE OF THE *Brāhmăns*,

BY

CHARLES WILKINS,

SENIOR MERCHANT IN THE SERVICE OF THE HONOURABLE THE EAST INDIA
COMPANY, ON THEIR BENGAL ESTABLISHMENT.

—————

LONDON:

PRINTED FOR C. NOURSE,
OPPOSITE CATHARINE-STREET, IN THE STRAND.

—————
M.DCC.LXXXV.

Preface

This book has been written to commemorate the two hundredth anniversary of the publication in 1785 of the first translation of the *Bhagavadgītā* into English. I first began the study of Western interpretations of that best-loved and most widely read of Hindu scriptures in 1977, shortly after my arrival in Australia. Since that time I have published three papers on various aspects of the question. A survey of the first hundred years of *Bhagavadgītā* interpretation in the West was read at the XIIIth International Congress of the International Association for the History of Religions, meeting in Winnipeg, Canada, in 1980, and was published in the official volume of Congress proceedings, *Traditions in Contact and Change* (ed. Slater and Wiebe), Waterloo 1983, pp. 65-85, as 'Some Western interpretations of the Bhagavad Gītā, 1785-1885'. This paper also appeared in *The Journal of Studies in the Bhagavadgītā*, volume 1 (1981), pp. 1-28. 'The early Theosophists and the study of the Bhagavad Gītā' was published in the journal *Theosophy in Australia* 43/3 (September 1979), pp. 50-9; and 'Protestant missionaries and the study of the Bhagavad Gītā' in *International Bulletin of Missionary Research* 6/4 (October 1982), pp. 155-9. Substantial traces of all three papers will be found in this volume, though none has been incorporated without alteration.

At Winnipeg I said – and I offer it as a justification for this exercise in the history of ideas:

> This present study is intended to be a modest exercise in the comparative, or intercultural hermeneutics of the [Bhagavad] Gītā ...
> ... in the end it may well prove to be the case that to study Western interpretations of the Gītā is in fact tantamount to studying in microcosm Western reactions to something much larger – Indian religion and culture in its entirety.

I would like to thank the Librarian of the Adyar Library, North Sydney, for help in obtaining material relating to the Theosophical Society; and John Cooper of Sydney for further supplementing these sources. Prof. Dr. H.-W. Gensichen of the University of Heidelberg drew my attention to, and sent me a photocopy of, the essay by R.D. Griffiths, quoted in Chapter 3, for which I am most grateful.

Several versions of the text have been typed by Margaret Gilet, with her customary speed and efficiency.

Sydney, November 1984   EJS

Introduction

In the modern world, sacred scriptures, whatever their origin, have at least one thing in common. Once they have been printed in large numbers no one can prevent them from being read by those for whom they were initially not intended. Translate them into other languages and their potential range is extended even further. Any scripture may fall into anyone's hands and be read not in the light of its 'original' religious, liturgical, philosophical or social setting but against the background of entirely different sets of presuppositions.

This process has been so widespread in the twentieth century that it is surprising that it has not aroused more attention among scholars. Certainly there has been an interest in such questions as 'Christian attitudes to Hinduism' (or Buddhism, or Islam, or whatever); but these have often suffered from the sheer vagueness with which questions have been posed and answered. In a manner of speaking there have been many Christianities and many Hinduisms, and the 'attitude' question has therefore been highly resistant to treatment in simple categories. No one can be prevented from asking the larger questions; but often much more might have been achieved if the encounter had been brought to a sharper focus.

It should be emphasised that the free interchange of scriptures is a problem belonging to the post-Enlightenment world. Before the turn of the nineteenth century or thereabouts scripture was not as a rule culturally mobile, nor was it often open to the scrutiny of a non-believer. True, sacred scripture – to the extent to which it actually was scripture, and not a collection of orally transmitted traditions – could be, and was, copied and translated whenever necessary, for the edification of the faithful in new linguistic areas. We may recall the various linguistic forms in which the Buddhist *Tripitaka* passed on its way from India, by way of the Himālayas,

Tibet and China, to Japan; or the translation of the New Testament into Syriac, Coptic, Latin and Gothic long before any strictly 'modern' translation was made. But in these cases the scripture in question was heard, read and interpreted only within the community of the faithful, along the lines laid down by that community's traditions. Perhaps outsiders might in some cases come into contact with some part of the sacred scriptural and liturgical tradition. What they could not do, save in exceptional cases, was to sit down in the privacy of their own studies and form their own opinion about the content of that tradition, merely by puzzling over the scriptural record. The sacredness, or holiness, of scripture demanded that those who were to be entrusted with its contents should themselves be 'holy', that is, initiated into the company of the faithful. Before initiation they would be taught only the barest essentials (as a rule, what to *do*, rather than what to think or believe); even after initiation, detailed knowledge of scripture among the laity would be extremely rare. Even the 'professionally' religious – priests, monks, nuns – would be taught only selectively, and always within a highly specific tradition of application and interpretation.

This pattern hardly obtains in our day. In the West it has vanished beyond recall, while in non-Western countries it has been greatly modified. The causes are not far to seek: increasing literacy on the one hand and the advent of mass-production printing on the other. Manuscripts and single printed copies of books can be guarded. Multiple copies, especially where they run into the hundreds of thousands, cannot. Nor can they be prevented from breaking free from a tradition of liturgical application and spiritual discipline and in effect taking on an independent life of their own. At this stage they become fair game for any and every interpreter who is able to procure a copy.

Since it is with Western interpretations of a Hindu scripture, the *Bhagavadgītā* (in what follows, abbreviated to 'Gita', without diacritical marks), that we shall be concerned in this book, a few words will be necessary about Western methods of interpretation on the one hand and about the Gita itself on the other.

Hermeneutics ('the science of scriptural interpretation') began life strictly within the Judaeo-Christian tradition and aimed initially at establishing why a given work should be understood in one way and not in another. Perhaps hermeneutics was never strictly a science, since it allowed a fair degree of subjectivity in its aims and methods. But it implied a scientific, historical approach to the material first of all. It was not content simply to record the opinions of the believing community but passed beyond this to the difficult area of establishing 'original' meanings, and of weighing these against ongoing traditions. This involved – and still involves – philological competence, a grasp of historical contexts and a capacity to weigh significant detail against totalities. Hermeneutics also tended to pass beyond the question 'What does this text mean?' to the question 'What *ought* this text to mean?' At this point, though, scholarship could easily give way to speculation of a kind which we shall encounter frequently in these pages.

In the post-Enlightenment period there arose an almost universal conviction that in matters of religion words and texts are of supreme importance. Seeking to grasp the role of religion in the history of the human race as a whole, generations of Western scholars have characteristically begun with the written record, believing it to be either a product of divine (and 'progressive') revelation or an account of human self-understanding. Year after year Western scholars threw themselves heart and soul into the collection, editing and translation of the sacred books of the world. A major landmark was the publication, between 1879 and 1910, of Friedrich Max Müller's fifty-volume series of *Sacred Books of the East*. It neither began nor ended there. A case might be made out for its having begun with the publication in 1785 of Charles Wilkins' *Bhagvat-Gēētā*, with which our account commences. But the underlying assumption was that the world as a whole ought to read its own sacred scriptures; that these could be understood, more or less as they stand, by anyone who cared to read them; and that their having originally had a far different religious and cultural setting than that of the modern West need not be a barrier to their appropriation.

Clearly, however, a scripture torn loose from its religious matrix will inevitably be different from that same scripture hedged about by rituals and rules, conventions and approved commentaries. In fact one of the strangest things about the Western tradition of Gita hermeneutics has been its almost total lack of interest in the Hindu world's own estimate of its own Gita. As we shall see in what follows, the West has approached the Gita from one of two angles: either as a piece of archaic literature, to be dissected, analysed and placed in an essentially remote religio-historical context, or as an exotic insight into the ultimate mystery of the universe – a scripture which is Hindu only incidentally.

The Western Orientalist has as a rule been proud of his own standards of philological and historical accuracy (which is not to say that he could not on occasion launch into flights of speculative fancy). Others who have written about the Gita have not always been so careful, and here and there writers have penned the most outrageous nonsense about the Gita. In a book published in America as recently as in 1970 the public was told (by an author who perhaps ought to be allowed to remain in decent anonymity) that a French translation of the Gita was produced by Burnouf in 1861 – so far so good. But then: 'Burnouf's *Gita* was translated into English by Charles Wilkins in 1846 with a preface by Warren Hastings. Hastings in 1786 recommended a translation of the *Gita* to the president of the East India Company and wrote a preface to it.' Seldom can such a gruesome collection of errors have crowded into two sentences! It is worth comparing, though, with the statement by an Indian writer that it was in 1775 that 'the first English translation by Wilkinson appeared in India'. Again it would be kinder not to name the author.

To assemble straightforward information about the impact of the Gita on the West is not too difficult, given a little time and effort; and I have been struck by the fact that what I am attempting to do in these pages has not been done before. Certainly most students of the Gita know some of the details of its Western history, but few have followed the subject very far. Paul Hubert (a French Theosophist) published in 1949 *Histoire de la Bhagavad-Gîtâ: ses diverses éditions de 1785 à nos jours*. And more recently there have been short articles on the inter-cultural hermeneutics of the Gita. In one of them, by the American scholar Gerald James Larson, there are two statements to which I should like to call attention. Larson points out that there are in a manner of speaking almost as many Gitas as there are readers of it, and that:

> What the *Gītā* is, finally, is inseparable from its many contextual environments, ancient and modern, Eastern and Western, scholarly and popular, corporate and personal, secular and sacred – contextual environments that have emerged in an on-going historical process and will continue to emerge as that historical process unfolds.[1]

And in a footnote he adds:

> An interesting monograph could be written on the *Gītā* as symptomatic of trends in nineteenth- and twentieth-century European and American scholarly thought.[2]

It is such a monograph that I am now attempting to write, though I

[1] Larson, 'The *Bhagavad Gītā* as cross-cultural process', in *Journal of the American Academy of Religion* 43/4 (December 1975), p.666.
[2] Ibid., p.666, n.45.

shall not impose *a priori* limits on what is, and what is not, 'scholarly thought'. The 'popular' is to my mind every bit as important as scholarship in forming images – in all likelihood more so – and in what follows, it is the Western image of the Gita with which I shall be chiefly concerned. For the most part I shall narrate rather than analyse, though in a concluding chapter I shall try to estimate the importance of the narrative, again taking up some of the points raised by Larson in his thought-provoking article.

*

A very brief word about the Gita itself may not be out of place at this point.

By Hindu standards, the Gita is not of great length, consisting of only seven hundred verses altogether, divided into eighteen 'books' or 'readings'. It takes the form of a dialogue between a prince, Arjuna, and his charioteer, Krishna (Kṛṣṇa) – actually the god Vishnu (Viṣṇu) in semi-human form – and is an episode in the vast epic the *Mahābhārata*. The epic tells the story of the struggles between two branches of the same family for temporal power; and at the point at which the Gita commences their respective armies are preparing to engage in battle. But Arjuna is overwhelmed by the thought that although as a warrior (*kṣatriya*) it is his duty (*dharma*) to fight when called upon to do so, equally it is his duty to uphold his family as a whole. Seemingly he cannot fulfil his duty in one direction without breaking it in another. Indecision paralyses him and he asks Krishna's advice. Initially, Krishna's answer is that he ought to fight, since in destroying human bodies he is not touching the soul, which is indestructible, and will in any case take on other bodies in due course. But soon the teaching leaves the practicalities of the warrior's dilemma and launches out into the vast area of the nature of reality on the one hand and human duty on the other. Eventually Arjuna is given to understand that he should engage in *karma yoga* (the discipline of works), doing his duty for its own sake, rather than for any benefits which may accrue; and that in the last analysis he should do everything for the sake of Krishna himself. At one point his devotion to Krishna is rewarded by a vision of the god as creator, sustainer and above all destroyer of all things. This scares Arjuna considerably, and he begs Krishna to return to his 'familiar four-armed form', after which the teaching resumes.

The name *Bhagavadgītā* may be taken to mean 'the song of the Adorable Lord' (*Bhagavat* = 'adorable'; *Gītā* = 'song'). The

Adorable Lord, or more strictly, Adorable One, is of course Krishna.

We shall have further opportunity to touch on the question of the dating of the work. Here we may simply say that Western scholars have generally opted for a date between 400 B.C. and A.D. 200 on purely philological grounds and have been reluctant to allow that there may ever have been a 'Krishna of history'. Hindu interpreters for their part have generally been uninterested in questions of dating, but when pressed almost always opt for a much greater antiquity. As with all ancient Hindu scriptures, absolute chronology cannot be arrived at by any means currently at our disposal; and relative chronology can only give the wide range of dates which we have mentioned.

I should like to emphasise that there is one aspect of the Gita's two hundred years of circulation in the West with which I shall not try to deal in this account. I shall make no attempt to compare and evaluate the various translations of the Gita which have been made into European languages. Perhaps the translator is always a traitor to the original; but degrees of treachery need not concern us. By Sanskrit standards, the language of the Gita is not of very great difficulty, and though there are certainly points of controversy here and there, I am simply assuming that any translation that is not hopelessly incompetent will convey at least a general impression of the Gita's contents to the inquisitive reader. Nor shall I be making more than passing reference to the formal commentaries on the text of the Gita which Western Orientalists have produced over the years. Even without this severely technical material, which can be appreciated only by the specialist, the record of the impact of the Gita on the mind of the West will prove to have been very great, and to have left deposits in some unexpected places.

In order to keep this book within manageable limits, I have chosen rather to select significant – or what seem to me to be significant – episodes along the path of Western Gita interpretation than to attempt to mention every last case. Some of these I shall discuss more fully than others. Perhaps my choice has been somewhat arbitrary, and I crave the indulgence of specialists for all the omissions which they will certainly notice. But the task has never been other than highly stimulating, and I hope that in what follows I can convey something of the fascination with which generations of Western readers have read the Gita – whether or not they have understood its even more profound hold on the mind and heart of Hindu India.

Part One
1785–1885

1

The First Translation

1. 'One of the greatest curiosities ever presented to the literary world'

In the spring of 1785, a London bookseller advertised the forthcoming publication of a remarkable Sanskrit work in translation, a series of dialogues between an Indian prince and his god. Modestly financed by the East India Company, the publication was aimed at the literary world. A curiosity it certainly was, for in 1785 Europe was practically unaware that India had a literary tradition of its own.[1] For many years, certainly, Europe had been interested in India as a source of wealth, but for its history, culture and religion there was as yet very little feeling, the best written sources being in a language which practically no European had mastered. For a century or more the learned had been producing treatises on subjects connected with India; these, however, had been based more on observation and hearsay than on solid first-hand evidence, with the result that an unhealthy emphasis had been placed on the bizarre and the horrific. This was perhaps inevitable, since the only prototypes which the West had on which to work were those of the biblical tradition on the one hand and Greece and Rome on the other; but it was hardly calculated to inspire respect. The sacred scriptures which India was reputed to possess in large numbers were still an unknown quantity, partly due to the language in which most were written, and partly because their priestly guardians were still reluctant to divulge their contents to foreigners.

By the 1780s, however, these guardians had been persuaded (the

---

[1] ' ... if anything was unexpected, it was the discovery of a literature in India, in distant India ... of a literature more ancient than Homer ... ', Max Müller, *Physical Religion* (London 1891), p.17f.

unsympathetic might say bribed) to relax their hold on at least some of their scriptures – at least those belonging to the class of 'tradition' (*smṛti*). At the same time it should be remembered that there was a still more authoritative category, that of *śruti*, or 'revelation', to which the Vedas proper belonged. In the eighteenth century, non-Hindu access to the Vedas was very difficult indeed. But the Gita, though authoritative, did not belong officially to that class.

There is some evidence that the Gita had actually been known to at least some Europeans since the sixteenth century, and that a manuscript translation of part of it into Portuguese had been made at that time.[2] But this translation seems not to have survived, and it was therefore in 1785 that the Gita first entered the European world of ideas, as

> The Bhagvat-Gēētā, or Dialogue of Kreeshna and Arjoon; in eighteen Lectures; with Notes. Translated from the Original, in the *Sanskreet*, or ancient language of the Brāhmans, by Charles Wilkins, Senior Merchant in the service of the Honourable the East India Company, on their Bengal Establishment.

At the time of its appearance, and for some years thereafter, Wilkins' translation made little impression on the mind of the West. Eventually, however, some very remarkable things were to be said about it. Just over a century later, in 1889, the Theosophist Charles Johnston was to write that, on account of that one publication, 1785 might be taken as marking 'an epoch in the intellectual history of the world', since there had then begun the 'westward flow of the wisdom of India' which by the 1880s had become a flood.[3] Étienne Lamotte observed in the late 1920s that since the publication of Wilkins' translation, the Gita had called forth 'an almost boundless admiration' in its Western readers, who had seen in it 'the masterpiece of Hindu thought, if not of universal literature'. At the same time, though, he was disposed to attribute its success in the West to 'the exaggerated admiration of certain dilettantes'.[4] In 1949 another Theosophist, Paul Hubert, was to write in glowing terms of Wilkins' translation as one of the 'striking events in the universal history of philosophy'.[5] A decade later we find George Hendrick

[2] Noted in Marshall (ed.), *The British Discovery of Hinduism in the Eighteenth Century* (Cambridge 1970), p.18.

[3] Johnston, 'Sanskrit study in the West', in *The Theosophist* (March 1889), p.338.

[4] Lamotte, *Notes sur la Bhagavadgītā* (Paris 1929), p.1f.

[5] Hubert, *Histoire de la Bhagavad-Gîtâ: ses diverses éditions de 1785 à nos jours* (Paris 1949), p.19.

noting on the one hand its 'antiquarian charm and historical importance', but stressing on the other that of all the early translations of the Gita, it had been this one which had had the greatest influence on the literature of the West.[6] And in 1979 Mary Lloyd wrote that Wilkins' translation 'marked the true beginning of Sanskrit scholarship in Europe'.[7] Of course all these testimonies were given, and could only have been given, in the light of much later developments. Wilkins for his part can have had no notion that in allowing himself to be persuaded to publish his Gita translation, he was doing anything more than adding one more small stone to the tiny cairn of Oriental scholarship.

*

Compared to some of his illustrious contemporaries, Charles (subsequently Sir Charles) Wilkins (1749-1836) was, and always remained, a somewhat obscure figure.[8] At the age of about fifty he was apostrophised by one John Collegins:

See patient Wilkins to the world unfold
Whate'er discover'd Sanscrit relics hold ...

But in 1785 he was a totally unknown quantity. He had been serving in Bengal since 1770 and had passed steadily through the ranks of the East India Company, becoming Senior Merchant in 1782. In the following year he had received from Warren Hastings, Governor of Bengal, permission to study Sanskrit at 'Benaris' – or rather to develop a study which he had begun in Calcutta a few years before. Evidently his ultimate objective was to translate into English the whole of the vast epic the *Mahābhārata*. By 1784 it was said that he had already completed more than a third of it 'with great accuracy and fidelity'. But it was never finished completely.

In a way even the publication of the Gita (which, as we have seen, is an episode in the *Mahābhārata*) may have been somewhat fortuitous. Wilkins apparently sent Hastings a manuscript copy, more or less as an example of his larger project, and Hastings was sufficiently impressed by what he read to write privately to the Chairman of the Court of the East India Company (Nathaniel

---

[6] Hendrick, Introduction to reprint edition of Wilkins (New York 1959), p.xiv.

[7] Lloyd, 'Sir Charles Wilkins, 1749-1836', in *India Office Library and Records: Report ... 1978* (London 1979), p.19.

[8] The best short account is that of Mary Lloyd, cited in the previous note.

Smith) recommending its immediate publication. Wilkins seems to have been genuinely surprised, writing to his patron that he was 'unconscious of the liberal purpose for which you intended the *Gēētā* ...'[9]

The role of Warren Hastings in the appearance of Wilkins' translation was thus a central one. Without this influential figure in the background as an enthusiastic (and knowledgeable) patron, not only Wilkins but others of the early British Orientalists – Halhead, Colebrooke, Jones – would have found their enterprises harder to sustain. Certainly Hastings was an expert in *Realpolitik*; but he was also an idealist. A century later it was possible for the Bengali nationalist Aurobindo Ghosh to call him a 'ruthless and monstrous tyrant', and the 'scourge of India'.[10] Tyrants, however, do not commonly further the culture of their victims as Hastings had done during his years in power. And even Aurobindo might have spared a thought for the Governor General's enthusiastic advocacy of the very same Gita which in 1907 was the bible of the Indian national movement.

Hastings, in forwarding Wilkins' manuscript to London, sent with it (again unknown to the translator himself) a long letter of commendation.[11] This was particularly necessary, since he knew very well that a philosophical discourse was unlikely to appeal to the hard-headed businessmen who administered 'John Company'. He admitted that its publication would hardly prove measurable in commercial terms: '... the study of the Sanskreet cannot, like the Persian language, be applied to official profit, and improved with the official exercise of it.' Nor was Wilkins making any claim concerning the profitability of his exercise. Perhaps, though, given continued support, '... the Translator may be encouraged to prosecute the study of the theology and mythology of the *Hindoos*, for the future entertainment of the curious'. He could hardly have set his sights lower.

Thanks to this letter of recommendation, we know rather more about Hastings' view of this curious new scripture than about Wilkins' own. 'Curious' was Hastings' own word; indeed, one of his first descriptions of the Gita was ' ... a very curious specimen of the Literature, the Mythology, and Morality of the ancient Hindoos'. The word 'ancient' is also worth noting. As yet there was no

[9] Wilkins, *The Bhagvat-Geeta* (reprint edition New York 1959), p.19.

[10] Aurobindo Ghosh, *Bande Mataram: Early Political Writings* I (Sri Aurobindo Birth Centenary Library I, Pondicherry 1972), p.464.

[11] Wilkins, op.cit., pp.5-16.

suggestion that the Gita could be of any *contemporary* significance, save as an unaccountable survival of the thought and manners of a bygone age. Its obvious parallels in the literature of ancient Greece and Rome had had to be resurrected by the scholars of the Renaissance; in India it appeared that the continuity had never been broken – as indeed it had not. Still, India's pundits were a small, select and jealous company who had only just been persuaded to yield up some of their secrets to the foreigner. The initial riddle of the Gita to the West was not why so many Hindus were still reading and interpreting it, but what its place might have been in India's classical age. This interested Hastings greatly.

Hastings knew that the Gita was part of a much larger work, the *Mahābhārata*, and took the opportunity both to tell London what that great Epic contained, and to record that it was superior in popular estimation to the (so far unknown) Vedas or to the *Purāṇas*. Whether Vyāsa had in fact written all the works attributed to him (the Epic included), Hastings permitted himself to doubt, though he considered that Vyāsa might have carried out some editorial function, reducing ancient Hindu ideas to 'a scientific and allegorical system'. This was the first time allegory had been mentioned in the West in connection with the contents of the Gita; it was not to be the last.

Having given a thumbnail sketch of the main plot of the *Mahābhārata*, Hastings ventured his own opinion of that part of it which he was recommending for publication. Here he had to show caution. There was no guarantee that the Court of the East India Company would be greatly interested in it, and he had to avoid being suspected of 'enthusiasm' (in the eighteenth-century sense). On some questions, particularly those having to do with religion, he therefore advised the suspension of judgment:

> Might I, an unlettered man [Hastings had little formal education], venture to prescribe bounds to the latitude of criticism, I should exclude, in estimating the merit of such a production, all rules drawn from the ancient or modern literature of Europe, all references to such sentiments or manners as are become the standards of propriety for opinion and action in our own modes of life, and equally all appeals to our revealed tenets of religion, and moral duty. I should exclude them, as by no means applicable to the language, sentiments, manners, or morality appertaining to a system of society with which we have been for ages unconnected, and of an antiquity preceding even the first efforts of civilisation in our own quarter of the globe, which, in respect to the general diffusion and common participation of arts and sciences, may now be considered as one community.

The Western reader Hastings believed was bound to find in the Gita 'obscurity, absurdity, barbarous habits, and a perverted morality'. This being so, the higher and nobler aspects of the work were to be welcomed as 'so much clear gain'. To distinguish between the two levels would demand the exercise of much imaginative tolerance on the reader's part: 'In effect, without bespeaking this kind of indulgence, I could hardly venture to persist in my recommendation of this project for public notice.'

Hastings then added a parenthesis on Yoga – 'this separation of the mind from the notices of the senses' – which he thought might be compared with some of the practices of the Church of Rome, and would certainly be hard (though not impossible) to grasp. And he went on:

> With the deductions, or rather qualifications, which I have thus premised, I hesitate not to pronounce the Gēētā a performance of great originality; of a sublimity of conception, reasoning, and diction, almost unequalled; and a single exception, among all the known religions of mankind, of a theology accurately corresponding with that of the Christian dispensation, and most powerfully illustrating its fundamental doctrines.

Hastings was of course not a theologian in any formal sense, and it is slightly difficult to tell what may have been in his mind in making this particular comparison. We may suppose, however, that in his somewhat Deist mind religion was a matter separate from mythology and 'theology' was concerned strictly with the nature, attributes and moral requirements of God. The Gita's insistence on the sacredness of moral duty – one of the many meanings of *dharma* – and the necessity for disinterested action therefore appealed to him, as did its vision of one God summing up in himself all the attributes of Deity. The late eighteenth century was quite capable of reading Christianity in a similar light.

Theology apart, Hastings' advocacy of Wilkins' translation was not without certain political implications, since he clearly hoped by such means to improve the already troublesome relations between the people of India and their new rulers. Sympathy for Hindu learning was certainly a virtue in itself; but, more than that, it was likely to prove indirectly profitable. In private he noted that Wilkins' work was 'part of a system which I long since laid down and supported, for reconciling the people of England to the natives of Hindustan'.[12] He made much the same point in his letter to the

---

[12] Cf. Mersey, *The Viceroys and Governors-General of India* (London 1949), p.18f.

Court. Although Wilkins could look forward to little more than 'the prospect of barren applause', the knowledge he was able to transmit was attractive and conciliatory:

> ... it lessens the weight of the chain by which the natives are held in subjection; and it imprints on the hearts of our own countrymen the sense and obligation of benevolence.

In any case, gazing with unusual foresight into the future, Hastings was convinced that writings such as the Gita

> ... will survive when the British dominion in India shall have long ceased to exist, and when the sources which it once yielded of wealth and power are lost to remembrance.

When he wrote this, he may have known that his days in India were already numbered. On 7 February 1785 he left India for England, home and impeachment (after nine years, he was acquitted). Probably few gave a thought to the small volume which went on sale at approximately the time of his arrival at Plymouth.

*

There is not a great deal that can be deduced from Wilkins' own short Preface to *The Bhagvat-Gēētā* about his own attitude to the document.[13] He did however make a few points. One was substantially political, a pragmatic point in Warren Hastings' favour which may not have been altogether true. The Brahmin, he said, who esteemed the Gita to contain 'all the grand mysteries of their religion', had been persuaded to make the text available by

> ... the liberal treatment they have of late years experienced from the mildness of our government, the tolerating principles of our faith, and, above all, the personal attention paid to the learned men of their order by him under whose auspicious administration they have so long enjoyed, in the midst of surrounding troubles, the blessings of internal peace ...

At least the East India Company had up to that time shown remarkable tolerance towards Hindu beliefs and practices, partly as a matter of deliberate policy, but partly also because of the minimal

---

[13] Wilkins, op.cit., pp. 23-6.

and unaggressive Christianity then favoured by most of the merchants and administrators. But it should be remembered that modest sums of money had also been involved, and that the Gita was not in the same class of 'grand mysteries' as were the Vedas.

Concerning the purpose of the Gita, Wilkins recorded that it appeared to be

> ... to unite all the prevailing modes of worship of those days; and, by setting up the doctrine of the unity of the Godhead, in opposition to idolatrous sacrifices, and the worship of images, to undermine the tenets inculcated by the *Vedas* ...

Its author's intention had in other words been ' ... to bring about the downfall of Polytheism ...' This again was true only up to a point, since the Gita denies not the existence, but the power, of deities other than Krishna. But in the climate of opinion of the 1780s this appeared to be a strong point in its favour, polytheism being regarded as an inferior and even infantile form of religion, suited only to those whom David Hume called 'monkies in human shape'.[14]

Otherwise Wilkins had little to add, save that the text was far from self-explanatory, being 'but imperfectly understood' by even the most learned Brahmins of his day; as to the existing commentaries (with which he appears to have had at least some acquaintance), these he held to be frequently 'more obscure than the original they were intended to elucidate'. The text must therefore be left to speak for itself, technicalities and all.

*

For the better part of a century, Wilkins' translation was the only version of the Gita available in English and, as we shall see, it was to exercise enormous influence on the mind of Europe and America. Interestingly enough, it was also re-translated from English into other European languages long before those languages had independent translations of their own. We may suspect, further, that some later translations were more re-worked versions of Wilkins than independent efforts. As an example of the extraordinary long-lasting influence of Wilkins' version we may note that it was being reprinted in India (by the Theosophical Society) more than a century after its first appearance. It was still in print in 1887, and may

---

[14] Hume, *The Natural History of Religion* (ed. Root, London 1956), p.75.

have survived longer. The journal *The Theosophist* noted in that year that it was still the cheapest edition available, but it already had competitors, and many more were to follow in the wake of the 'Krishna renaissance' (of which more later).[15] By that time, too, it had entered into a world of ideas vastly different from anything that either Charles Wilkins or Warren Hastings could possibly have visualised.

2. 'The essence of all Shastrus'

During the first century of Gita interpretation in the West, beginning with Charles Wilkins in 1785 and ending with Edwin Arnold in 1885, discussion and debate was conducted almost entirely in the geographical West, on a basis of Western ideas and assumptions. Hindus contributed comparatively little, and it is not likely that there was much awareness in India itself of what was being said about the Gita away in Europe and later in America. Hindu *pandits* were forbidden to cross the 'black waters' on pain of losing caste status. But even if there had been a Hindu presence in the West at this time, it is doubtful whether the Gita would have played much part in their interests and concerns. Gradually, as Hindus began to write and debate in English (mostly from the 1830s on), statements were made about the authoritative sources of Hindu belief and practice; these seldom contained any explicit mention of the Gita. Authority rested on the Veda, and the Gita was not part of the Veda. An example will serve to emphasise this point.

By common consent the first international figure in Indian intellectual history was Ram Mohun Roy (1772/4-1833), compiler of *The Precepts of Jesus, the Guide to Peace and Happiness* (1820), active social reformer, educationalist and founder in 1828 of the Brahmo Samaj.[1] From his writings as a whole it would seem that the Gita played very little part in the formation of his theology, which was broadly theistic and even in a sense 'unitarian': here Muslim influence was important, while in Hindu terms he drew chiefly on the witness of the Upanishads. He was utterly opposed to 'idolatry' in any shape or form, and hence was uninterested in the *Purāṇas*.

Roy was also a frequent controversialist, often on matters of social concern within the Hindu community, and it was in the course of one of his debates, on the subject of the immolation of Hindu widows

[15] Notice in *The Theosophist* (1887), p.61. The publisher was Tukaram Tatya.
[1] On Roy, see Hinnells and Sharpe, *Hinduism* (Newcastle-upon-Tyne 1972), p.80ff.

('suttee'), that he appealed to the authority of the Gita. (It is also believed that he wrote a commentary of his own on the Gita, though this has now been lost and we cannot tell what it might have contained.)[2]

In *A Second Conference between an advocate for, and an opponent of, the practice of burning widows alive* (1820),[3] Roy answered the argument which claimed that in immolating herself on her husband's funeral pyre the pious Hindu widow gained an entirely specific reward, namely, an honoured name on earth and eternal bliss in heaven by her husband's side. But this Roy believed to be contrary to the teachings of the Gita, which stated that works should be performed, not for the sake of any rewards to which they might give rise, but entirely for their own sake, without thought of reward. To self-immolate for the purpose of obtaining immortal bliss clearly contradicted the principle of *nishkāma karma* (selfless endeavour). He wrote:

> Without entirely rejecting the authority of the Geeta, the essence of all Shastrus, no one can praise rites performed for the sake of fruition, nor recommend them to others; for nearly half of the Bhuguvud Geeta is filled with the dispraise of such works, and with the praise of works performed without desire of fruition.[4]

The phrase 'the essence of all Shastrus' is significant. The 'Shastrus' (*śāstras*) were and are the Hindu scriptures in their entirety, though divided into various categories and possessing varying levels of authority. In all matters of controversy the higher takes precedence over the lower, *śruti* (revelation) over *smṛti* (tradition), that which points to the innermost meaning over that which prescribes what is to be done in a given instance. In support of this separation of categories Roy quotes from the 'Moonduk' (Muṇḍaka) Upanishad: 'Shastrus are of two sorts, superior and inferior; of these the superior are those by which the Eternal God is approached.' And immediately he cites further: 'In the Bhuguvud Geeta Krishna says: "Amongst Shastrus, I am those which treat of God." '[5] Thus although in one sense the Gita, as part of the Epic, belongs in the category of 'tradition', Roy's argument shows that it

[2] My informant on this point is Professor S.N. Mukherjee of the University of Sydney.

[3] Roy, *Translation of several Principal Books, Passages, and Texts of the Veda, and of some Controversial Works on Brahminical Theology* (2nd ed. London 1832), p.215ff.

[4] Ibid., p.222.

[5] Ibid., p.231.

is actually being treated as 'revelation' and as supremely authoritative.

Hindu society is similarly divided, into the 'ignorant' and the 'learned', the former being dependent upon the latter for guidance and instruction: 'Learned men should endeavour to withdraw all those ignorant persons from works performed with desire, but should never, for the sake of profit, attempt to drown them in the abyss of passion.'[6] The 'learned', then, are expected to follow the explicit teachings of the Gita on this point and to communicate their understanding to those – the vast majority – to whom the Gita's teachings are presumed to be inaccessible. At one point Roy says to his opponent: 'The Geeta is not a rare work, and you are not unacquainted with it.'[7] And again: 'The Geeta and its Commentaries are both accessible to all. Let the learned decide the point.'[8] But the fact that the argument was couched in these terms does rather suggest that at that time appeal was not necessarily always made to the Gita in matters of dispute.

Since it will be argued at a later stage that the Gita became 'popular' in the fullest sense only after the 1880s, it must be emphasised that 'popular' is not a synonym for 'authoritative'. This example from the 1820s shows that among the 'learned' the Gita was approached as a final court of appeal in matters of scriptural interpretation. It enshrined the essence of the Hindu scriptural record. But by implication it did so only among the very small number of those who had been educated along traditional lines. To such persons, the Gita was easy of access, and controversial issues could be referred to it – though its 'essential' teachings could also be overlaid by legalisms derived from other *śāstras*.

On this occasion Roy was speaking, not to the masses, but to those in whose hands the everyday conduct of Hindu affairs still lay – the brahmins on the one hand and the British administrators on the other (the 'Conference' was first published in Bengali and subsequently translated into English). In India in 1820 the machinery of popular education had hardly begun to be set up; literacy was uncommon; the Gita, though fully accessible and supremely authoritative to 'the learned', was not yet a 'popular' writing, nor had it begun to be coupled with the political process. Its *Sitz im Leben* was within the intricacies of *dharma* in all its aspects, day-to-day practices as well as ultimate goals. Arvind Sharma has

---

[6] Ibid., loc.cit.
[7] Ibid., p.233.
[8] Ibid., p.239.

argued that on this occasion the Gita played an important role in the abolition of suttee, alongside the social and political forces which have been more commonly acknowledged.[9] In this he is surely right. Roy's 1820 argument was founded on the Gita's doctrine of 'desireless action', and the Gita thus made, it might be argued, its first entry into the field of modern Indian politics. Over half a century was to elapse, however, before it assumed a dominant role in that volatile area.

[9] Sharma, 'The Gita, Suttee and Rammohun Roy', in *The Indian Social and Economic History Review* xx/3 (1983), pp.341-7.

2

Romantics and Transcendentalists

3. 'A more comprehensive soul'

Within twenty years of the Gita's first appearance in the English language, a subtle but in the end dramatic change had come over the intellectual face of Europe. Provoked in part by the outburst of the French Revolution and by a reaction against the increasing urbanisation and industrialisation of the major European countries, in literary terms it took the form of the 'romantic' revival. From form for form's sake, the new generation turned to the cultivation of feelings. Classical rigidity gave way to an emotional flexibility, rules to impressions, the Augustan lawmaker to the common man as the arbiter of fashion. Among the *literati* at least, the emphasis in religion also shifted, from obedience to divinely-instituted law to instinctive response to a Deity revealed more gently in the world of Nature.

The romantic movement, wrote Nirad Chaudhuri,

> ... stimulated every aspect and kind of mental activity, passional, ratiocinative, scholarly, imaginative and artistic, and gave to each a special motivation, method and expression. Under its influence people loved and worshipped differently, studied and taught differently, wrote books and composed music differently, and all these departures from the established pattern were made possible because, in the first instance, it created a different type of European mind which would not stay within the limits set by the eighteenth century.[1]

Those limits had been rational, orderly, moral – and to a great

[1] Chaudhuri, *Scholar Extraordinary: the life of Professor the Rt. Hon. Friedrich Max Müller, P.C.* (London 1974), p.84.

extent cultural and geographical. To the romantics all authority was to be located within the thinking and feeling individual human consciousness, accepted as a matter of inward conviction rather than out of fear of punishment or censure, here or hereafter.

Demagogues aside (for the age had its Napoleons), the early nineteenth century set greater store by its poets than by its lawgivers. The poet, wrote Wordsworth, in his celebrated Preface to *Lyrical Ballads*,

> ... is a man speaking to men: a man, it is true, endowed with more lively sensibility, more enthusiasm and tenderness [to the previous generation, 'enthusiasm' had been a failing rather than a virtue], who has a greater knowledge of human nature, and a more comprehensive soul, than are supposed to be common among mankind; a man pleased with his own passions and volitions, and who rejoices more than other men in the spirit of life that is in him; delighting to contemplate similar volitions and passions as manifested in the goings-on of the Universe, and habitually impelled to create them where he does not find them.[2]

India was just beginning to assume its role in the romantic drama, thanks to the trickle of translations which were beginning to become available in the West. Laws, dramas, philosophical treatises of the order of the Gita – all had their part to play in titillating the romantic imagination. Again according to Wordsworth, the poet sees '... the mind of man as naturally the mirror of the fairest and most interesting properties of nature'.[3] But 'man' in this case is no longer the frequenter of coffee-houses and clubs; rather he is universal man, Rousseau's 'noble savage' as well as the London 'wit', the dweller by the Ganges as well as the Seine or Thames. The purpose of the poet and the desire of those who read poetry was henceforth to see man *in* nature, declining in power and perception the farther he drew away from nature, but still capable of learning lessons from nature, should he so choose.

In one respect, however, the legacy of the Age of Reason remained in force: that at the heart of religion there is a sense of moral obligation, a compulsion to do one's duty at the command of God (or Nature) for the good of all. The 'sense of absolute dependence' which Schleiermacher in Germany identified as the heart of all religion was also a sense of obligation to act in accordance with nature's *numen*. In some ways this was as much a Stoic as a Christian interpretation of life: but already the hold of many in the West on the more abstruse

[2] *The Complete Poetical Works of William Wordsworth* (London 1950), p.854.
[3] Ibid., p.855.

details of Christian theology, particularly on the supernatural side, was being loosened; and in any case, there appeared to be no reason why moral truth should be restricted by time or place. India in particular fulfilled all the conditions for a source of timeless wisdom; and the Gita could not have been improved upon as a compact compendium of Indian wisdom.

*

Oddly enough, although Wilkins' translation had been published in London and paid for by the East India Company, the British for a number of years showed very little interest in it. Doubtless this was in part a reflection of the usual British attitude to India during most of the period of the Raj: that India as a whole was a profitable nuisance, which could be left in the safe-keeping of those civil servants, administrators and soldiers who were compelled to spend time there in the line of duty. Certainly the poet Robert Southey (1774-1843) had read the Gita in the preparation of his lurid narrative poem *The Curse of Kehama* (1810), though his reading did little to improve the final result.[4] A much more typical British reaction to India was that of Thomas Babington Macaulay, who was President of the Committee of Public Instruction in the India of the 1830s, pined for England during the whole of his 'exile' and in the end poured scorn on the whole of the edifice of Indian traditional learning (' ... medical doctrines, which would disgrace an English farrier – astronomy, which would move laughter in the girls at an English boarding-school – history, abounding with kings thirty feet high, and reigns thirty thousand years long – and geography made up of seas of treacle and seas of butter.')[5] It was in 1835 that the issue of English-language *versus* vernacular higher education in India was settled in favour of the 'Anglicists', largely due to Macaulay's advocacy.[6] In such circles as these the Gita was a political irrelevancy and could therefore be safely ignored – as indeed it was.

In the absence of political and commercial considerations, early nineteenth-century Germany was able to look on India in a far more idealised light than was possible to many in Britain. The first German philosopher to devote his attention to India had been Immanuel Kant (1724-1796), who for many years lectured on

[4] Bearce, *British Attitudes to India, 1784-1858* (Oxford 1961), p.103.

[5] Trevelyan, *The Life and Letters of Lord Macaulay* (London 1908), p.291.

[6] For a summary of the Anglicist-Orientalist controversy, see Monier-Williams, *Modern India and the Indians* (4th ed. London 1887), p.289ff.

physical geography in Königsberg, and took up India in this connection.[7] His information, however, was acquired at second or third hand from the classical writers and from travel books, and he made no use of any Hindu scripture. The image of India as the home of consummate wisdom and virtue, and as having the capacity to make all its devotees virtuous and mild, appears to have been launched first by Johann Gottfried von Herder (1744-1803), who had certainly read the Gita by the late 1780s and quoted from it in his *Ideen zur Philosophie der Geschichte* ('Thoughts on the philosophy of history'). But to Herder, 'the Christian Brahmin', the Gita was only one of the sources on which his romantic image of India was based; a far greater impact appears to have been made by Sir William Jones' translation of the drama *Shakuntalā* (1789), which also inspired Goethe to lyrical flights.

In the area of speculative philosophy, the impression provided by the Gita was greatly reinforced by the publication of Anquetil Du Perron's Latin translation (from Persian) of a number of Upanishads.[8] Du Perron's *Oupnek'hat* appeared in two volumes in 1801 and 1802. In 1808 one of the Upanishads from this volume, the *Chhandogya*, was rendered into German by Thaddae Anselm Rixner. In the absence of any other Vedic texts or commentaries, which did not become available to the West for many years thereafter, the study of Hindu religious thought was still not soundly based. The Romantics, however, were scarcely aware of any such limitations.

The next step in German Gita interpretation was taken by August Wilhelm von Schlegel (1769-1845), who in 1818 became Germany's first Professor of Sanskrit (at the University of Bonn).[9] A decade earlier Schlegel's younger brother Friedrich (1772-1829) had published a book on the language and the wisdom of India, *Über die Sprache und Weisheit der Indier*, which in the end became a personal renunciation of the Indian dream, though that is a matter which need not concern us further. In 1825 the elder Schlegel published the second direct translation of the Gita from Sanskrit into a European language, in this case Latin.[10] In the same year, on 30 June 1825,

---

[7] von Glasenapp, *Das Indienbild deutscher Denker* (Stuttgart 1960), pp.5-13.

[8] Ibid., p.25. Cf. Söderblom, *Gudstrons uppkomst* (Stockholm 1914), p.328ff.

[9] *Die Religion in Geschichte und Gegenwart* (1st ed. Tübingen 1913), vol.5., cols. 300-2.

[10] According to Humboldt: 'This translation is so masterly and at the same time so conscientious and faithful, it treats so intelligently the philosophical content of the poem, and is such good Latin besides, that it would be a great pity if it were used only for a better understanding of the text, and not read for its own sake as well, by all those who are interested in philosophy and archaeology [antiquities].' Cowen, *Humanist without Portfolio* (New York, 1963), p.175.

Wilhelm von Humboldt lectured to the Berlin Academy of Sciences on the Gita, placing it firmly in the mainstream of the scholarship of the period.

Humboldt's lecture, *Über die unter dem Namen Bhagavad-Gītā bekannte Episode des Mahābhārata* ('On the episode in the Mahābhārata that goes under the name of Bhagavad-Gītā'), was published in 1826, and comprised mainly a summary of the Gita's contents. However, it is worthy of more than a passing mention.

Humboldt had begun the serious study of the Gita only a couple of years previously, partly as a result of having visited Paris and meeting certain Indologists, among them Eugène Burnouf.[11] He saw the contents of the Gita less as religion than as philosophical poetry, *Naturdichtung*, not essentially different from what he had found in Schiller; or perhaps in Schubert, for it was later said of him that he listened to the Gita's verses as he might have listened to music.

It is perhaps not surprising, then, to find Marianne Cowen stating that Humboldt found in the Gita his own 'spiritual ancestors'. Basically, she says, that is a matter of 'the Perennial Philosophy', the essential message of all mysticism, Eastern and Western, past and present.[12] But this seems hardly likely. Certainly Humboldt may have read the Gita with an eye to the perception of the oneness of all things, or to the finding of the Romantics' 'blue flower'. But his was equally a deeply moral insight – understandably so, for anyone brought up within the range of Kantian ideas of duty and the categorical moral imperative was bound to respond in some way to the Gita's emphasis on the immutable *dharma*, as well as to the depths of *bhakti* devotion and the person of Krishna. In this respect, there was an Enlightenment legacy in the midst of Romanticism. Otherwise, what chiefly appealed to Humboldt in the Gita was its originality and its apparent simplicity, at least when compared to the intricacies of the Brahmanical systems. Krishna's doctrine, he wrote,

> ... develops in such a peculiarly individual way, [and] it is, so far as I can judge, so much less burdened with sophistry and mysticism, that it deserves our special attention, standing as it does as an independent work of art ...[13]

[11] Haym, *Wilhelm von Humboldt* (repr. Osnabrück 1965), p.575: 'Fast alles, was den deutschen Sprachforscher in den letzten Jehren am lebhaftesten interessiert hatte, war durch die Forschungen der Pariser Gelehrten an ihn herangebracht worden.'

[12] Cowen, op.cit., p.23f.

[13] Ibid., p.169.

To avoid misunderstanding, it should be emphasised that Humboldt was here using the word 'mysticism', not to express the heights of spiritual attainment and insight, but in a pejorative sense, meaning an unhealthy reliance on the irrational and the emotional. We shall return to this subject later.

Of Humboldt's enthusiasm for the Gita there could be no doubt. He wrote to a friend that its ideas were the deepest and the most elevated which the world had to offer ('... wohl das Tiefste und Erhabenste, was die Welt aufzuweisen habe'),[14] and he sought to make those ideas, as he understood them, his own. This may fairly be described as the Romantic consensus on the Gita, to the extent to which it was actually known, that its contents were universally human, and not Hindu or Indian only, and that its message was a message of oneness – with God and with Nature. These sentiments were nowhere treated with more seriousness than among the 'New England Transcendentalists'. To these we must now turn.

4. 'The first of books'

Nowhere did Charles Wilkins' translation make a deeper impression than on the company of eclectic amateurs generally called the 'New England Transcendentalists' – their centre, Concord, Massachusetts, and their acknowledged leader, Ralph Waldo Emerson (1803-1882),[1] who epitomised the Transcendentalist position in these words:

> Mind is the only reality, of which man and all other natures are better or worse reflectors ... The Transcendentalist adopts the whole connection of spiritual doctrines. He believes in miracle, in the perpetual openness of the human mind to new influx of light and power; he believes in inspiration, and in ecstasy ... Our American literature and spiritual history are, we confess in the optative mood; but whoso knows these seething brains, these admirable radicals, these unsocial worshippers, these talkers who talk the sun and moon away, will believe that this heresy cannot pass away without leaving its mark.[2]

---

[14] Haym, op.cit., p.580f.

[1] The literature of New England Transcendentalism is vast. Among general works, see Matthiessen, *American Renaissance* (New York 1941), and Christy, *The Orient in American Transcendentalism* (New York 1932).

[2] Emerson, 'The Transcendentalist', in Atkinson (ed.), *The Selected Writings of Ralph Waldo Emerson* (New York 1950), pp.89, 90, 94.

Writing in 1873 to Max Müller in Oxford, Emerson recalled how his interest in the wisdom of India had been aroused first of all by the reading of '[Victor] Cousin's sketch, in his first Lectures, of the Dialogue between Krishna and Arjoon, & I still prize the first chapters of that Bhagavat as wonderful ...'[3] This was in 1832 or thereabouts, Cousin's *Cours de philosophie* having been published in 1828 and translated into English by H.G. Lingberg in 1832 as *Introduction to the History of Philosophy*.

Victor Cousin (1792-1867) has been acclaimed by posterity, not for the brilliance of his philosophical method, but for turning philosophy in France from the materialist excesses of the post-Revolutionary period toward his own brand of eclectic idealism. A voracious reader, he had ample opportunity to widen his interests during a period of political exile during the greater part of the 1820s. It was at this time that he made the acquaintance of the Gita, perhaps during a visit to Germany, where he met Hegel and Schelling among others. And in the first course of lectures delivered on his restoration to the *École Normale* he touched briefly upon the Gita. It was this brief reference which had fired Emerson's imagination.

In India, Cousin announced, there is a 'universal symbolism': but what does it express? There is doubtless an idea: but in what does it consist? He himself had been disturbed and disoriented by his encounter with Indian thought and Indian monuments, but 'a few pages of a philosophical work' had quickly restored order to his mind. Briefly he sketched the argument (or at least the setting) of the Gita, and summarised what he understood to be its central message. Arjuna is a warrior (*Kshatriya* is here spelt by Cousin 'Schratrias'!), condemned to do battle. Very well, then; he must fight. Tomorrow, whatever the outcome, the sun will again shine on the world, and 'the eternal principle' will still be there. Beyond this principle there is nothing but illusion, and those who attack value to that which is illusory, are in error. Even action itself is an error and an illusion: 'The beauty, the merit of action, is that it should be undertaken with a certain indifference to whatever results it might produce. Doubtless one must act, but as though one did not act. Nothing exists but the eternal principle, being itself.'[4]

This Cousin evidently found appealing, since it placed all purely human effort in its right position and its right proportions – to be undertaken, certainly, but without reference to material results or rewards (and bearing in mind that Cousin himself had been in exile

---

[3] Rusk (ed.), *The Letters of Ralph Waldo Emerson* (New York 1939), vol. 1, p.lix.
[4] Cousin, *Cours de Philosophie* (Paris 1841), pp.71-5.

for several years, he could hardly be expected to have embraced a philosophy of irresistible progress). Where India was concerned such a philosophy had led man to mistrust himself, had prevented him from developing practical interest and true morality and had made him to care little for the actions of the past, 'for there is no human history in India, and consequently no chronology'. Having said that, Cousin passed somewhat abruptly to the Greece of Pericles.

*

Actually Emerson's reading of Cousin, though it introduced him to the Gita, was not his first encounter with India; in the early 1820s he had read what the Unitarians had had to say about Ram Mohun Roy, the 'Hindoo convert' (he was actually nothing of the kind, though he was a Unitarian of sorts), and had transcribed into his diary some lines from 'A Hymn to Narayena'. But it was certainly the reading of Cousin which brought the Gita to his attention.

Not until 1845 – sixty years after its first publication – did Emerson actually acquire his own (if it was his own) copy of the Gita. As late as May 1845 he was still writing that he wanted a copy, and was prepared to pay the going rate for it. In the end, a copy arrived in Concord, evidently on loan from James Elliot Cabot, and on 17 July 1845 he wrote to Elizabeth Hoar, in the middle of a letter otherwise devoted to trivia:

> The only other event is the arrival in Concord of the 'Bhagvat-Geeta', the much renowned book of Buddhism, extracts from which I have often admired but never before held the book in my hands.[5]

Ralph L. Rusk notes caustically, with 'Buddhism' in mind, that Emerson was 'still uncertain of his bearings in the Orient'.[6] Certainly he was, though his later friendship with Max Müller cured him of the grosser inaccuracies. But, once having arrived, the book captivated him. On 1 September 1845 he was writing apologetically to Cabot of his inability to part with it,[7] and at the end of the month announced that at last he had his own copy, which had cost him £1: 'I have been so fortunate as to procure a copy of the Bhagvat Geeta

---

[5] *The Letters* ... vol.3, p.290.
[6] Ibid., n.40. However, at that time the West generally was still very unfamiliar with Buddhism, and Emerson was perhaps no worse informed than others of his contemporaries.
[7] Ibid., p.299.

from London, so I return yours with hearty thanks.'[8] He was soon lending his new treasure out among his friends; in November 1846 we find him writing to John Boynton Hill, 'In the absence of the Bhagvat Geeta, I have torn from a commonplace book this fine sketch of Cousin, which you must put together & read.'[9] Perhaps it was the same copy which was lent in 1851 to Emily Mervine Drury of Canandaigua, N.Y. And in 1852 to John Greenleaf Whittier, who wrote:

> I feel guilty in respect to the *Bhagvat Geeta*: but it is too late to repent: & I will een keep it until I restore it to thee personally in exchange for Geo Fox. It is a wonderful book – & has greatly excited my curiosity to know more of the religious literature of the East.[10]

At about this time Emerson appears seriously to have contemplated producing an American edition of Wilkins' Gita translation. But if so (and there would seem to have been nothing to prevent it) it never materialised. Apparently still in 1845 he had only one copy, which had passed through many hands, for in December of that year he wrote to a friend on tour in Europe:

> You will help me much if you can bring home with you a copy of the Bhagvat Geeta such as mine ... I bought it for a pound sterling, & could easily have bought another. Now Conway and various persons have ordered it in vain.[11]

It may be, therefore, that the initial impact of the Gita on the New England Transcendentalists came through not more than two copies – though parts were doubtless transcribed into many commonplace books and journals.

It was characteristic of the circle around Emerson to take and use whatever sources of wisdom presented themselves as parts of their own deeply-felt but unsystematic view of life. But though eclectic their constructions were not self-indulgent – at least not initially. In his celebrated essay on 'The Over-Soul' (the Transcendentalists' substitute for God), Emerson wrote:

---

[8] Ibid., p.303.
[9] Ibid., p.361.
[10] *The Letters* ... vol.4, p.336.
[11] Ibid., p.479.

Let man then learn the revelation of all nature and all thought to his
heart; this, namely, that the Highest dwells with him; that the sources
of nature are in his own mind, *if the sentiment of duty is there* [my
italics].[12]

It was this sense of duty, Wordsworth's 'stern daughter of the voice
of God', which acted as a brake on the Transcendentalists'
speculations. Certainly thinking was important; but thinking which
did not issue in right action was valueless. It was precisely this
combination between theory (*sāmkhya*) and action (*yoga*) under the
canopy of duty (*dharma*) which Emerson found in the Gita and
absorbed into his system. But the Gita, though to be prized as 'the
first of books', was only one source among many. In 1836 Emerson
described his 'method' in the following terms:

Each new mind we approach seems to require an abdication of all our
past and present empire. A new doctrine seems at first a subversion of
all our opinions, tastes, & manner of living. So did Jesus, so did Kant,
so did Swedenborg, so did Cousin, so did Alcott seem. Take
thankfully & heartily all they can give, exhaust them, leave father &
mother & goods, wrestle with them, let them go until their blessing be
won ...[13]

Describing a 'magnificent day' spent with the Gita, Emerson felt
and confided to his journal that

It was the first of books; it was as if an empire spoke to us, nothing
small or unworthy, but large, serene, consistent, the voice of an old
intelligence which in another age and climate had pondered over and
thus disposed of the same questions which exercise us.[14]

Not long before, he had copied into his journal two verses of the Gita:

Children only, and not the learned, speak of the speculative and the
practical doctrines as two. They are but one, for both obtain the
self-same end, and the place which is gained by the followers of one, is
gained by the followers of the other. That man seeth, who seeth that
the speculative doctrines and the practical are but one.[15]

[12] Emerson, 'The Over-Soul', in *Selected Writings*, p.276.
[13] Sealts (ed.), *The Journals and Miscellaneous Notebooks of Ralph Waldo Emerson*
(Cambridge, Mass. 1965), vol.5, p.178f.
[14] Quoted by Christy, op.cit., p.23.
[15] Gita V:4–5 (Wilkins' translation).

This was a neat expression of his own philosophy, and of his deep conviction that the approach to the Over-Soul and the development of individual perfection were one and the same.

Otherwise, references to the Gita are for the most part limited to Emerson's journals, letters and private notebooks, and are not to be found in his voluminous published writings. There is however one notable and celebrated exception, the poem 'Brahma'.

If the red slayer think he slays,
    Or if the slain think he is slain,
They know not well the subtle ways
    I keep, and pass, and turn again.

Far or forgot to me is near;
    Shadow and sunlight are the same;
The vanished gods to me appear;
    And one to me are shame and fame.

They reckon ill who leave me out;
    When me they fly, I am the wings;
I am the doubter and the doubt,
    And I the hymn the Brahmin sings.

The strong gods pine for my abode,
    And pine in vain the sacred Seven;
But thou, meek lover of the good!
    Find me, and turn thy back on heaven.[16]

This poem, so obscure and enigmatic to anyone unversed in Hindu tradition (and those who have not understood it have for that reason often laughed at it), is based in part on a verse found in both the Gita and the *Katha Upanishad*. The main point of the poem centres on two doctrinal issues: first, that killing and being killed are 'real' only on the lower level of phenomena, but that neither has any relevance on the level of pure Being; though the body may be killed, the soul remains untouched, merely passing on to join itself to other bodies like new suits of clothes; and secondly, that the same applies to all other human distinctions between pairs of opposites, such as 'far and near' and 'shadow and sunlight': all these are phenomenal qualities, and behind and beyond them there is that eternal principle which Emerson called 'The Over-Soul' but which might also be called (on Emerson's eclectic principles) 'Brahma'. For the finding of this even 'heaven' is a poor substitute. In Evangelical Christian terms, Emerson had indeed turned his back on heaven, and still

[16] *Selected Writings*, p.809.

more on heaven's guardians and messengers. For that they forgave neither him nor his admirers and followers.

However much Emerson may have admired the Gita, he absorbed no more than its general atmosphere. He did not interpret it. His philosophy had been formed before he had read it, and he accepted it as a valuable confirmation of what he had already come to believe about the innermost essence of the universe. One did not need to invent the 'Over-Soul', one had to learn to perceive it. And where better to perceive it than in the pages of the Gita? As F.O. Matthiessen has written about *Brahma*,

> ... all the severing details of man's existence, all the distinctions between shadow and sunlight, between the Brahmin and his hymn, indeed, between life and death, are caught up and reconciled and obliterated in the sweep of the divine mind.[17]

*

Interpreter or not, Emerson made of the Gita a piece of required reading for all those who were in rebellion against the confines of Evangelical Christianity and who sought for evidence of the Over-Soul in a world context. In the light of the transcendental vision, the Gita was Hindu only incidentally, and what it might have meant to India the Transcendentalists scarcely knew, nor did they care. This essentially Romantic view of India and the Gita has persisted ever since in persons of a certain cast of mind, to the despair of the professional Orientalist. It was never to do the Gita much harm. But, by cutting its Hindu roots and transplanting it into far different soil, it was ultimately to make of it a scripture different from anything India had previously known.

5. 'In every man's brain is the Sanscrit'

Henry David Thoreau (1817-1862) was in his late twenties when the Gita arrived in Concord, the town (or rather village) where he had been born. Unlike Emerson, he was a man who lived in a circumscribed world; his weapon was less the voice than the pen, but it was turned as frequently upon himself as upon the materialist world around him: he was, it has been said, 'the true and faithful

---

[17] Matthiessen, op.cit., p.44.

reporter of a rare spirit, his own'. The difference between the respective approaches of Emerson and Thoreau has been pointed out as resting, first, on Emerson's love for Plato – a love which Thoreau did not share – and secondly, on something more practical. As Claude Gayet has rightly observed, 'Emerson had integrated Hindu concepts on an abstract level within the totality of his philosophic structure of thought. But Thoreau's confrontation with the Hindu world view was in the main a practical one; Hindu thought provided him with elements for the formation of an articulate philosophy of life.'[1] Thoreau was far more interested in living a disciplined life than was the intellectual Bostonian Emerson. His enthusiasms were, if anything, greater. And he too, having met the Gita, built a version of its teachings on *karma yoga* ('the discipline of works') into his own life-style and philosophy.

Thoreau's thoughts on the Gita were expressed most fully in an eight-page meditation incorporated into his early work *A Week on the Concord and Merrimac Rivers* (written 1840-4, but not published in full until 1849).[2] These pages are not easily summarised, though they rest in part on the contrast drawn by Thoreau between the 'pure morality' of Christian scripture and the 'pure intellectuality' of Hindu scripture in general, and the Gita in particular. The Hindu qualities he saw as being 'buoyancy, freedom, flexibility, variety, possibility' – all of these 'qualities of the Unnamed'. Christianity by contrast is 'humane, practical, and, in a larger sense, radical'.[3] Thoreau was of course no enemy of radicalism as such. But in his early years he set far greater store by thoughts than by actions, and in the realm of thought he was convinced that the Gita was unsurpassed: 'The reader is nowhere raised into and sustained in a higher, purer, or *rarer* region of thought than in the Bhagvat-Geeta.' This is far superior to any merely human action.

> What, after all, does the practicalness of life amount to? The things immediate to be done are very trivial. I could postpone them all to hear this locust sing. The most glorious fact in my experience is not anything that I have done or may hope to do, but a transient thought, or vision, or dream, which I have had. I would give all the wealth of

---

[1] Gayet, *The Intellectual Development of Henry David Thoreau* (Uppsala 1981), p.38f. Cf. Matthiessen, op.cit., p.102.

[2] The edition I have used was published in London in 1906. It may be worth noting that *The Portable Thoreau* (ed. Bode, Harmondsworth 1977) includes only an abridged version of *A Week on the Concord* ... ,from which all references to the Gita have been deleted. One is left wondering why.

[3] *A Week* ... (1906 ed.), p.116f.

the world, and all the deeds of all the heroes, for one true vision. But
how can I communicate with the gods who am a pencil-maker on the
earth, and not be insane?[4]

Thus the reading of the Gita emphasised for Thoreau above all the
difference between Oriental and Occidental ways of thought: 'The
former has nothing to do in this world; the latter is full of activity.
The one looks in the sun till his eyes are put out; the other follows
him prone in his westward course.'

> I would say to the readers of Scriptures, if they wish for a good book,
> read the Bhagvat-Geeta ... translated by Charles Wilkins. It deserves
> to be read with reverence even by Yankees ...[5]

Above all, the East is the home of philosophical thinking and of
vision, and in comparison with this, Europe has little or nothing of
which to be proud. Even the greatest of Europeans (and here he
names Goethe) lacked the 'universality of genius' with which to
approach India aright, while

> Beside the vast and cosmogonal philosophy of the Bhagvat-Geeta, even
> our Shakespeare seems sometimes youthfully green ... *Ex oriente lux*
> may still be the motto of scholars, for the Western world has not yet
> derived from the East all the light which it is destined to derive
> thence.[6]

Thoreau saw the Gita as being 'less sententious and poetic' than
some other Oriental works that he had read; but as against this its
genius is more sustained and developed. Its 'sanity and sublimity'
had impressed the minds of 'soldiers and merchants' – here he is
evidently thinking of Hastings and Wilkins, though Hastings was
not a soldier. It is capable of appealing, to all sorts and conditions of
men, whether they be practically or philosophically minded, 'as
either the traveller may wet his lips, or an army may fill its
water-casks at a full stream'.[7]

Perhaps it was the atmosphere, rather than the actual content, of
the Gita which appealed chiefly to Thoreau. He was entranced by the
thought of a Hindu wisdom which 'never perspired' but unfolded
naturally. As to its contents, what did it matter that parts were

[4] Ibid., p.120.
[5] Ibid., p.121.
[6] Ibid., p.122f.
[7] Ibid., p.126.

difficult to grasp: 'Give me a sentence which no intelligence can understand. There must be a kind of life and palpitation to it, and under its words a kind of blood must circulate for ever.'[8] In its very vagueness and impressionism this statement shows the spirit in which the Transcendentalists approached the Gita – not to learn from it about India; but rather to obtain confirmation of what they already believed about the universe as a whole: namely, that it is a fascinating web of interrelated meanings. What those meanings are, can be discovered by any who will make the attempt. Never better expressed than in the Gita, even there they strike a chord, for 'in every man's brain is the Sanscrit'.[9]

The Gita is also mentioned once in Thoreau's celebrated *Walden* (1854), in a passage prompted by the harvesting from Walden Pond by 'a hundred men of Hyperborean extraction' (not Swedes but Irishmen!) of ice for use in refrigeration on the high seas.

> Thus it appears that the sweltering inhabitants of Charleston and New Orleans, of Madras and Bombay and Calcutta, drink at my well. In the morning I bathe my intellect in the stupendous and cosmogonal philosophy of the Bhagvat-Geeta, since whose composition years of the gods have elapsed, and in comparison with which our modern world and its literature seem puny and trivial; and I doubt if that philosophy is not to be referred to a previous state of existence, so remote is its sublimity from our conceptions. I lay down my book and go to my well for water, and lo! there I meet the servant of the Brahmin, priest of Brahma and Vishnu and Indra, who still sits in his temple on the Ganges reading the Vedas, or dwells at the root of a tree with his crust and water jug. I meet his servant come to draw water for his master, and our buckets as it were grate together in the same well. The pure Walden water is mingled with the sacred water of the Ganges. With favouring winds it is wafted past the site of the fabulous islands of Atlantis and the Hesperides, makes the periplus [circumnavigation] of Hanno, and floating by Ternate and Tidore and the mouth of the Persian Gulf, melts in the tropical gales of the Indian seas, and is landed in ports of which Alexander only heard the names.[10]

In Thoreau's reading of the Gita and a very few other Hindu works, what chiefly appealed to him was the aspect of discipline – the ideal of the *yogin*. In 1841 he wrote in his journal that 'one may discover the root of the Hindoo religion in his own private history, when, in the silent intervals of the day or the night, he does

---

[8] Ibid., p.129.
[9] Ibid., p.131.
[10] Thoreau, *Walden* (New York 1964), p.198f.

sometimes inflict on himself like austerities with a stern satisfaction'.[11] Material poverty was one facet of this discipline, while others were solitude, chastity and a measure of personal austerity. In the Gita's own terms, discipline was a means to an end, the ideal of carrying out detached work in the world. The disciple was urged to turn his back on the materialistic values of the world, on comfort and pleasure, and to impose on himself an inward discipline the better to find his own soul.

What appeared to be missing from this idealistic vision was a programme of precise and practical social action. By the time he came to write *Walden*, Thoreau had begun to turn toward social practicalities, though the detachment he had read in the Gita was still a strong influence upon him. In later years he was to move more and more in a practical direction, to become more concerned with the question of slavery, and to launch the idea of 'civil disobedience' in a celebrated essay of 1848 – an essay which is well known as having influenced Gandhi's mode of political thought. Here again we have an example of an idea partly derived from Indian sources – in this case the ideal of a 'natural' society, as opposed to a society created out of mere political and economic expediency – passing through a Western mind and then being fed back into India. In his later writing, though he never again dealt with the Gita as he had done in *A Week* and *Walden*, one can trace the mature consequences of his earlier reading in the Hindu sources.

In respect of Thoreau's later writings, Gayet sums up:

> This move from abstract thought to action included the rejection of several aspects of Hindu philosophy that had been extremely important in Thoreau's early thought. Thoreau could no longer conceive of virtue as a knowing, not a doing; nor could he conceive of the moral good as the quality of a mind slumbering, never active in the ways of the world.[12]

It is interesting to reflect that something very similar was to take place, forty or fifty years later, in Hindu thought generally – a movement away from contemplation (often called by the West 'quietism') and toward positive socio-political action. In Thoreau's case, the process involved the leaving behind of the Gita, though it might equally be argued that he was exchanging the ideal of the *muni*

[11] Quoted by Gayet, op. cit., p.44.
[12] Ibid., p.127.

for that of the *karmayogin*. And half a century or so later a new generation of Hindu interpreters were able to urge that this was what the Gita had been teaching all along.[13]

---

[13] As a final footnote, in 1971 Jay Bremyer published a little book, '*Walled-in' Soul in Nature*, subtitled 'A synthesis of "Walden" and the Bhagavad-Gita'. Leaving aside the atrocious pun of the title, the book is evidence that the connection between Thoreau and the Gita was being pursued once more by the neo-transcendentalists of the late 1960s and early 1970s.

3

Missionaries and Mystics

6. 'There are wounds within, which Hindooism cannot heal'

As we have seen, the Gita first came to the serious attention of the West not in the years immediately following its first publication in English, but approximately half a century later, in the wake of the Romantic Movement. Often those who read and commented upon it were concerned less with its meaning to India than with the impression it made upon their own 'feelings' (to use a Romantic term in an essentially Romantic situation). Mostly their personal religion was indistinct and impressionistic, certain only of the necessity of obeying a sense of duty and moving steadily in the direction of a conception of religion later epitomised by Matthew Arnold as 'morality tinged with emotion'.

The 'transcendental age' in matters of religion lasted for perhaps three decades between the 1830s and the 1850s, being brought symbolically to an end by the publication in 1859 of Darwin's *Origin of Species*. It was an age which believed in progress without having been introduced to the categories of evolution and natural selection. It believed in the powers of the human reason while setting bounds to its possibilities by recognising the power of the emotions. It had a burning historical curiosity. In the wake of the industrial revolution it was politically unstable, the instability culminating in the 'year of revolutions', 1848. Therefore as some of the old certainties were called in question by assorted prophets – Strauss, Marx, Engels, Kierkegaard – the individual emphasis became dominant in some quarters while being totally denied in others. It was also an age of discovery and saw the beginnings of many a new science.

In religion, however, it was most of all an age of conflict. Battles were being fought on many fronts simultaneously, but almost all resolved themselves into questions of *authority*. What, in matters of faith, is finally trustworthy? A sacred scripture? A historical community? Or the exercise of the human reason alone, following the evidence wherever it might lead?

These, roughly, were the questions. But the answers were seldom unambiguous, and various combinations and permutations were possible. Unlike the Roman Catholics, most Protestants (with the exception of the Lutherans in northern Europe and Saxony) placed little reliance on the historical community of faith. The liberals were at least beginning to relinquish their hold on the infallible word of the Bible – though this movement was not to accept all the consequences of its position much before the end of the century. The Age of Reason had at the same time left its mark, first by insisting on ethical conduct as the major identifying feature of true religion,[1] and secondly by constructing a logical system of tests and proofs by which religious truth was to be recognised. Alongside these trends there was the irregular, but on the whole growing, influence of Evangelicalism, which affirmed the literal truth of Scripture with utter conviction, while making use of rational argument to buttress its position wherever possible.

Contact with the non-Christian world was to a considerable extent in the hands of the Evangelicals, through the major Protestant missionary societies, most of which were founded during these same years. With very few exceptions their use of the Bible dictated the terms on which they viewed that world – as 'fallen', 'idolatrous' and, as a whole, condemned to final destruction. For the scriptures of (in this case) the Hindu tradition they had very little time, except as evidence of the depths of human depravity. Most had practically no access to them; nor, in all likelihood, would they have availed themselves of the opportunity, even had it presented itself. Free access was not to come much before the end of the century.

In the absence of such evidence, those Christian missionaries who spent time in India were forced to judge Hinduism, not by the contents of its scriptures, but by its popular practices. Much of what

---

[1] Maurice, *The Religions of the World* (5th ed. London 1877), p.236: 'Englishmen in the last [eighteenth] century seem for the most part to have persuaded themselves that man is not a mysterious being; that the Gospel does not address him as such; that its main use is to check disorders which the law cannot entirely redress, to make servants respectful of their masters, to keep the humble classes from interfering with the privileges of their superiors; that the kingdom of heaven is a place where certain rewards are bestowed hereafter for decency of conduct here.'

they saw fascinated and horrified them in equal measure.[2] This, most thought, could not be the 'natural theology' of the textbooks, but rather the plain and unvarnished work of the devil. Deist theories could not meet the case; only the Bible had the right words to describe it.

During these same years, however, there were other voices which demanded a hearing. Orientalism was a rapidly expanding industry. Hindu scriptures were becoming more and more available, with the Gita at their head. Certainly the average missionary could dismiss these as of no concern. But to others, there was clearly a case for a Christian response, a response which would concentrate, not on the subjective feelings of the reader, but on what were taken to be the objective 'facts' of revelation. The case which we shall consider was, it must be allowed, extremely unusual – a polyglot text of the Gita produced by a missionary organisation, with an introductory essay which, although critical, steers well clear of the denunciation customary at the time.

In Europe, even in Christian circles, the 1840s had seen the first real mitigation of the denunciatory tone in respect of the other great religious traditions of the world. F.D. Maurice's Boyle Lectures of 1845-6, subsequently published as *The Religions of the World and their Relations to Christianity* and reprinted many times during the remainder of the century, marked something of a watershed in this regard. But in discussing India and Hinduism (which he does repeatedly), Maurice makes no reference whatever to the Gita, which he appears not to have read and may not even have heard of. Maurice was of course no Indologist, but the absence of the Gita from his list of references may indicate that by the 1840s, copies of Wilkins' translation were rare and difficult of access. (Emerson, too, as we have seen, had difficulty in procuring a copy of his own.)

Maurice did however state a principle which was to prove very tenacious among liberal Christians confronted with an alternative scheme of salvation: that the Hindu asks important questions concerning human nature and destiny, but that only the Christian Gospel can provide adequate answers to those questions. The time has come, wrote Maurice, when the Hindu

> ... cannot be questioning merely; he must have answers. I contend
> that he who is able to give them is not a destroyer, but a preserver:

---

[2] The most celebrated example of this is still perhaps l'Abbé Dubois' *Hindu Manners, Customs and Ceremonies* (written in its final form around 1815, but not published until 1897).

that he will have a right to boast of having upholden all that was strongest and most permanent in the Hindoo life and character, while English influences in general were, however innocently and inevitably, threatening to undermine them. I concede with equal readiness, that if Christianity do not offer these answers, it cannot make this boast; it must leave to some other instrument the work of regenerating Hindostan.[3]

Although the Gita was not brought forcefully to the attention of Christian missionaries in India until the years of the 'Krishna renaissance' in the 1880s and 1890s (to which we shall return), the earliest missionary evaluation of the Gita was written half a century earlier by the Rev. R.D. Griffith of the Wesleyan Missionary Society. In 1849 the Wesleyan Mission Press of Bangalore published, under the editorship of J. Garrett, a remarkably handsome 'polyglot' edition in Sanskrit, Canarese and (Wilkins') English, with a prefatory essay by Griffith.[4]

Protestant missions in British India had at that time only a relatively short history, and they still had not taken on their dominant later characteristics of numerical accessions by way of mass movements, on the one hand, and a concentration on higher education on the other. Neither Hinduism nor Christianity had as yet taken on 'modern' characteristics. Despite the work of Ram Mohun Roy (who had died in England in 1833) and his followers in the Brahmo Samaj, the Hindu revival had scarcely begun. Christians for their part still believed that success would in time come through the marshalling of rational arguments and 'evidences' for Christianity and against Hinduism. These evidences, in the exposition of which Paley was still the chief authority, were however all drawn from Judaeo-Christian sources: as Griffith put it in his essay, ' ... the glorious Gospel of the blessed God' is free from 'confusedness and contradictions', being verified ' ... by miracle and prophecy: proofs that wall it about with divine defences'.[5] These of course made no impression on most Hindus. Still less of an impression was made by the use – to which this age was still prone – of supportive quotations from the great men of the Graeco-Roman past. This too was a characteristic of Griffith's essay.

Griffith, like many another later Christian commentator on the

---

[3] Maurice, op.cit., p.59f.

[4] Garrett (ed.), *The Bhagavat-Geeta, or dialogues of Krishna and Arjoon; in eighteen lectures. Sanscrit, Canarese, and English: in parallel columns* (Bangalore 1849). It begins with 'An essay on the Bhagavat-Geeta,' by the Rev. R.D. Griffith (pp.xxxvii-lvii).

[5] Griffith, in op.cit., p.xxxix.

Gita, confessed at the outset that he had ambivalent feelings about its contents:

> Truthful and animating as are some of its principles, and irresistible and ennobling as are some of its precepts, we look upon the system propounded by Krishna, with painful feelings.[6]

Certainly the Gita was treating some fundamental questions with high and therefore admirable seriousness, Griffith thought; but religious value is to be found, not in the asking of the correct questions, but in the acceptance of divinely authorised answers. In some respects mankind might well be able to arrive at adequate answers by the exercise of the unaided human reason – the position of 'natural theology', of which the Gita might be regarded as a specimen. In this limited sense, it contains a proportion of the truth:

> Every error presupposes some truth, and every system of mythology, however speculative, superficial or ill-informed, has for its nucleus and support, principles which lie deep and inalienable in the convictions, and destinies of humanity, and in the order and constitution of the government of the Most High.[7]

But whatever of good might be found in the Gita, commendations receive 'a disagreeable and unlooked-for check' by other aspects of its setting and teachings.

First, its narrative framework is unconvincing. How could 'the dogmas of an occult philosophy ... a series of abstruse lectures on speculative theology' be communicated 'amid the tumult and excitement of two powerful armies breathless to be avenged on each other'?[8] The communication of the Law on Sinai seemed to Griffith to have been given a far more convincing setting, while the teachings of Jesus had been given the best setting of all.

Secondly, the internal consistency of the Gita leaves somewhat to be desired. Given the known structure of Hindu belief, its specific teachings cannot be equally acceptable to all Hindus. The basis of Hindu doctrine Griffith believed to be the philosophy of Patanjali. This being so, some Hindus were bound to object to some of the Gita's teachings. Griffith went further, claiming (with what now appears to be a most remarkable exaggeration) that

---

[6] Ibid., p.xxxvii.
[7] Ibid., loc.cit.
[8] Ibid., p.xxxviii.

The orthodoxy of the Geeta in many of its fundamental tenets, much less as a whole, no intelligent Hindu would allow.[9]

No intelligent Hindu? The most that can be said is that in the mid-nineteenth century the Gita did not occupy the position which it was later to assume as the epitome of all Hindu teaching, and that it was even then more firmly anchored in Vaishnava *bhakti* than in any *smārta* tradition.

Thirdly, Griffith was profoundly unconvinced by the ethical aspect of the Gita's teachings. 'It would seem [he wrote] that men have always been slower in coming to moral truth, than they have been in arriving at metaphysical truth.' The moral teachings of the Gita he considered to be both unclear and impracticable: ' ... confused to no small extent, and in practice such as are never, and can never be realised'.[10] The trouble was that in his view the exercise of morals is always inseparable from the consequences of morals and simple obligation is powerless to provide the motive for right action. Bad acts call forth retribution; good acts lead to their reward – a central pillar in the Deist view of religion[11] and common at the time among many who were not Deists, Griffith included. The Gita's doctrine of *nishkāma karma* therefore simply will not work.

But this leads to a further consequence, to which Humboldt had already drawn attention: the consequence of 'fatalism'. If actions are unavoidable, then they are predetermined; there is nothing which man can do to escape from them. It may be objected that at this point Griffith was misinterpreting the implications of the Gita's teachings, the emphasis of which lay less on the unavoidable nature of actions than on the absence from them of personal desire. None the less, to the missionary this doctrine seemed 'repulsive' and its consequences 'dreary and uninviting'. Even should we cast all our works on God (as the Gita certainly enjoined), this improves matters not at all:

The transference of our actions on condition to Deity, subtracts from our moral feelings all healthful stimulus; it sheds upon us an unmanly indifference; it disorganises the probationary and tentative economy with which we are allied; it blasts the charities of man's heart; it strips the spirit of ardour – it paralyses its elasticity; – it breaks the wing.[12]

[9] Ibid., p.xxxix.
[10] Ibid., p.xlii.
[11] On Deism, see Sharpe, *Comparative Religion: A History* (London 1975), p.16ff.
[12] Griffith, op.cit., p.xliii.

At this stage in Western history Christianity on the Protestant side was nothing if not 'strenuous', even at times 'muscular' (a word, and a sentiment, usually attributed to Charles Kingsley). It emphasised the faithful performance of duty in obedience to the will of God, the rolling up of sleeves, the mastery of feelings (especially those of a sexual nature) and obedience to properly constituted authority. It also believed, still some time before the publication of Darwin's *Origin of Species*, in progress. Therein lay another point of contrast with the Gita, or at least the doctrine of rebirth which it expounded.

Of the notion of progress Griffith could find no trace in the Gita. Instead there was the doctrine of 'Metemsychosis' [*sic*], which explicitly contradicted 'the tendency of every thing to advance itself'. 'The cycles and epicycles of the heavy thinkers of antiquity, have been displaced for ever, by the fact that the march of nature, is progressive, and not self-evolving.'[13] Nature never halts, nor does she reverse her direction. The same applies to man's moral view, as stated in the Gita; there is no possibility to strive for any upward and onward motion. On the contrary, such motion as there is, may be in any direction, depending on the exigencies of *karma*. Man therefore is an exception to a universal rule. He may struggle upward, but is forever liable to fall:

> Transmuted into a reptile, or a beast, his better feelings are ruinously mortified, and of all that was noble, and hopeful, and divine in him, he is miserably defrauded. Such things surely cannot be![14]

And again Griffith contrasts this doctrine with Christian teachings concerning the future life, and death as 'a state of intense self consciousness' – though he admits that the state of the dead between death and the final resurrection is a matter 'wrapt in the profoundest obscurity'.[15]

In face of this catalogue of doctrinal objections, it may be hard to see what could remain of (in Christian eyes) positive value. But, on one point at least, Griffith was warmly appreciative: namely, in respect of the principles of yoga as bodily and spiritual disciplines. He did not wish to be thought actually to be advocating 'Hindoo austerities', but he did state that 'the Yoga doctrine is founded upon a deep acquaintance with the human constitution and wants': and of

13 Ibid., p.li.
14 Ibid., p.lii.
15 Ibid., p.liii.

these, the chief was discipline.[16] The human mind he considered to be a weak and worthless instrument unless brought under subjection. But: 'Energised and purified by rigorous persevering discipline, what barrier would obstruct its progress? what problem baffle its penetration?'[17]

Griffith concluded that it would be unjust to condemn Hinduism out of hand on a basis of some of its practices on the popular level – a habit of mind which was very common at the time among the early Christian missionaries, of whom the Abbé Dubois may serve as a representative example. Certainly there was in his view much that was unattractive in the world of Indian religion: but that could not apply to everything. And in any case, it invited the *tu quoque* argument against Christianity. But, having recognised as much, there remained the impression that although India had long been capable of formulating the right questions, it was unable to give the right answers to those questions:

> There are wounds within, which Hindooism cannot heal; distempers which it cannot eradicate. This *desideratum* in all its fulness, is announced to us, in the Gospel of Jesus Christ.[18]

In this respect Hinduism was of a piece with all natural theology. It had enough knowledge to state the problem of human nature and destiny, but not enough to lead to the solution of the problem. For that, there was need, not of speculation, but of revelation – which the Gita, all its virtues and high seriousness notwithstanding, did not contain.

Earlier in his essay Griffith had stated that for the missionary to employ only 'rude declamation and ridicule' in his attempt to convince the Hindu of the superiority of Christian teachings to his own was bound to be a failure. Such an approach would have precisely the opposite effect to that desired: it would merely 'exasperate their temper and outrage their prejudices'.

> The transition to Christianity would be easier (much easier than we are wont to consider) on pointing out the doctrinal correspondences between their system and our own, than by denying the former those claims, which history and the constitution of our common nature so obviously warrant.[19]

[16] Ibid., p.lv.
[17] Ibid., loc.cit.
[18] Ibid., p.lvi.
[19] Ibid., p.xlv.

In the middle years of the nineteenth century the quest for 'correspondences' and 'points of contact' (in German, *Anknüp-fungspünkte*) between pre-Christian and Christian belief-systems was becoming slightly more common. Still, however, it had to be balanced against the biblical witness against 'idolatry' and Christian exclusivity generally.[20] In this present case, the Gita could be viewed under the categories of 'natural theology'. As such, it could not be without its insights and positive values, which insights and values could be used as points of departure for the proclamation of the Christian message. No Christian (and certainly no Christian missionary in India) could expect to find the fulness of religious truth in a Hindu scripture. But, for a time at least, it gave some Christians the possibility to place whatever value they could upon the Gita, while reserving for their own tradition the right to have the last word on matters concerning man's salvation.

7. 'The odious indifference of these orientals'

The word 'mysticism' is so much a part of the everyday vocabulary of the study of religion in our day that it is hard to conceive of a time when it was both novel and somewhat outrageous, at least to Christians of the evangelical persuasion. But this was certainly the case in the middle years of the nineteenth century. At that time the words 'mystic' and 'mystical' were certainly current in the English language, but they were used only as synonyms for 'strange', 'mysterious' and 'inexplicable'.[1]

For those few who read German, things were complicated by the existence of two words, *Mystik* and *Mystizismus*. Though obviously derived from the same Greek source, they nevertheless had entirely different meanings. *Mystik* was a legitimate category in the world of religion, referring to a type of theology common enough (though always regarded as slightly dangerous) in the Catholic Church – that which saw the ultimate goal of all spirituality as the *unio mystica* of the soul with God. *Mystizismus*, on the other hand, was used in a derogatory sense by religious rationalists to refer to a type of quasi-religion of which they emphatically did not approve – a type

[20] For a fuller treatment, see Sharpe, *Faith meets Faith* (London 1977), pp.1-18.

[1] 'Mystic', 'mystical' and 'mysticism' are such common words that it is surprising that they have not been more thoroughly investigated from the standpoint of the history of ideas. For a preliminary discussion see however Sharpe, 'Christian mysticism in theory and practice', in *Religious Traditions* 4/1 (1981), p.19ff.

which elevated the non-rational above the rational, feelings above the exercise of the intellect. Translated into English, both became 'mysticism', a potential source of the most terrible confusion. What they had in common was of course an emphasis on the hiddenness of spiritual life in 'the secret place of the most high'; where they parted company was perhaps more in the eye of the beholder than in any measurable quality of faith, though what it amounted to was a belief that in *Mystik* the human reason is transcended, whereas in *Mystizismus* it is either bypassed or ignored altogether.

In the years around 1900 in the English-speaking world it was to become something of an intellectual fashion to write and speak about the nature and qualities of mysticism, the implication being always that this was the highest form of religion attainable by man. This did not mean that previously there had been no trace in the world of religion of what was later *called* 'mysticism': clearly all its main features – ranging all the way from visions, voices, trances and other 'altered states of consciousness' to a simple sense of peace, contentment and pleasure – had always been there. But in the 1850s the sights of the religious community in the West were set at a different level, and in any case there was no word to describe these phenomena. In 1900 everything of a 'transcendental' nature could be classified as one form or another of mysticism. In 1850 such phenomena were still uninteresting, and still indescribable.

*

Robert Alfred Vaughan (1823-1857) may be regarded as the one who introduced the concept of 'mysticism' to the English-speaking public, in a book first published in 1856 and entitled *Hours with the Mystics: a contribution to the history of religious opinion*.[2] Vaughan was the son of the Principal of a Congregational theological college in Manchester – perhaps an unlikely place from which to expect the emergence of a pioneer book on mysticism. The outward aspect of Manchester could hardly have been more unattractive. Another Manchester resident of the 1850s, George MacDonald, described the 'chimneyed city' in these words:

---

[2] Vaughan, *Hours with the Mystics: a contribution to the history of religious opinion* (6th ed. London 1893), with a memoir of the author by his son.

> ... the smoke is caught,
> And spreads diluted in the cloud, and sinks,
> A black precipitate, on miry streets,
> And faces gray glide through the darkened fog.
> Slave engines utter again their ugly growl,
> And soon the iron bands and blocks of stone
> That prison them to their task, will strain and quiver
> Until the city tremble.[3]

Manchester, however, did have an intellectual and 'liberal' face, and through the person of A.J. Scott, the first Principal of Owens College (the embryo of Manchester University) there were points of contact with the great liberal thinkers of the time – Ruskin, F.D. Maurice, Carlyle and behind them the German circle of the disciples of Goethe.

Vaughan himself died young but may be counted as another of the same school of independent liberal Christians of the period. His personal ambition was to be both a Christian minister and a man of letters, and in quest of a subject on which to write he rejected Leo the Great and Savonarola for a book on the mystics, which he recognised as in all probability ' ... rather less popular but more novel'.[4]

Novel it certainly was. It was not on the other hand uncritical, and in later years another authority on the subject of mysticism, W.R. Inge, was to accuse it of not treating with sufficient reverence ' ... the highest quest to which the human spirit can devote itself'.[5] This was perhaps partly a matter of the rather artificial dialogue form in which the book was cast – though that is by the way. What is important from our point of view is that in a section on 'Early Oriental Mysticism' Vaughan cast a brief and not particularly friendly eye on the Gita.

It is just possible that Vaughan may have had access to the edition of the Gita produced in India in 1849, which we have previously discussed. At least it is evident that his main point of criticism was identical with that of Griffith: namely, that due to the doctrine of metempsychosis the Gita advocates moral indifference and the disregarding of the consequences of one's actions. He wrote:

[3] Quoted in Greville Macdonald, *George Macdonald and his Wife* (London 1924), p.191.
[4] Vaughan, op.cit., p.xi.
[5] Inge, *Vale* (London 1934), p.42. A similar opinion was expressed by Evelyn Underhill, who found Vaughan's book 'supercilious and unworthy': Underhill, *Mysticism* (12th ed. London 1930), p.xiii.

I find here not a 'holy indifference', as with the French Quietists, but an indifference which is unholy. The *sainte indifférence* of the West essayed to rise above itself, to welcome happiness and misery alike as the will of Supreme Love. The odious indifference of these orientals inculcates the supremacy of selfishness as the wisdom of a god ...[6]

Vaughan's trouble was of course that he was in no way qualified to appreciate, or even to understand, any of the premises on which the Gita's arguments rested. In the absence of such understanding, he was forced to judge on the basis of data derived from another tradition altogether: namely, those of a 'social Christianity' which placed the utmost value on conscious and purposeful moral action in the world. To Vaughan, it seemed that the Gita provided the Hindu with a sanction for setting aside the distinction between good and evil. Hence: 'Mysticism ... is born armed completely with its worst extravagance.'[7] And the absence of responsibility is the beginning of insanity.

8. 'Ce livre est probablement le plus beau qui soit sorti de la main des hommes'

The first original translation of the Gita direct from Sanskrit into French did not appear until 1861. This is itself somewhat surprising, bearing in mind the level of French interest in matters Indian throughout the century and the very high level of Indological scholarship achieved by French *savants*. It was not the Gita's first appearance in French, however, which took place only two years after the publication of Wilkins' translation.

In 1787 the Abbé Parraud of the Académie des Arcades de Rome produced the first French version:

> Bhaguat-Geeta (Le) ou Dialogue de Kreeshna et Arjoon: contentant un précis de la morale des Indiens traduit du sanscrit, la langue sacrée des Brahmes, en Anglois, par Ch. Wilkins et de l'Anglois en François par Parraud.

It received a mixed reception, according to Paul Hubert, though as a first version in French Hubert regards it as worthy of honourable mention.[1] In subsequent years there were other translated

---

[6] Vaughan, op.cit., p.52.
[7] Ibid., loc.cit.
[1] Hubert, *Histoire de la Bhagavad-Gîtâ* (Paris 1949), p.19f.

translations. In 1832, for instance, Jean Denis, Comte de Lanjuinais, rendered August Wilhelm von Schlegel's Latin translation into French; and a similar service in respect of Friedrich von Schlegel's German translation of a selection taken from the Gita's first seven books was performed by Mazure, in his *Essai sur la langue et la philosophie des Indiens* (1837). Victor Cousin's brief account of the Gita in his *Cours de philosophie* (1828) we have already noted.

French scholarly interest, however, was fixed chiefly on the Vedas, partly, it has been said, as a result of the 'aryanising anticlericalism' of the post-revolutionary period.[2] On this view sheer antiquity was of the utmost importance, and the Vedas, being so much older than the Gita (and apparently older even than Homer), took up a great deal of time. Eventually, though, it was a noted Vedic scholar, Émile-Louis Burnouf (1821-1907) – not to be confused with his still more celebrated older brother Eugène (1801-1852) – who turned his attention to the Gita. The Gita he believed to be 'probably the most beautiful book which the hand of man has ever produced', and his text, comprising a transliterated Devanagari text and a prose translation, was entitled *La Bhagavad-Gîtâ ou le chant du bienheureux: poème Indien* (1861).

In a preface Burnouf explained why he had undertaken this publishing venture. Science, politics and commerce, he said, were all calling us towards the Orient; but knowledge is a necessary prerequisite to understanding. And the Orient *is* India: by the superiority of its race, its language and its two religions (Hinduism and Buddhism) India dominates the Orient. 'Now the civilisation of India is expressed entirely in Sanskrit'[3] – a statement which is by no means true, but which at that time appeared to be true and which the West accepted without question. To understand that language (and hence the culture with which it is inextricably bound up) three things were necessary – a grammar, a dictionary and a text. The grammar Burnouf had already published, in 1859; the dictionary was to follow in 1863; the Gita provided the most suitable text.

Burnouf was therefore offering the Gita to the French public as a model of Sanskrit verse, and not merely as a philosophical treatise. Although he certainly set a high value on its contents, and in the preface to the second edition of his translation (1895) stated that 'ce livre est probablement le plus beau qui soit sorti de la main des hommes',[4] he was perhaps prepared to leave speculation about its

---

[2] Eliade, *No Souvenirs* (Eng. tr. London 1978), p.267f.

[3] Burnouf, *La Bhagavadgîtâ* ... (Paris 1961), p.vi.

[4] Hubert, op.cit., p.6.

ultimate meaning to others: its beauty was formal and aesthetic rather than metaphysical. The Gita's metaphysical content was however useful, in its way. He wrote:

> Because of the metaphysic which is developed in it, the poem offers an abundant variety of compound and abstract words, of which the elements have between them correspondences less easy to grasp than in the picturesque words of the epic language; as a result of which the study of the Bhagavad-gîtâ is, from the point of view of language, much more profitable than that of the epics: so much so, that anyone who possesses a thorough knowledge of this little poem may regard himself as having taken a great step in the knowledge of Sanskrit. Furthermore, whatever may be its theoretical value and the date of its composition, the Bhagavad-gîtâ contains the very essence of the brahmanical philosophy and gives us a sure-footed entry into the knowledge of India: for in India this poem is venerated equally with the holy scriptues; divided into eighteen readings, it is the object of the daily meditation of pious persons.[5]

In the remainder of his preface Burnouf occupied himself mainly with arguing in detail for the practice which he had adopted, following Lassen and Schlegel, of separating the words of the Sanskrit text, rather than printing them continuously in accordance with Indian practice. He ended, however, with a political point. The study of Sanskrit, he wrote, must not be left to students in the privacy of their own garrets but must be publicly funded by the State. Only when this had happened would France be able fully to enter upon the road on which other European nations (Britain and Germany) were already so far advanced. His own modest work he trusted would hasten the coming of that day.[6]

The political implications of Orientalism need to be borne in mind. The reason why East India Company in London had been prepared to fund the first translation of the Gita was partly that they had allowed themselves to be persuaded that it might prove politically expedient for them to do so. At least it was hoped that it would assure men of influence in India that British rulers were prepared to support local cultural and religious institutions. Max Müller's text of the *Rig Veda* was funded by the same commercial company on the same grounds. So too was Haileybury College. It was all very much a matter of *Realpolitik*, and a proportion at least of Western interest in Hinduism was prompted by the desire to govern the country more

[5] Ibid., p.vii (my translation).
[6] Ibid., p.xi.

efficiently. The same principle was capable of being extended to the practice of Christian missions in India – as in Max Müller's prospectus for the *Sacred Books of the East* series.[7] Without adequate knowledge, he argued, there could be no understanding; and without understanding, the missionary would be beating the air. Hence it was necessary to enter as far as possible into the mind of the East, the better to be able to influence it.

This undoubtedly was also in Burnouf's mind in producing his Gita translation. France might yet gain a share in the Indian market, and in the meantime she must prepare. What better means of preparation than by learning India's sacred language? And what better and more convenient example of the use of that language could there possibly be than the Gita?

---

[7] *The Life and Letters of the Rt. Hon. Friedrich Max Müller*, edited by his wife (London 1902), vol.2, p.9.

4

Theories of Origin

9. 'More than a mere hypothesis'

In the West's encounter with the Gita it is inevitable that there should have been frequent comparisons between the Gita's teachings and those religious ideas which the West knew best: namely, those of the Christian Bible. As a rule considerations of history did not play any particular part in those comparisons. Most readers and commentators had their sights set at a different level and were looking for eternal truth, independent of the changes and chances of human history. Rationalists and Romantics alike believed in universal values, values capable of being recognised by anyone, given certain conditions, and obviously independent of time and place. If the Gita and the Bible exhibited resemblances, then that was so much clear gain – for if the two spoke with one voice, the voice could the more easily be accepted as that of God (or 'the Over-Soul').

There were however important historical questions to be faced where the Gita was concerned. When had it been composed? And in what kind of world had its message first been proclaimed? By the 1850s there was beginning to emerge some kind of consensus among Western scholars as to some aspects of these questions. The Gita was a composite, eclectic work, bringing together elements of the three philosophical schools of Vedānta, Sāṁkhya and Yoga, and perhaps echoes of Buddhism, all under the canopy of *Krishna-bhakti*. It had been compiled within a couple of centuries either way of the beginning of the Christian era – precise dates were impossible to determine (as indeed they still are). Hindu scholars, it is scarcely necessary to add, worked on different principles and generally believed the Gita to have been composed (or rather transmitted) *in illo tempore*, in the dawn of time, without wishing to relate that time to Western chronologies.

To Western scholars matters of history were central. In the world of ideas, culture and institutions, new impulses were demonstrably transmitted from one region to another – by armies, along trade-routes, by missionaries, and in less easily measurable ways. The discovery of the relationship between Sanskrit and the classical European languages, Greek and Latin, had caused much speculation about an 'original' Indo-European language and about who might once have spoken it. The link between India and Greece was already known and had certainly led to the transmission of ideas in one direction or another (in *which* direction was another matter entirely). In short a strong case could be made out for the principle of diffusion in matters of religion and culture – in many ways a stronger case than for the competing principle of unilinear evolution.

There was in India a persistent tradition linking the coming of Christianity with the name of the Apostle Thomas, and claiming that there had therefore been a Christian presence in India perhaps as early as the middle of the first century A.D. Even should this prove to be legend, the Syrian 'Thomas Christians' had most certainly been well established in India before the end of the second century.[1] But this opened up an intriguing possibility. Might the Gita have been compiled subsequent to that date, and might it exhibit, alongside its Hindu-Buddhist elements, some trace of Christian influence? In 1869 a book published in Germany made precisely this suggestion.

To raise the question of a possible Christian influence on the Gita produces a predictable reaction today, a century or more later. In 1961 an orthodox Hindu, Nataraja Guru, asserted that the suggestion that the Gita 'might have borrowed its teachings from the Bible' is 'a notion which is hardly worth treating seriously'.[2] Certainly it is, if expressed in these terms: at the time of the Gita's probable compilation there was no New Testament in the modern sense to borow from, and thus there can be no question whatsoever of wholesale 'borrowing'. The impatient dismissal of the possibility of an *indirect* Christian influence on the Gita, on the other hand, may well be as much the product of Indian national pride as an evaluation of evidence. Mesopotamian, Persian, Greek, Roman and Germanic

---

[1] Whether the Apostle was, or was not, ever actually in India is not a question I am able to discuss in this context. But see Brown, *The Indian Christians of St. Thomas* (Cambridge 1956), p.63-5: 'The evidence ... does not prove the apostolic mission of St Thomas in south India. It does show that there was no physical reason why Christian traders, or the Apostle himself, could not have come to Malabar in the first century.'

[2] Nataraja Guru, *The Bhagavad Gita: a sublime hymn of dialectics* (London 1961), p.8.

influence on Christianity cannot well be denied. Why then should not the possibility of influence in an eastward direction be at least considered?

In 1869 Dr Franz Lorinser published a new translation and commentary on the Gita, *Die Bhagavad-Gita: Uebersetzt und erläutert.* Lorinser confessed himself to be a relative newcomer to the field of Indology, and stated his intention as being to produce a version 'adapted to the spirit of the German language'.[3] But, much more seriously, in the course of his studies he had arrived at the firm conviction

> ... that the author of the Bhagavad-Gita not only knew and frequently made use of the books of the New Testament, but that he also worked Christian ideas and views into his system ...[4]

Lorinser therefore believed that the Gita, which the world already regarded as 'one of the fairest flowers of heathen worldly wisdom', actually owed its 'purest and most greatly praised teachings' to the New Testament! The possibility had first suggested itself in comparing the theophany of Krishna with the transfiguration of Christ; at that stage he had followed Schlegel in supposing the Gita to be of a very great age. Later authorities, however, had convinced Lorinser that it might have been composed at a much more recent date. He gradually became convinced that ' ... the theory of a Christian and particularly a New Testament influence on the composition of the Bhagavad-Gita is more than a mere hypothesis'.[5] Initially he claimed not to have expected to arrive at such a conclusion, but quoted for his comfort from Max Müller:

> If, after years of tiresome labour, we do not arrive at the results we expected – if we find but spurious and unimportant fabrications of individuals, where we thought to place ourselves face to face with the heroes of an ancient world, and among ruins that should teach us the lessons of former ages, – we need not be discouraged or ashamed, for in true science even a disappointment is a result.[6]

But having once made up his mind on the issue, Lorinser's enthusiasm knew no bounds, and in the end every resemblance

---

[3] Lorinser, *Die Bhagavad-Gita* ... (Breslau 1869), p.iv.
[4] Ibid., p.v.
[5] Ibid., p.vi.
[6] Müller, *History of Sanskrit Literature* (London 1859), p.8, quoted by Lorinser, op.cit., p.ix.

between the Gita and any part of the New Testament, however superficial, became an incontrovertible proof of direct borrowing – more than one hundred passages in all. No purpose would be served by listing them.

It might perhaps have been expected that Christians, and particularly Christian missionaries, would have showed some interest in Lorinser's theory. But they did not – at least not on the level of publications. I have been unable to find any mention of the theory in any missionary literature before 1903, and even then it was mentioned only to be rejected.[7] It was on the other hand discussed briefly by a number of Western Orientalists in the later nineteenth and earlier twentieth centuries, though again it was for the most part treated coolly and even with some contempt, perhaps because Lorinser was not an acknowledged Sanskritist. One or two scholars were prepared to allow the theoretical possibility of some slight degree of indirect influence.[8] Sir Edwin Arnold went farthest, suggesting that since in his day the weight of evidence placed the composition of the Gita in the third century A.D. '… perhaps there are really echoes in this Brahmanic poem of the lessons of Galilee, and of the Syrian incarnation'.[9] Paul Deussen, in *Der Gesang des Heiligen* (1911), also thought that a case might perhaps be made out for Christian influence on at least *five* passages (4:4-5, 9:29, 9:32 as mentioned by Lorinser, and 4:35 and 6:30, which were not among his texts). The New Testament texts involved, incidentally, were John 8:57-8, John 14:20 (three times) and Galatians 3:28.[10] Most, however, did not believe that the Christian presence in India could have antedated the compilation of the Gita. Representative was Garbe, in *Indien und das Christentum* (1914), who thought that Christianity arrived in India in the early third century at the earliest; if the Gita were a third-century compilation, as a few scholars believed, then there was *a remote possibility* of influence from that direction, but no more than that.[11]

[7] There was however a favourable note in Robinson, *History of Christian Missions* (Edinburgh 1915), p.61f.

[8] A stronger case could be argued for some degree of Christian influence on the *bhakti* movement generally. See Grierson, 'Hinduism and early Christianity', in *The East and the West* (April 1906), p.143: 'I do not myself doubt that this great step forward of the Hindu soul [*bhakti*] was due to the influence of the Christians who were then settled in the country.'

[9] Arnold, *The Song Celestial* (5th ed. London 1891), p.ix.

[10] Discussed in detail by Garbe, *Indien und das Christentum* (Tübingen 1914) p.247f.

[11] Ibid., p.249f.

10. 'A rather popular and exoteric exposition of Vedantic doctrines'

As the end of the first century of Gita interpretation in the West approached – a centenary which to the best of my knowledge no one considered celebrating – the Romantic period was declining into aestheticism. Individual quests for cosmic enlightenment were being pursued with less passion, interest having shifted to the (apparently) much firmer categories of history, progress and evolution. Following the upheavals of the late 1850s, India had settled down into the temporary role of a British commercial asset, a laboratory of imperial theory and – and on the emotional level – a proud jewel in the crown of the Queen-Empress. By the 1870s and 1880s, Western Orientalists had at their disposal rather more Indian material than they could comfortably cope with. Most of this was literary, in keeping with an age which still set supreme value on the written word, though it was coming to be complemented by the varied fruits of first-hand observation on the part of travellers, soldiers, administrators, missionaries and casual visitors.

Between about the 1850s and the 1880s, the Gita occupied a comparatively modest place in the agenda of Western Orientalism. Certainly new translations were being made, and theories were being advanced to account for its origins – Lorinser's being the most controversial. But, from the 1860s on, the Orientalists were able to concentrate on the much older and much more extensive and intriguing Vedic texts, in comparison with which the Gita appeared to be late and derivative.

The story of the discovery and appropriation of the *Veda* by Western scholars might well be told in a manner similar to this present study, though it would be less extensive. It would not on the other hand be less controversial.

There were two interrelated lines of scholarship involved. One was linguistic: the discovery, as we have noted, that Sanskrit belonged to the same 'Indo-European' family of languages as did Greek and Latin. First recognised by Sir William Jones in the late eighteenth century, the nature and extent of the relationship first emerged in 1816, with the publication of Bopp's comparative grammar. Henceforth there was every reason for scholars to see Sanskrit literature, not as an isolated phenomenon, but in relation to Graeco-Roman (and perhaps other) parallels.

At this stage, however, India appeared to have no Homer. That there existed a body of sacred material called the *Veda* (=

knowledge) was known, but its contents were not. For one thing, the *Veda* was of such sacredness that the Brahmins whose duties involved the memorising of various parts of it simply would not divulge it to *mlecchas* (= foreigners). Gradually, however, ways were found to overcome this difficulty and, from about the 1830s on, texts became available, as did the major Vedic commentary, that of Sāyaṇa. The existence of this commentary was actually something of a hindrance, since it gave interpretations of the Vedic hymns which were traditional without necessarily being historical. The actual text, too, was excessively difficult linguistically, and the would-be student who approached the hymns for the first time had to achieve a transition not unlike that between, say, Macaulay and Chaucer. For that reason alone Western students were few.

Actually, in Hindu terms the *Veda* was an extensive and complex body of material, comprising 'hymns', commentaries and various speculative writings, sorted into a number of traditional divisions. To Hindu India, the *Veda* was, and has remained, a unity, in which each part has to be interpreted in the light of all the rest.[1] To the West, on the other hand, there was apparently a clear historical and functional sequence within this material, and at the head of the category stood the 1028 'hymns' of the *Rig Veda* (the word 'hymns' is often used, though this is misleading: they were chanted by priests in the performance of rituals, not by a congregation bent on 'having a good sing'). But whatever they were, the verses of the *Rig Veda* were not, according to Max Müller, who put them into print for the first time, 'revelation' in the fullest sense:

> ... anybody who came to know them at first hand had to confess that they seem quite unfit to satisfy the religious cravings of a later generation. They contain praises of the physical gods [i.e. deified natural phenomena], they implore their help, they render thanks for benefits supposed to have come from their hands ... All this is historically and psychologically full of interest, but there is little, except here and there, of exalted religious thought, of poetry or philosophy, still less of any records of historical events.[2]

Nevertheless there was a kind of intoxication in the study of these obscure sources. Someone has spoken of 'the expulsive power of a new affection', and during the second half of the nineteenth century most Western Indologists – who had never been as interested in the Gita

---

[1] For a concise statement of the 'holistic' Hindu approach to the Veda, see Knipe, *In the Image of Fire* (Delhi 1975), passim.

[2] Müller, *Auld Lang Syne*: second series (New York 1899), p.200.

as were the Transcendentalists – moved more and more in a Vedic direction, and away from the comparative simplicity of the Gita.

Histories of Sanskrit literature written during the second half of the nineteenth century are instructive less for what they say about the Gita than for what they do not say. In most the Gita is mentioned briefly as an episode in the *Mahābhārata* but scarcely discussed in its own right.

Histories written early and late in this period both give the same impression, that the Gita was much less interesting than the Vedic literature. Albrecht Weber's history of Indian literature, dating in its first edition from the 1850s and in a later revision from 1875 (English translation 1878) devotes some 175 pages to the various branches of the Vedic literature – more than the rest of 'Sanskrit literature' in its entirety. Epic poetry rates only 13 pages, while the Gita receives only half a dozen passing references and is nowhere considered in detail. In a footnote Weber touches on Lorinser's theory of Christian influence, without actually rejecting it: chronologically, Weber stated that there was 'no forcible objection' to it, though he clearly thought that Lorinser had overstated his case.[3]

By 1900 the position had not greatly altered, to judge from A.A. Macdonell's *A History of Sanskrit Literature*. Again the Epic literature does not put in its appearance until page 233, and although more attention is paid to the *Mahābhārata* there are only four passing references to the Gita. Certainly at one point Macdonell acknowledges that 'the beauty and the power of the language [of the Gita] ... is unsurpassed in any other work of Indian literature'.[4] But that is all.

In between Weber and Macdonell we have a similar book by the Boden Professor of Sanskrit at Oxford, Monier Williams (later Sir Monier Monier-Williams), *Indian Wisdom* (1875), which includes 18 pages on the Gita. Here again the Gita is placed at the very end of the development of Indian religious literature, 'at the close of the subject of philosophy'. Williams had no theory of composite authorship; its unknown author, he wrote, was ' ... probably a Brāhman and nominally a Vaishṇava, but really a philosopher whose mind was cast in a broad and comprehensive mould'.[5] From this point on Williams gives little more than a summary, with apposite quotations, of the contents of the Gita. Williams, however, was a Christian of

---

[3] Weber, *The History of Indian Literature*, (Eng. tr. London 1878), pp.169, 235, 238, 242.

[4] Macdonell, *A History of Sanskrit Literature* (reprint Delhi 1976), p.344.

[5] Monier-Williams, *Indian Wisdom* (2nd ed. London 1875), p.136f.

warm Evangelical convictions (in 1860 he had been elected Boden
Professor in competition with Max Müller, for that very reason), and
it was only to be expected that he should take up Lorinser's theory. It
might equally be expected that he found it congenial. This was far
from so, however, though he evidently felt that his readers might
have wanted him to take a pro-Lorinser stance:

> To any one who has followed me in tracing the outline of this
> remarkable philosophical dialogue, and has noted the numerous
> parallels it offers to passages in our sacred Scriptures, it may seem
> strange that I hesitate to concur in any theory which explains these
> coincidences by supposing that the author had access to the New
> Testament or that he derived some of his ideas from the first
> propagators of Christianity.[6]

To his credit Williams was not prepared to engage in special
pleading on this issue. Resemblances were not proof of influence of
the kind that Lorinser had seen everywhere. And in addition there
was the problem of the apparent 'pantheism' of so much of the Gita.
Surely, Williams argued, any contact with Christianity must have
eliminated (or at least very much modified) this. Similar
resemblances could be pointed out from the writings of Seneca,
Epictetus and Marcus Aurelius. Otherwise Lorinser had not,
apparently, considered that 'fragments of truth are to be found in all
religious systems, however false' and that the Bible is 'a thoroughly
Oriental book, cast in an Oriental mould, and full of Oriental ideas
and expressions'. Although 'something may be said for Dr Lorinser's
theory',[7] Williams does not say precisely what, and one is left
wondering whether he may not have wanted to support it for
Christian reasons but was unable to for the sake of his Orientalist
conscience.

On the matter of authorship and dating of the Gita Williams
considered it to be the work of a creative individual, bent on shaping
an 'Eclectic School' of his own somewhere between the second
century B.C. and the second century A.D. This was no less plausible
than other theories concerning origins. But one feels that in the end
his interest in the Gita was very much prompted by its religious
contents and particularly by its insistence on personal devotion to a
personal God. Perhaps this made of the Gita a specimen of Hindu
Protestantism, with *bhakti* as the counterpart of *agapé*, Krishna as the

[6] Ibid., p.152f.
[7] Ibid., p.143, n.1.

counterpart of Christ, and faith dominant in both. Other
Orientalists had their sights set at a different level.

*

Towards the end of the first century of Gita interpretation in the
West there could be no doubt as to who was the most widely
acclaimed of scholarly Indologists. Friedrich Max Müller
(1823-1900) was German by birth, the son of the Romantic poet
Wilhelm Müller.[8] He studied classics and philosophy in Leipzig
moving later to Berlin (where he met the Upanishad enthusiast
Schopenhauer) and later still to Paris, where he studied under
Eugène Burnouf and determined upon his *magnum opus*, a complete
Sanskrit text of the *Rig Veda*. As with Wilkins' translation of the
Gita, the Directors of the East India Company were persuaded to
defray the high cost of printing and publication, and the four massive
volumes of the *Rig Veda*, with Sayana's commentary, appeared in
1849, 1853, 1856 and 1862 respectively. The remainder of his life
Müller spent in Oxford. His close personal friendship with the Royal
family brought him honours, culminating in his election to the Privy
Council. After applying unsuccessfully in 1860 for the Boden
Professorship in succession to H.H. Wilson, he was appointed a few
years later, in 1868, to a personal chair of comparative philology.
From this undemanding post he produced a long series of books and
lectures dealing with the interconnected subjects of language,
mythology, religion and human thought generally, always with the
closest of reference to his beloved and idealised India (which,
however, he never visited).

Müller's attitude to the Gita will hardly be understood apart from
his attitude to the development of Indian literature in general. At the
head of the Indian literary hierarchy stood the *Rig Veda* (from which
the other Vedas derived most of their important material).
Conceived at the dawn of man's religious awareness, they contained
a primal revelation of the Infinite, perceived if not altogether
understood:

> We see in the Vedic hymns the first revelation of Deity, the first
> expression of surprise and suspicion, the first discovery that behind this
> visible and perishable world there must be something invisible,
> imperishable, eternal or divine. No one who had read the hymns of the

---

[8] The most recent biography is Chaudhuri, op.cit.

Rig-veda can doubt any longer as to what was the origin of the earliest Aryan religion and mythology. Nearly all the leading deities of the Veda bear the unmistakable traces of their physical character. Their very names tell us that they were in the beginning names of the great phenomena of nature, of fire, water, rain and storm, of sun and moon, of heaven and earth. Afterwards, we can see how these so-called deities and heroes became the centres of mythological traditions, wherever the Aryan speakers settled, whether in Asia or in Europe. This is a result gained once for all ...[9]

It was during this 'afterwards', when pure insights were being transmuted into the crudities of mythology by means of a strange process which Müller called a 'disease of language', that the Epics had emerged, and with them, the Gita. The Vedic age had been a time of clarity, close to the dawn of things. The second period of Sanskrit literature, on the contrary, was a time of confusion and obfuscation, not without its beauties, but notable rather for its gargoyles than its graces.

Max Müller, then, although his personal background was very much in the German Romantic tradition, in no way shared the Romantic admiration for the Gita. For a greater source of inspiration than the Gita had arisen in the shape of the Veda. In retrospect he clearly believed the Gita to have been overrated. In 1882, lecturing to candidates for the Indian Civil Service, and speaking of the development of Sanskrit literature, he observed that it was a pity that this literature had first come to the attention of the West through products of this second, somewhat degenerate period in its history, which had aroused far more interest than they had properly deserved:

> It was a real misfortune that Sanskrit literature became first known to the learned public in Europe through specimens belonging to the second ... period. The Bhagavad-gîtâ ... [and other writings of the period] ... are, no doubt, extremely curious ... [and when they were discovered appeared to be of great antiquity] ... But all this has now changed.[10]

It had changed simply because of the discovery of the importance of the Veda, in comparison with which the Gita was of little practical significance.

---

[9] Müller, *Three Lectures on the Vedanta Philosophy* (London 1898), p.25f.
[10] Müller, *India, what can it teach us?* (2nd ed. London 1892), p.90.

Although the specimens of this modern Sanskrit literature, when they first became known, served to arouse a general interest, and serve even now to keep alive a certain superficial sympathy for Indian literature, most serious students had soon disposed of these compositions, and while gladly admitting their claim to be called pretty and attractive, could not think of allowing to Sanskrit literature a place among the world-literatures, a place by the side of Greek and Latin, Italian, French, English and German.[11]

It had been Burnouf in the Collège de France who had brought about the change in the West's view of the matter. Burnouf was '... the last man to waste his life on mere Nalas and Sakuntalâs', or on 'pretty Sanskrit ditties'. He had bypassed all this later literature, and had gone to the Veda and to early Buddhism, ' ... the two stepping-stones in the slough of Indian literature'.[12] Müller might have added, though he did not, that Eugène Burnouf's younger brother Émil-Louis had been left to produce a French translation of the Gita as an exercise for students of Sanskrit.

Müller was not of course saying that the Gita was to be classified among the 'pretty Sanskrit ditties' on which no scholar of repute would waste his time. He did after all commission a new translation and commentary on the Gita for his *Sacred Books of the East* series (which we shall consider shortly). But he did sum up his view of the matter in a lecture of 1882, in which he called the Gita ' ... a rather popular and exoteric exposition of Vedântic doctrines'.[13] This was hardly adequate, if only because the Gita contains a great deal which is not *Vedānta*. Doubtless also the notion of the teachings of the Gita as 'popular and exoteric' would have annoyed very many Hindus and every last Theosophist, for whom the Gita was esoteric or it was nothing.

Lecturing in a series of Gifford Lectures in Glasgow in 1888, Müller again mentioned the Gita on a couple of occasions. He repeated his point about the relative age of the Hindu sources, stating that: 'The periods which succeed the Vedic in the history of the Brahmanic religion are of much smaller interest to us [than the Vedic period proper]'.[14]

He also made brief mention of Lorinser's theory of Christian influence on the Gita. Clearly he had no strong objection on purely chronological grounds; but even if Christian influences on the Gita

[11] Ibid., p.93f.
[12] Ibid., p.94f.
[13] Ibid., p.252.
[14] Müller, *Natural Religion* (London 1889), p.541.

should prove to have been chronologically possible 'there is no necessity for admitting them'.[15] This seems a slightly odd statement as it stands. But the reasoning behind it was simple. The notion of the love of God, and of love (*bhakti*) directed toward God, had certainly 'developed' in the Semitic area out of sterner notions. Why then could it not have 'developed' equally well in India?

> It is strange that these scholars [Lorinser *et al.*] should not see that what is natural in one country is natural in another also. If fear, reverence, and worship of the Supreme God could become devotion and love with Semitic people, why not in India also?[16]

Müller's view, then, appears to have been that Christian influence might and could have been operative; but that there is no way in which it could be demonstrated, and in any case the formation of the Gita's *bhakti* doctrine could be explained perfectly well without recourse to such extreme theories.

*

Max Müller, though a fascinating figure in his own right, has relatively few readers today. The fifty volumes of *Sacred Books of the East*, however, which he conceived and edited between 1879 and 1900 are still widely used. In this series a new translation of the Gita appeared in 1882 as Volume VIII. It is interesting to note that this volume was the only one in the whole series to be undertaken and completed by a non-European.

Earlier, in 1875, Kāshināth Trimbak Telang had produced a Western-style verse translation of the Gita, with a lengthy introduction. His *SBE* volume contained, as well as the Gita, two other episodes from the *Mahābhārata*, the *Sanatsujātīya* and the *Anugītā*, each supplied with a shorter preface. His 36-page introduction to the Gita occupied a point midway between Western and traditional Indian modes of interpretation. It took a moderately conservative position on matters of date, while lamenting the lack of 'that reliable historical information ... which one naturally desires, when entering upon the study of any work'. He admitted that precise information about the age and origin of the Gita was impossible to come by:

[15] Ibid., p.99.
[16] Ibid., p.97

... there is no exaggeration in saying, that it is almost impossible to lay down even a single proposition respecting any important matter concerned with the Bhagavadgîtâ, about which any ... consensus can be said to exist.[17]

The Gita may or may not have been a genuine part of the original *Mahābhārata*, the textual problems being similar to those surrounding the Homeric question.

On the whole, Telang was content to defer to his editor Max Müller in locating the Gita among the later Upanishads, at a time prior to the formation of philosophical systems in India. This explained (after a fashion) the existence of 'several passages in the Gîtâ which it is not very easy to reconcile with one another'.[18] The author of the Gita seems not even to be conscious that these inconsistencies exist. Thus: ' ... the Gîtâ is a non-systematic work, and in that respect belongs to the same class as the older Upanishads'.[19] Linguistically it is in a different class from classical Sanskrit literature. It maintains a certain distance from the Vedas, but mentions (in 9:17) only three, and not four, Vedas, the *Atharva* being omitted. But on internal grounds, Telang thought it pre-Buddhist, though not necessarily earlier than the Buddha himself:

> The Upanishads, with the Gîtâ, and the precepts of Buddha appear to me to be the successive embodiments of the spiritual thought of the age, as it became more and more dissatisfied with the system of mere ceremonial then dominant.[20]

Telang was reluctant to speculate about the *earliest* date at which the Gita might have been composed. Concerning the *latest* date, he went back much farther than most Western scholars, however:

> We may ... lay it down as more than probable, that the latest date at which the Gîtâ can have been composed, must be earlier than the third century B.C., though it is impossible to say at present how much · earlier.[21]

---

[17] Telang, *The Bhagavadgîtâ* ... (2nd ed. Oxford 1898), p.1f.
[18] Ibid., p.11.
[19] Ibid., p.13.
[20] Ibid., p.27.
[21] Ibid., p.34.

11. 'So have I read this wonderful and spirit-thrilling speech,
    By Krishna and Prince Arjun held, discoursing each with each;
    So have I writ its wisdom here, – its hidden mystery,
    For England; O our India! as dear to me as She!'

In 1885, the Gita had been in Western hands for a century, and it was in a way appropriate that the unofficial centenary should have been marked by the publication of what is perhaps the most celebrated, and in some ways the most influential, of Gita translations, Edwin Arnold's *The Song Celestial.*

Sir Edwin Arnold (1832-1904) was one of those many Victorian authors and poets who enjoyed enormous fame in their heyday but are little read today.[1] In fact almost the only thing for which he is remembered now is the indirect role he played in introducing Gandhi to the Gita. In his autobiography, Gandhi wrote: 'I have read almost all the English translations of it [the Gita], and I regard Sir Edwin Arnold's as the best. He has been faithful to the text, and yet it does not read like a translation'.[2] It is also significant that Gandhi was persuaded to tackle the Gita by certain Theosophical friends since, as we shall in due course see, the Theosophists were particularly well disposed toward the Gita and, not unnaturally, regarded Arnold as an ally.

Arnold's sympathies were, however, Theosophical only indirectly and by implication. He might perhaps be characterised as the broadest of a notable generation of broad-church Anglicans. Influenced by such men as F.D. Maurice and F.W. Farrar, while at Oxford he had been tutored by A.P. Stanley, later Dean of Westminster and a close friend of Max Müller. In 1852, at the age of twenty, he won the Newdigate Poetry Prize for a poem entitled 'The Feast of Belshazzar', which began:

Not by one portal, or one path alone
God's holy messages to men are known.[3]

The years 1857-60 he spent in India as the Principal of the Government School (Deccan College) in Poona, after which he returned to England and a career in journalism and freelance writing. His interests were worldwide, and his personal philosophy

---

[1] Wright, *Interpreter of Buddhism to the West: Sir Edwin Arnold* (New York 1957).
[2] Gandhi, *The Story of my Experiments with Truth* (Ahmedabad 1969), p.50.
[3] Wright, op.cit., p.18.

tended more and more in the direction of a form of Transcendentalism. In 1868 he married the great-niece of William Ellery Channing, and he was a friend of Emerson and of Walt Whitman. It is perhaps also worth noting that his youngest son became a convert to Theosophy.

Arnold's most celebrated excursion into the world of Oriental thought, his poem on the Buddha, *The Light of Asia* (1879), was written, so a recent biographer tells us, 'as a witness for religious liberalism'.[4] Not unnaturally this gained him a considerable following among the Theosophists, for whom the most extreme liberalism was part of the very air they breathed; and he was very well received by the Theosophists (many of whom were at this time crypto-Buddhists) on a visit he paid to India and Ceylon in 1885-6. But by this time he had further added to his reputation as a literary Orientalist through his version of the Gita.

In preparing to write his version, Arnold worked chiefly with the English translation of John Davies (1882), which he stated to be 'truly beyond praise for its fidelity and clearness', and appears not to have used Wilkins. *The Song Celestial* is of course a free verse paraphrase rather than a literal translation (though it does embrace a few minor ventures in textual criticism). It has been said that

> ... there is no literary translation that has superseded this one. Today it is the only one of Arnold's poems that is still regularly read and the one on which his future reputation must rest.[5]

It is sometimes pointed out that, subsequent to this effort, Arnold 'reverted' to Christianity when he wrote *The Light of the World* about the life of Jesus. Was it because he had gone too far in his expressions of sympathy for the East, and wished to try to redeem a heretical reputation? I hardly think so. Certainly he was aware that he had been criticised for his involvement with Islam, Hinduism, Buddhism and Japan. But to assume that he came to believe that there had been an imbalance in his religious life which was in need of correction is to misunderstand the nature and ethos of late-nineteenth-century liberal Christianity, which in fact saw the great non-Christian traditions less as competitors to the Christian Gospel than as legitimate preparations for its message. The Gita therefore had its own integrity and value, just as had the life of the Buddha; but it was not, in Arnold's view, sufficient of itself, since it

[4] Ibid., p.71.
[5] Ibid., p.127.

needed to find its fulfilment in Christ. Significantly, in *The Light of the World* Arnold makes the Magi who brought their gifts to the infant Jesus not Zoroastrians (or whatever) but Buddhists!

Perhaps Arnold's personal religion was 'magnificently unorthodox', at least by the officially accepted standards of his day; but he was not alone among Christians in seeing the Gita as 'celestial' and therefore as worthy of the deepest respect. That he finally, in *The Light of the World*, appeared to be moving back to what his contemporaries mostly regarded as uniquely revealed Truth is to misread the evidence. He was not moving back, but (as he saw it) onward and upward, in the manner of all nineteenth-century religious evolutionists.

*

With the publication of *The Song Celestial* we have come to the end of the first century of Gita interpretation in the West. It is worth noting that practically everything on which we have reported actually took place, geographically speaking, *in* the West, and as the result of a series of more or less adequate translations. Two things have perhaps emerged from the survey thus far. On the one hand – and leaving the early Deists on one side – we have seen a resolute attempt on the part of some readers to build the central message (or what appeared to be the central message) of the Gita into a system of instinctive, 'transcendental' philosophy, and to find in it support for a world-view already held for other reasons; to this enterprise, questions of authorship and dating were strictly irrelevant. On the other hand, we have seen the beginnings of an attempt to subsume the Gita under the categories of literary criticism. Approached from this angle, the general view appears to have been that although nothing could be said with certainty about the absolute age or the origin of the poem, it had apparently begun life as an Upanishad. Its philosophical and religious foundation had therefore seemingly been Vedāntic, though it had afterwards had elements of Sāmkhya, Yoga and Bhakti incorporated into it. In neither case was the Gita considered as a *living* Hindu scripture, part of the on-going religious tradition of Hindu India.

At about this time, however, a great change developed, due almost entirely to the new role which the Gita began to play, from the 1880s on, in the life of the Indian national movement. Certainly some of the old questions continued to be asked and answered by Western scholars; but to their number were added many new questions about the capacity of the Gita to continue to be a source of religious and political inspiration. Two new interpretative schools emerged, in support of or in response to the challenge of what some called 'the neo-Krishna movement': the Theosophists on the one hand and the Christian missionaries on the other. A characteristic of Gita interpretation from now on was that it centred in India itself rather than in the West; also, it was characterised by a new spirit of give-and-take (at its best, dialogue, at its worst, mud-slinging). Before 1885, remarkably few Hindus were prepared to rise up and challenge the West's reading of the Gita. After 1885, not only did the Gita rapidly become the supremely authoritative, and in some respects all-sufficient, holy scripture for the whole of 'educated India'; it became equally the nationally-aware Hindu's declaration of independence, a symbol of nationhood on which the *mleccha* might comment only with the greatest circumspection. The Western interpreter therefore was apt to find his theories and his constructions challenged and contradicted – perhaps most notably in respect of the Gita's unity and with regard to the questions of 'the Krishna of history'.

In short, while from 1785 to 1885 the Gita appeared to the West as a fascinating document, after 1885 it became a powerful symbol, to which the older canons of interpretation were capable of answering only in part.

Part Two
1885–1985

5

Renaissance, Radicalism and Theosophy

12. 'A common and well-read scripture for the whole of educated India'

That the Gita was not always the universally read source of Hindu learning, spirituality and devotion which it appears to be today is a statement still capable of inspiring some incredulity (not to say hostility) both inside and outside India. The question at issue, however, is not whether before the 1880s the Gita was known, revered and interpreted within India – clearly it was all three – but whether it was *widely* known, and by whom. Traditionally the Gita had been accessible to the learned, to the *pandits*, as 'the essence of all the Shastras'. In popularity, however, the Krishna of the *Purāṇas* had the upper hand of the charioteer-god of the Gita in the wider community of Vaiṣṇavism; while in Shaiva and Shakta circles the emphasis lay elsewhere.

In the India of the mid-to-late nineteenth century, access to the higher reaches of scholarship, or even to the vestibule of literacy, was becoming more common than before; but thanks to the deliberate policy of the British administration to offer higher education only through the medium of the English language, traditional Hindu learning was still kept separate from the official educational process. This led to two consequences: on the one hand, to the creation of a newly-literate class, who were at least capable of absorbing impulses and impressions through the medium of the printed page; but on the other, to the separation of that same class of young men from the roots of their own religious tradition. To the orthodox, these were 'men without a *dharma*'; they were problems to themselves and their families; but by the turn of the century they were also becoming a problem to the administration, since they provided a fertile soil for the growth of nationalism and anti-British feeling generally.

Before about the 1880s, radical political agitation was not a great problem. Certainly there was national sentiment, but it was generally felt that it could be reconciled with loyalty to the British Crown, and that political activity could be contained within constitutional limits. In 1866, for instance, the Brahmo leader Keshab Chandra Sen was cheered in Calcutta when he expressed his nation's 'deepest gratitude and loyalty to the British nation and Her Most Gracious Majesty Queen Victoria' and spoke of her 'beneficient Christian administration', which had proved 'not only a political, but a social and moral blessing' to India.[1] Twenty, and still more, forty years later this type of language was no longer acceptable.

*

By common consent, the beginnings of the 'renaissance' in Hindu thought, and of its active alliance with the Indian national movement, are taken to date from 1875, the year in which both the Árya Samáj and the Theosophical Society were founded. Interestingly enough, neither was particularly influential in Bengal, then or later; nor did either make any great use of the Gita. To Dayánanda Sarasvatī, the founder of the Árya Samáj, the Gita was not properly part of the canon of Hindu scripture at all;[2] the Theosophists for their part awoke to the significance of the Gita (as we shall see shortly) only after their removal from New York to Adyar, by way of Bombay. This was not until 1883. But by then the Gita was beginning to fulfil a new role in India, a role not altogether dissimilar from that of the *Thoughts of Chairman Mao* in the China of the Cultural Revolution.

It is slightly odd to reflect that in, say, 1880 the Gita was almost as easily accessible to the West as it was to the average Hindu in India. Some at least of those Hindus who were later to give their unstinting devotion to the Gita and its teachings first read it in an English translation. Gandhi certainly did; so too in all probability did Sri Aurobindo.

---

[1] Sen, *The Brahmo Somaj: four lectures by Keshub Chunder Sen* (London 1870), p.17.

[2] Dayánanda was passionately opposed to image-worship in any form, and appears to have rejected the Gita (though the matter is somewhat disputed) on the grounds of its non-Vedic character on the one hand and its links with the popular worship of Krishna on the other. On Dayánanda, see Jordens, *Dayánanda Sarasvati, his Life and Times* (Delhi 1978).

From the early 1880s, however, this situation changed. At first slowly, and after 1900 with the force of an avalanche, the Gita came to occupy a position (which in the popular mind it has since that day never lost) as the undisputed statement of all that is most central and most important in the Hindu world of ideas. That this movement more or less coincided with the period during which Swami Vivekānanda was acknowledged as Hinduism's major world spokesman (some indeed going so far as to claim that 'Hinduism' – as a relatively simple, unified concept, that is – was actually created by Vivekānanda at the World's Parliament of Religions in Chicago in 1893) is not without interest. For just as Vivekānanda reduced Hinduism to a set of relatively simple, though all-embracing, principles, so there emerged a Scripture which possessed those same qualities of drama, simplicity and comprehensive scope. That scripture was the Gita. By 1912 C.F. Andrews was able to write that, *within living memory*, the Gita, ' ... which a century ago was scarcely known outside the learned circle of the pandits ... has been elevated from a position of comparative obscurity to that of a common and well-read scripture for the whole of educated India'.[3] A few years earlier, in 1907, another liberal Christian missionary, Bernard Lucas, had recorded that although among the common people of India the Krishna of the *Purāṇas* still held sway over the heart, 'amongst the more thoughtful classes it is the Krishna of the Bhagavad Gita who embodies the highest thought and the most profound wisdom'.[4] By this time, however, the popularisation of the Gita had been in process for something like thirty years.

*

This is not the place to enter into a detailed account of the early years of the Indian national movement, the history of which has been fully documented, both from the Indian and the British angles. Commonly it is held to have begun in the 1880s with the formation of the Indian National Congress – interestingly enough, on the initiative of Theosophists and Theosophist sympathisers. The Congress's medium of debate was English, its constituency middle-class and its political stance nothing if not constitutional. But its progress was slow, and for many years it had a minimal influence on India's masses. This did not escape the attention of a younger and

[3] Andrews, *The Renaissance in India* (London 1912), p.146.
[4] Lucas, *The Empire of Christ* (London 1907), p.100.

more radical generation of Indian nationalists, who at the turn of the century threw themselves into the task of mobilising the Indian proletariat and freeing the movement from what they regarded as being its constitutional shackles. The trouble was that the common people of India had no political consciousness and no notion of India as a single country. Above all there appeared to be no common symbols around which the common people could be gathered for political action. This the radicals set themselves to remedy.

In the event two separate but interconnected groups of symbols were pressed into service as a matter of political expediency.[5] One was centred on the notion of the holy Motherland as a goddess, a *shakti* (power, emanation) of the Supreme – this view was canvassed chiefly in Bengal – the other on the idea of the *avatāra* (descent, incarnation) of the Supreme, sent to earth to free the country from moral corruption and the neglect of *dharma* (law, custom), and on Krishna as the chief of those *avatāras*. Since it was in the Gita that the *avatāra* idea had reached its fullest fruition, the Gita acquired in the process a new status as a manual of political action. We must now look at this development in a little more detail since, had it not taken place, the next phase of Western interest in the Gita would not have been provoked in the way it was.

*

Leaving the Indian National Congress on one side, the radical nationalists of the 1890s and after were found to be chiefly in two parts of India. One was Bengal, the other Maharashtra. In Maharashtra there was a military tradition which Bengal, generally speaking, had never possessed. Consequently the Maharashtrian movement, led by Bal Gangadhar Tilak (1856-1920), had a markedly military character and stressed qualities of bravery, warfare, physical strength and (of course) independence from foreign rule.[6] Initially the Bengali movement was more literary than overtly military, though a measure of guerilla warfare was subsequently generated there too, partly in imitation of the Maharashtrian ideology of action; but in both there was the tendency which we have already mentioned – the quest for powerful symbols of national

---

[5] For a fuller discussion, see Sharpe, 'Avatāra and Śakti: traditional symbols in the Hindu renaissance', in Biezais (ed.), *New Religions* (Uppsala 1975), pp.55-69.

[6] On Tilak, see Cashman, *The Myth of the Lokamanya: Tilak and Mass Politics in Maharashtra* (Berkeley 1975).

endeavour. Some of the radical movement's prototypes were found in Russia, Italy and Ireland; the symbols, however, had to be Indian.

Tilak's device was to create new popular festivals in honour of figures from India's mythical and historical past. The most important of these festivals was for a seventeenth-century Maratha chieftain and general, Shivaji, who had fought against Muslim armies, partly (so Tilak claimed) inspired by the Gita. But there was a problem here. The exploit for which Shivaji was chiefly renowned could so easily be seen as an act of base treachery. In 1659 his army was besieged in the fortress of Pratapgarh by the Muslim forces of Afzal Khan. Shivaji arranged a truce in order to meet Afzal Khan face to face, ostensibly to discuss the terms of a surrender; but he was armed, and he killed his defenceless counterpart, leaving his army without a leader so that it was easily overcome.

Now this was perhaps of little enough consequence in itself. In time of war no one has ever been seriously expected to adhere to every last standard of civilised behaviour. But no state of declared war existed in India in the 1890s. More seriously, Tilak claimed that in acting as he did Shivaji was adhering strictly to the precepts of the Gita, and perhaps implied that others who read the Gita might also be permitted to act in the same way.

The moral and ethical aspects of the assassination of Afzal Khan were widely discussed at the Shri Shivaji Coronation Festival of 1897 and were reported in Tilak's journal *Kesari* for 15 June 1897. The only part of the discussion that need concern us here is that in which the Gita entered the argument. Tilak is recorded as having said:

> Great men are above the common principles of morality. These principles fail in their scope to reach the pedestal of great men. Did Shivaji commit a sin in killing Afzal Khan? The answer to this question can be found in the *Mahabharata* itself. Shrimat Krishna's teaching in the *Bhagavad Gita* is to kill even our teachers and our kinsmen. No blame attaches to any person if he is doing deeds without being motivated by a desire to reap the fruit of his deeds. Shri Shivaji Maharaja did nothing with a view to fill the small void of his own stomach [from interested motives]. With benevolent intentions he murdered Afzal Khan for the good of others ... [This may be legally wrong, but it is morally defensible.] ... Do not circumscribe your vision like a frog in a well. Get out of the Penal Code, enter into the extremely high atmosphere of the *Bhagavad Gita*, and then consider the actions of great men.[7]

[7] Cited in McLane, *The Political Awakening in India* (Englewood Cliffs, 1970), p.56.

It could be, and was, argued that Tilak had not actually instructed anyone to behave in this violent way. Nevertheless the possible implications were clear enough (or seemed so, to the British authorities), and Tilak was shortly to spend eighteen months in gaol. It was not many years before hot-eyed revolutionaries (whom we might perhaps style 'freedom fighters') went into battle, and some even to the gallows, accompanied by at least the memory of some verses of the Gita.

The impression made by Tilak's speech on the Government of India was confined to its possible consequences in the realm of law and order. Summing up in the 1920s – by which time Tilak had died in exile and the leadership of the national movement had passed to Gandhi – Sir Valentine Chirol wrote:

> This was the first public glorification of political murder under British rule. Government ... paid no serious attention to it, even when Tilak was chosen shortly afterwards to be a member of the Bombay Legislative Council; but it was to bear fruit.[8]

The murder of Mr Rand and Lieutenant Ayerst on the day of Queen Victoria's Diamond Jubilee (27 June 1897) was attributed by Chirol directly to Tilak's influence; the murderer, Damodar Chapekar, Chirol described as ' ... a young Chitpawan Brahman whom Tilak's fiery denunciation of British oppression had worked into a state of murderous frenzy'. This may or may not have been strictly true; but at least a connection had been established, and for the first time (though not for the last) the Gita had come to be associated with revolutionary violence.

It might be as well to point out, however, that the question of 'killing in a righteous cause' had been taken up in other no less authoritative Hindu scriptures, notably the Laws of Manu (*Mānavadharmaśāstra*). In view of the widespread post-Gandhian Western assumption that all Hindus subscribe to the notion of *ahimsā* (non-violence), it may be useful to quote some verses from *Manu*:

> Twice-born men may take up arms when (they are) hindered (in the fulfilment of) their duties, when destruction (threatens) the twice-born castes (*varṇa*) in (evil) times.
> In their own defence, in a strife for the fees of officiating priests, and in order to protect women and Brāhmaṇas; he who (under such circumstances) kills in the cause of right, commits no sin.
> One may slay without hesitation an assassin who approaches (with

[8] Chirol, *India* (London 1926), p.100ff.

murderous intent), whether (he be one's) teacher, a child or an aged
man, or a Brāhmaṇa deeply versed in the Vedas.

By killing an assassin the slayer incurs no guilt, whether (he does
it) publicly or secretly; in that case fury recoils upon fury.[9]

The Sanskrit word here translated as 'assassin' is *ātatāyin*, literally
'one whose bow is drawn (to take another's life)' and, by extension,
'one who is bent on inflicting harm upon one's person, property or
family'. If and when an *ātatāyin* can be identified, then the person
threatened has the absolute right in Hindu law to use violence in his
own defence, regardless of the status of the 'assassin' concerned.
This was what Shivaji had done in respect of Afzal Khan; the
implication was that other Hindus might do likewise in respect of
some other *ātatāyin*.

But *Manu* was, despite everything, a less well known scripture than
the Gita; and what was needed was less a code of conduct, however
heroic, than an example to emulate. Krishna was one such example;
Shivaji was another.

Tilak's mature exposition of these principles was not written down
until he had been sent into exile in Burma by the British government
in India. In late 1910 and early 1911 he compiled his massive
commentary on the Gita, *Srimad Bhagavadgītā-Rahasya*, first published
in Marathi in June 1915, though not in English until 1936. The Gita,
Tilak announced, is 'essentially a treatise on Right or Proper
Action'; it 'expounds the root principles of the present Vedic
Religion'; further, ' ... there is no other work in the whole of
Sanskrit literature, which explains the principles of the present Hindu
Religion in as succinct and yet as clear and unambiguous a manner
as the Gītā'.[10] Not surprisingly, perhaps, Tilak made no claim to have
followed any of the traditional interpretations. Above all his
commentary concentrated, not on metaphysics, but upon action –
action which might well involve the use of violence in a just cause.
Quoting *Manu* VIII on the question of the *ātatāyin*, Tilak claimed
that such an assailant might well be one who harms minds, and not
merely the one who attacks bodies; that self-protection is of more
importance than *ahimsā*; and that the nation needs warriors:

> In short, the ordinary rules of morality are not always sufficient, and
> even the most principle (*sic*) maxim of Ethics, namely that of

[9] Bühler, *The Laws of Manu* (Sacred Books of the East, vol.25, reprint New York
1969), p.314f. (Manu VIII:348-51).
[10] Tilak, *Srimad Bhagavadgītā-Rahasya* (3rd ed. Poona 1971), p.xxv.

Harmlessness, does not escape the necessity of discrimination between the duty and the non-duty.[11]

The heart of the matter is to act in accordance with one's own duty, without the desire for personal reward. Passivity will achieve nothing: 'That by which everybody will be harmed is neither Truth nor Harmlessness.'[12] And: 'The law of Truth consists in performing one's promises and vows.'[13]

*

In Bengal, where the political focus of the national movement was to be found, around 1880 the dominant ideas among the Hindu intelligentsia were still basically Western – a combination of rationalism and individualism which had little taste or time for nationalist agitation. The eclectic and intellectual Brahmo Samaj was still a power to be reckoned with. But new impulses were just beginning to be felt. In the words of Bipinchandra Pal:

> … the conflict of political interests between the new generation of English-educated Indians and the British officialdom in the country, and the more fundamental cultural conflict between European modernism and Indian mediaevalism soon provoked a revolt against this foreign domination in the wake of which rapidly followed a national self-consciousness which, in the first flush of its recently found pride of race and culture, commenced to repudiate whatever was foreign, irrespective of the intrinsic reason and value of it, and set up a defence even of those social institutions and religious and spiritual tendencies that had previously been openly repudiated as false and harmful.[14]

The Brahmo Samaj itself was becoming more and more traditional. The Theosophical Society began in the 1880s to affirm ancient Hindu values in a way which to Hindus was both welcome and unexpected. And, most important, there grew up in Bengal itself a literary school, led by Bankim Chandra Chatterjee, in which fresh attention was drawn to the life and character of Krishna, and to the Gita as the supreme record of Krishna's teachings. Interestingly

[11] Ibid., p.44.
[12] Ibid., p.47f.
[13] Ibid., p.52.
[14] Pal, *Memories of my Life and Times* (Calcutta 1973), p.343f.

enough, Bankim Chandra's approach to the Gita was intended to be thoroughly 'modern', and his prototype was Ernest Renan's *Life of Jesus*. Again according to Bipinchandra Pal,

> Bankim Chandra followed, or more correctly closely imitated Renan in his presentation of Shree Krishna ... Bankim Chandra ... first formed in his own mind a picture of Shree Krishna as the Ideal Man; he applied this picture to his examination of the Krishna legend current among our people, and rejected everything that did not harmonise with it.[15]

Bankim Chandra's major contribution was his *Krishnacharitra* (1886, 2nd ed. 1892), which as well as depicting the historical Krishna as the 'ideal man', also argued for an extremely early date for the composition of the Gita, on what appear to be totally inadequate grounds. In 1887 there appeared an epic poem on Krishna's youth, *Raivatak*, by Nobin Chandra Sen, and many further such publications became available down to the turn of the century, culminating in S.C. Mukhopadhyaya's *The Imitation of Sreekrishna* (1901), a collection of daily readings combining texts from the Gita, the *Mahābhārata* and the *Bhāgavata Purāṇa*. Throughout this literature, Krishna was presented along the lines laid down by Bankim Chandra as a hero, a philosopher-statesman, an example for emulation and above all as the spiritual champion of the people of India in her time of trial.[16]

That time of trial arguably began with the passing in 1883 of the Ilbert Bill, an apparently insignificant move to remove the distinction between Indian and British members of the Covenanted Civil Service, but a move which aroused violent opposition from the European community in India. Racial feeling, always latent, burst violently to the surface. Speeches were made by Europeans against Indians, and increasingly by Indians against the British administration. At this time, relations between India and the British administration suffered their first serious blow since the 1850s, and Indian politicians became more and more convinced that agitation – even violent agitation – was the only political method likely to achieve results. For Bengal's part, this new approach was to reach a climax in the years between 1900 and 1910 and an especial point of violence in connection with the 1905 partition of Bengal. Throughout these twenty or so hectic and tragic years the message of the Gita

---

[15] Ibid., p.345.
[16] Farquhar, *Gita and Gospel* (Calcutta 1903), p.67ff.

was to serve as an inspiration and an exhortation to selfless service on behalf of India.

An important passage was that in which Krishna says: 'For whensoever right (*dharma*) declines ... and wrong (*adharma*) uprises, then I create myself. To guard the good and to destroy the wicked and to confirm the right (*dharma*), I come into being in this age and in that (*yuge-yuge*)' (Gita 4:7f.). *Adharma* could so easily be identified as foreign rule, *mleccha dharma*, and Krishna's cause as the nationalist cause. Indeed, as we shall see shortly, not only was Krishna seen as the nation's own *avatāra*; the national movement as such could equally be seen as an *avatāra* of the supreme.

But the Gita was only one of the sources in which the character of Krishna is delineated; and previously the Gita had been overshadowed in popular devotion by the *Bhāgavata* and *Viṣṇu Purāṇas*. The Bengali literary movement was eclectic in its use of sources, drawing from Gita and *Purāṇas* impartially; but by the end of the century the Gita had gained the upper hand in point of popularity, especially among the educated and half-educated classes from which the nationalist cause in Bengal was mainly recruited.

One important reason for this was simply that the Gita was of a convenient size and could therefore be marketed cheaply and sold widely to a new reading class, that of students and ex-students. The masses, of course, continued to receive their teachings orally rather than through the medium of the printed page, and were in any case extremely hard to arouse to political action, but there were good reasons why the Gita should have been made available to the intellectuals. One was simply to counteract the already widespread influence of Christian missionary literature directed at that same class.[17] Another was that the Gita provided an intellectual, and not merely an emotional, justification for political action – though admittedly the emotional dimension was of great importance as a form of *bhakti* directed toward the cause of the motherland.

A second major reason for the growing popularity of the Gita was that, in the Gita, Krishna was depicted as a mature leader of men and not simply as a youthful and mischievous 'trickster'. As such he could not but appeal to budding politicians.

A third reason was a matter of content. The Gita of course contained many strata of doctrine, but one of its central teachings was the doctrine of *nishkāma karma*, or selfless endeavour. This in the situation of the time was the ideal complement to personal devotion

---

[17] On the Christian missionary movement of the time, see Sharpe, *Not to Destroy but to Fulfil* (Uppsala 1965), p.194ff.

to Krishna – a total commitment to the cause of the restoration of *dharma*, that cause with which Krishna himself had always been identified as an *avatāra*. This commitment, ideally at least, did not aim at personal rewards or personal profit: the cause itself was all-in-all. Other closely related political lessons derived from the Gita included the notion (hinted at, as we have seen, by Tilak) that killing in the pursuit of a righteous cause did not bring guilt upon the killer. This at least some nationalists undoubtedly believed.

Thus there emerged a string of political and semi-political commentaries on the Gita. But it was enough in many cases simply to display a picture of Krishna instructing Arjuna on the battlefield of Kurukshetra, the field of *dharma*, in order to convey the desired meaning. This was the case with Aurobindo Ghosh's journal *Karmayogin*, while the revolutionary paper *Juguntur* had Gita 4:7 as its motto.

13. 'Our chief national heritage'

Among India's political interpreters of the Gita in the first decade of the twentieth century, by far the most persuasive and the most radical was Aurobindo Ghosh (1872-1950).[1] Born in Calcutta as the third son of a surgeon, he had been sent to England at the age of seven to receive a western education. From 1879 to 1885 he lived with an English family in Manchester, proceeding thereafter to St. Paul's School in London and King's College, Cambridge. He did not return to India until 1893. In one respect he was by that time thoroughly westernised: namely, in his complete mastery of the English language, which always remained his chief medium of communication. But in another important sense during his years at Cambridge he had become a fervent Indian patriot. He chose not to enter the Indian Civil Service (the story was that despite high academic marks, he had deliberately failed the riding test) and returned to India to teach and write. Until 1906 he worked in Baroda, moving in that year to Calcutta, where he became the undisputed intellectual leader of the radical wing of the Indian national movement. He was jailed for a year in 1907-8 for suspected complicity in a bomb incident, and in February 1910, probably fearing further imprisonment, he fled to the French territories of, first, Chandernagore and later Pondicherry, where he remained for

---

[1] See Karan Singh, *Prophet of Indian Nationalism: a study of the political thought of Sri Aurobindo Ghosh* (Bombay 1970).

the rest of his life. Although many suspected that he was still politically active behind the scenes, it was as the sage Sri Aurobindo that he was known. He continued to write voluminously from the shelter of his Ashram, building up a universal philosophy and eventually creating the 'city' of Auroville as the physical heart of an emerging world union based on heightened consciousness. India's independence day was celebrated (though by design or accident it is hard to say) on his seventy-fifth birthday, 15 August 1947, and he died five years later.

During the years of his most active political involvement (1905-10) Aurobindo wrote and spoke repeatedly about the Gita, and undoubtedly did much to continue the impulse begun twenty years earlier and promote further the Gita's role in the Indian national movement. Others might echo his words and his sentiments; others before him might have made similar use of some of its verses and teachings; but in no other writer of the period do we find the same combination of force and lucidity. The Aurobindo of this period was the supreme political idealist, though at the same time he was acutely aware of the needs of *Realpolitik*.[2] Desiring freedom for his country above all else, he was prepared to seek ideological support wherever he could find it. His Indian prototypes included Ramakrishna, Vivekānanda and Tilak. Vivekānanda he commended for his 'plan of campaign' of attempting to make India 'the first power in the world' ('Who else has the undisputed right to extend spiritual sway over the world?' he asked.)[3] Tilak's Shivaji festivals he saw as being helpful, not as excuses for open revolt, but certainly for 'the cultivation of courage'.[4] Annie Besant he also praised as ' ... the cultured and eloquent lady whom the Mahatmas have placed at the head of the new Theosophist Church ...'[5]

From time to time before his imprisonment in 1907 we find Aurobindo apostrophising the Gita in terms generally reminiscent of Tilak. For instance he asserted in a celebrated article on 'The morality of boycott' (*Bande Mataram*, 26 December 1906) that 'the Gita is the best answer to those who shrink from battle as a sin, and aggression as a lowering of morality', and that 'politics is the ideal of the Kshatriya [warrior], and the morality of the Kshatriya ought to govern our political actions'.[6] But this was hardly a new departure,

[2] Ibid., p.112: 'No way for achievement of the main object was abhorrent or unwelcome to him.'

[3] Aurobindo, *Bande Mataram: Early Political Writings* vol.1 (Sri Aurobindo Birth Centenary Library I, Pondicherry 1972), p.428.

[4] Ibid., p.476.

[5] Ibid., p.234f.

[6] Ibid., p.124f.

and at this time Aurobindo was more concerned with the image of India as the sacred *shakti* (power, emanation) of the Eternal than with any details of Gita interpretation. Where he mentioned Krishna in these years, it was almost always the youthful, popular Krishna of the *Bhāgavata Purāṇa* he had in mind. In the almost one thousand pages of the first volume of the *Sri Aurobindo Birth Centenary Library* (covering his writing during the period down to May 1908) there is virtually no mention of the Gita. Indeed one might almost conclude that up to this time Aurobindo scarcely knew the Gita, or at least that he was far too much of the sceptic to pay it much attention.

After May 1909 all this changed. His acquittal in the Alipore Conspiracy Case (which the British insisted was less a matter of his proven innocence than of the non-availability of concrete evidence of complicity) was early in the month. On 30 May he delivered in Uttarpara a speech under the auspices of an organisation called the *Dharma Rakshini Sabha* (Society for the Protection of Dharma) in which he told of an experience which had come to him as a result of reading the Gita. Previously he had been a secular young man. But now he saw things differently:

> Then He placed the Gita in my hands. His strength entered into me and I was able to do the Sadhana [spiritual discipline] of the Gita. I was [able] not only to understand intellectually but to realise what Sri Krishna demanded of Arjuna and what He demands of those who aspire to do His work ... to renounce self-will and become a passive and faithful instrument in His hands ... I realised what the Hindu religion meant.[7]

Krishna, who had granted him this vision, had said to him:

> 'I am in the nation and its uprising and I am Vasudeva, I am Narayana, and what I will, shall be, not what others will. What I choose to bring about, as human power can stay.'[8]

The heart of Krishna's message to Aurobindo in gaol, however, had been that the core of Hindu religious teaching – the *Sanātana Dharma* – was true and universal. ('When it is said that India shall be great, it is the Sanatan Dharma that shall be great. When it is said that India shall expand and extend herself, it is the Sanatan Dharma that shall expand and extend itself over the world.')[9] And since it

[7] Aurobindo, *Karmayogin: Early Political Writings* vol.2 (Sri Aurobindo Birth Centenary Library II, Pondicherry 1972), p.3.
[8] Ibid., p.6.
[9] Ibid., p.8.

was in the Gita that this teaching was most clearly, comprehensively and concisely stated, the role of the Gita in this new phase of India's religious life was self-evident. Certainly Aurobindo's discovery of the universality of the Gita was somewhat belated, but once the revelation had been made it was never again to leave him.

An intriguing possibility presents itself at this stage. What *version* of the Gita had Aurobindo read in gaol? It was almost certainly not a Sanskrit or Bengali text, for a couple of months later he was still confessing his own inability to address a Bengali audience in their own language: English was still his means of communication. A few years earlier Gandhi had read the Gita for the first time in Arnold's English translation. It may well be that Aurobindo too owed his first encounter to an English translation: namely, that of the Theosophist leader Annie Besant. The first of her translations had been available since 1904, with an emphasis strikingly similar to Aurobindo's. Pre-dating both, in 1903, she had written, and the Board of Trustees of the Central Hindu College, Benares had published, 'an advanced text book of Hindu religion and ethics', under the title *Sanātana Dharma*.

This may of course be the merest coincidence, but we cannot dismiss the possibility that the politically experienced and resourceful Annie Besant may at this critical stage have opened up to Aurobindo some of the possibilities latent in the Gita. Aurobindo's frequent use of the phrase *sanātana dharma* ('the eternal law') – hardly common earlier – is one pointer in this direction. But, more generally, the activist tone of Annie Besant's writings can hardly have been unattractive to Aurobindo at this time; her evolutionism too may well have appealed to him. But Mrs Besant was still, despite everything, an upholder of the values of the British Empire, and this Aurobindo can only have found distasteful.

Be all this as it may be, during his last couple of years of activity in Bengal Aurobindo lost no opportunity to proclaim the message of the Gita and to hold up for emulation its ideal of the *karmayogin* – one who works for the restoration of *dharma* without thought of personal reward. He also emphasised the dimension of *bhakti* (loving devotion) in the message of the Gita as an attitude of mind equally applicable to the patriot's feeling for his sacred motherland. *Bhakti* is far more an emotional than a rational matter; Bankim Chandra Chatterji had been born 'in a country surcharged with *bhakti*', wrote Majumdar, and Aurobindo too in the political sphere attempted 'to open the flood-gate of emotion'. For a time he succeeded:

... to Aurobindo's call the Hindus responded from all over India. *Ananyā-bhakti*, or unswerving devotion, henceforth became the basis of nationalism: not patriotism based on a pride in the past history of this ancient land.[10]

The father of Bengali literature, Bankim Chandra Chatterjee, had published in 1882 a novel, *Ananda Math* (Eng. tr. *The Abbey of Bliss*, 1906), set in the days of the 'Sannyasi Rebellion' of the 1770s.[11] It told the story of a band of ascetics, consecrated to the service of the sacred Motherland, and included the poem 'Bande Mataram', which became the motto, the slogan and the anthem of the national movement. In Aurobindo's translation from 1909 it read in part:

Mother, I bow to thee!
Thou art wisdom, thou art law,
Thou our heart, our soul, our breath,
Thou the love divine, the awe
In our hearts that conquers death.
Thine the strength that nerves the arm,
Thine the beauty, thine the charm.
Every image made divine
In our temples is but thine.[12]

This was the ideal face of the national movement – passionate, sentimental, devoted to the divine images of the holy motherland (as Durga) and the powerful hero (Krishna). But from the *Western* point of view there was another face – a face of contempt for constituted authority, ever liable to resort to the use of violence and not averse to quoting the Gita in its attempted justification. It may well be that, as Sumit Sarkar has said, ' ... the conventional image of the Bengal revolutionary as advancing with a bomb in one hand and the Gita in the other seems more than a little overdrawn'.[13] And yet this same author acknowledges that at the 'combined religious school and bomb factory' set up in 1908 by Barindrakumar Ghosh (Aurobindo's brother) at Muraripukur (otherwise Maniktala or Maniktola), a suburb of Calcutta, spiritual exercises based on the Gita 'were given almost as much importance as bomb-manufacture'.[14] For a time vows were also taken on the Gita during initiation into revolutionary

[10] Majumdar, *Bhakti Renaissance* (Bombay 1965), p.77f.
[11] Farquhar, 'The fighting ascetics of India', in *Bulletin of the John Rylands Library* (Manchester 1925) p.431ff.
[12] Langley, *Sri Aurobindo* (London 1949), p.124.
[13] Sarkar, *The Swadeshi Movement in Bengal, 1903-1908* (New Delhi 1973), p.484.
[14] Ibid., p.486.

secret societies.[15] Small wonder then that as these circumstances became known the British authorities came to view the Gita with grave suspicion, less for anything it contained than for the symbolic use that was being made of it.

On the eve of his departure from the political scene, Aurobindo penned this defence of the Gita:

> Mr. Risley repeats a charge we have grown familiar with, that the Gita has been misused as a gospel of Terrorism. We cannot find any basis for this accusation except the bare fact that the teaching of the Gita was part of the education given by Upendranath Banerji in the Maniktola garden. There is no evidence to show that its tenets were used to justify a gospel of Terrorism. The only doctrine of the Gita the Terrorist can pervert to his use, is the dictum that the kshatriya must slay as a part of his duty and he can do it without sin if he puts egoism away and acts selflessly, without attachment, in and for God, as a sacrifice, as an offering of action to the Lord of action. If this teaching is in itself false, there is no moral basis for the hero, the soldier, the judge, the king, the legislature which recognises capital punishment. They must all be condemned as criminals and offenders against humanity. It is undoubtedly true that since the revival of religious thought in India the Gita has ceased to be what Mr. Risley calls it, a transcendental philosophy, and has been made a rule of life. It is undoubtedly true that selflessness, courage, a free and noble activity have been preached as the kernel of the ethics of the Gita. That teaching has in no country been condemned as ignoble, criminal or subversive of morality, nor is a philosophy of any value to any sensible being if it is only transcendental and cannot be lived. We strongly protest against the brand of suspicion that has been sought to be placed in many quarters on the teaching and possession of the Gita, – our chief national heritage, our hope for the future, our great force for the purification of the moral weaknesses that stain and hamper our people.[16]

The overtly political period in the history of Gita interpretation was not of long duration and its extremist phase was even shorter, lasting for no more than half a dozen or so years. This was chiefly because, as a repository of revolutionary doctrine, it lacked immediate appeal. Its doctrine that one ought not to strive after precisely determined goals was not calculated to appeal to the impatient; and its metaphysics were obviously distasteful to the socialist wing of the national movement. The figure of Krishna might well serve as a

---

[15] Ibid., p.485.
[16] Aurobindo, *Karmayogin* ... (Pondicherry 1972), p.400f.

national hero; but the attitude of subservience which the Gita also taught inspired far fewer heroic deeds than the group around Aurobindo and his brother might have wished – quite apart from the cloak-and-dagger atmosphere of the time and the sheer chaotic inefficiency which so often seemed part of Bengali politics. The masses simply would not react in the desired way; as Sumit Sarkar says, even before 1910 'the contradiction between subjective desires and objective conditions almost inevitably pushed the movement into the path of political dacoity and individual violence'.[17] The revolutionaries turned their back on religion; the religious lost whatever interest in revolution they might perchance have had. Sarkar is surely right, that the use made during this period of the Gita and other traditional symbols was a curious phenomenon, representing the effort of a group of intellectuals 'utterly westernised in outlook and way of life striving by a tour de force to turn overnight into orthodox Hindus, imparting to age-old rituals and symbols a political content which was in fact quite untraditional'[18] – and being ignored by the truly orthodox in so doing! They also alienated more internationally-minded Hindus, notably Rabindranath Tagore.

This was not the way ahead for India. And yet, when all this has been said, the radicals did succeed in bringing the Gita even more forcefully to public attention, inside and outside India.

14. 'The Krishna stories belong to what is least admirable and moral in Indian religious literature'

By the first decade of the present century the Gita was universally acknowledged in India (and especially in Bengal) as the Hindu Scripture *par excellence*, the concentrated summary of all that was most central in Hindu doctrine and experience. It was likewise in process of becoming an element in a political manifesto, a religious support for a movement of national liberation. There were four interlocked attitudes involved, which we may summarise:

1. Hindu *dharma* is threatened by *mleccha dharma*, and the Gita is a treatise about the restoration of *dharma*. In the Gita, Arjuna was in the end told that he ought to fight in the name and for the sake of Krishna: so too should all those who hold their motherland dear.

2. If violence is involved, then so be it. The *Laws of Manu* had always laid down that if a person could be identified as an *ātatāyin*,

---

[17] Sarkar, op.cit., p.488.
[18] Ibid., p.495.

that is, a man of violence who is threatening one's family and property, then one has the absolute right to kill him without guilt or penalty accruing. British rule is a collective *ātatāyin* and may therefore be disposed of by whatever means are appropriate.

3. In any case, according to Krishna in the Gita, one cannot harm the eternal soul of an enemy by killing him: only his body. The warrior has no cause to grieve over being in this way part of a natural process.

4. Actions carried out without the desire for personal reward are never registered negatively in the bank of *karma*, nor are actions carried out in the name and for the sake of Krishna. As an *avatāra*, Krishna's function was the restoration of *dharma*. But this is equally the function of the national movement, which thereby becomes an *avatāra* itself.

It was not to be expected that the majority of Westerners – and in this case for 'Westerners' we may read 'British' – in India would be able to react positively to this cluster of ideas. The British administration found it more of an irritant than a real threat and reacted predictably by jailing anyone suspected of 'subversion'. But there were two other groups of Westerners whose reactions were much less predictable and who were in any case opposed to each other on almost every point. On the one hand there were the members of the Theosophical Society, who had no history of involvement in things Indian before the 1880s, but who at the turn of the century came out firmly on the side of the Indian national movement while remaining supportive of the British imperial ideal (this at least was the view of Annie Besant, who led the movement). On the other there was the Protestant Christian missionary corps, active in India for many years already, many of whom might have been able to support the national movement, had it not chosen to ally itself with the Hindu revival, but saw in Hinduism 'the old enemy', which could do nothing but harm to the Indian national cause. It should be added that Theosophists and missionaries disliked one another intensely and continued to do so for many years.

What the two had in common, however, was that both were forced to react to what the national movement was doing, and both were compelled to take up the study of the Gita in the process.

The longer history of Protestant missions in India needs to be borne in mind, for one important reason. In the earlier part of the nineteenth century, as we have seen, the Gita was hardly a 'popular' scripture in the full sense of the word. The central figure of Krishna, on the other hand, *was* well known as a focus of popular Hindu piety. For the Gita is not the only Hindu Scripture in which Krishna appears. He is equally the central figure in the vast narratives of the *Bhāgavata* and *Viṣṇu Purāṇas*. There, however, he is not the mature warrior, philosopher and statesman, but the youthful 'trickster', the supernaturally-born child whose divine powers had been revealed in a succession of extraordinary exploits. It was this youthful Krishna of the *Purāṇas* who had long been the focus of popular Hindu devotion on the Vaiṣṇava side, not least in Bengal, where he had been celebrated in festivals involving human intimacy and the relaxation of normal social restraints. There was a powerful erotic side to this type of Krishna devotion, and this was reason enough for Christian missionaries in the nineteenth century to react against it with horror and disgust.

Thus when Christian missionaries spoke of Krishna they tended inevitably to speak of him with the Krishna of the *Purāṇas* in mind. They could have read the Gita in one or another translation, but there is practically no evidence that most of them did. Griffith's polyglot edition of 1849 seems to have made little impression, perhaps because of its size and consequent expense. And in any case there was always the trickster-figure in the background to disturb the image. Thus when we read in 1855 that India's population 'is morally unhealthy, nor can we be surprised that they are so when the deteriorating influences to which, under the name of religion, they are subjected, are brought to remembrance',[1] we may surmise that the anonymous writer has been either contemplating a *lingam*, or the sculptures on the Khajuraho temple, or a *Holi* festival – or possibly all three.

Lest it should be thought that this was merely an exercise in Victorian prudery, it may be worth pointing out that Hindu reformers could be equally scathing. As early as 1817 Ram Mohun Roy had composed *A Defence of Hindoo Theism* in which he had this to say about the popular worship of Krishna, 'the most adored of all the incarnations, the number of whose devotees is exceedingly great':

> His worship is made to consist in the institution of his image or picture, accompanied by one or more females, and in the contemplation of his history and behaviour, such as his perpetration of murder upon a female of the name of Pootna; his compelling great number of married and unmarried women to stand before him denuded; his debauching them and several others, to the mortal affliction of their husbands and relations; his annoying them, by violating the laws of cleanliness and other facts of the same nature.

---

[1] *Church Missionary Intelligencer* vol.6 (1855), p.76.

The grossness of his worship does not find a limit here. His devotees very often personify (in the same manner as European actors upon stages do) him and his female companions, dancing with indecent gestures, and singing songs relative to his love and debaucheries. It is impossible to explain in language fit to meet the public eye, the mode in which Muhadéva, or the destroying attribute, is worshipped by the generality of the Hindoos: suffice it to say, that it is altogether congenial with the indecent nature of the image, under whose form he is most commonly adored.

The stories respecting him, which are read by his devotees in the Tuntras [Tantras], are of a nature that, if told of any man, would be offensive to the ears of the most abandoned of either sex.[2]

Of course this diatribe, though it began with Krishna, ended with Śiva (Mahādeva). Nevertheless the point of criticism was the same: the flouting in *Purāṇas* and *Tantras* alike of the ground rules of morality, especially sexual morality. If Krishna was bad, then Śiva was worse.

No missionary ever had a good word to say about the Krishna of the *Purāṇas*, and if the Krishna of the Gita were the same Krishna then the youthful exploits attributed to him ruled him out as a hero, let alone as a god. A people whose main need in life was for moral purpose needed to look elsewhere for guidance. Protestant missionaries in India between the 1880s and 1930s maintained a consistent angle of attack and in the end a fairly monotonous chorus of abuse. At a missionary conference held in London in 1888 an American Presbyterian, F.F. Ellinwood, having characterised Krishna as 'a good-natured, rollicking Bacchus, romping with the shepherdesses [the Gopis were not shepherdesses, but an American could scarcely have said 'cowgirls'] around their camping fires, and setting at defiance all laws of decency and morality', went on to assert that, in answering mankind's need for a mediator in this way, 'the father of lies has given a stone for bread, and a serpent for fish'.[3] In 1906 another Christian described Krishna as an immoral rogue, 'a compound of Lothario and Jack the giant-killer'.[4] A couple of years later, when the British Congregational missionary Sydney Cave came to India, he found that a prescribed Christian textbook in the Tamil language contained the following: 'You say that Krishna

---

[2] Roy, *Translation of the Veds*, etc. (2nd ed. London 1832), p.149f.

[3] *Report of the Centenary Conference of the Protestant Missions of the World ... London, 1888* (London 1889) vol.1, p.54.

[4] Grierson, 'Hinduism and early Christianity', in *The East and the West* (April 1906), p.150.

gave lofty teaching to Arjuna, but who was that Krishna? – a murderer, an adulterer, a thief.'[5] In 1912 we find Charles Freer Andrews, who could hardly be accused of lack of sympathy for India and things Indian, and was later to become one of Gandhi's closest friends, writing that 'there has been no more potent source of degradation in the whole of Hindu religious history than the vile legends concerning Krishna in the *Purānas*. They have corrupted the imagination of millions of the human race, and their evil influence is still potent in India at the present time.'[6] Two decades later Edgar W. Thompson was still writing in practically identical terms: 'The Krishna stories belong to what is least admirable and moral in Indian religious literature. They are not merely unethical and offensive to the conscience: they appear silly and tedious to the reason and taste of the modern man.'[7] In 1938 a German missionary of the Leipzig Missionary Society, Gustav Staehlin, described the Krishna of the *Purānas* as 'a mighty hero who performs a number of astounding heroic deeds, surrounded by a halo of grotesque miracles' and as 'more an emancipation from all moral laws than an ideal pattern'.[8] And as a final example we may refer again to Sydney Cave, who spoke in his Haskell lectures of 1939, *Hinduism or Christianity?* of 'the lewd Krishna of the later *Purānas*'.[9]

The point need not be elaborated further, except to say that whatever most missionaries in India in the earlier part of the twentieth century may have thought about the Krishna of the Gita, always at the back of their minds was the image of the sexually hyperactive Krishna of the *Purānas*, 'the very incarnation of an oriental sensualist'.[10] Before about 1900 practically no missionary was prepared to allow that the two Krishnas might have little or nothing to do with each other, or that the Gita could be read without referring to the *Purānas* at all.

Of course, Protestant missionaries of the period were almost all the products of the Evangelical revival. Most had little formal education and no training in Sanskrit or Indian thought generally. To them religion was largely a matter of public and private morals,

[5] Cave, *Hinduism or Christianity?* (London 1939), p.22.
[6] Andrews, *The Renaissance in India* (London 1912), p.81f.
[7] Thompson, *The Word of the Cross to Hindus* (London 1933), p.147f.
[8] Staehlin, 'Avatar and Incarnation', in *The Way of Christ* (January 1938), p.15f.
[9] Cave, op.cit., p.22.
[10] Jhaveri, 'Krishna, the Hindu ideal', in *East and West* [a different journal from that quoted in n.4 above] (April 1902), p.657. It should perhaps be added that on this occasion, the words were written by a Hindu bent on presenting Krishna as 'the ideal man', and pouring scorn on the missionary stereotype in the process.

and to the extent that Hindu scriptures appeared to sanction moral laxity approval was almost bound to be withheld. Trained to be literal-minded in matters of faith and uncompromising in matters of conduct, the realms of myth, symbolism and esoteric meanings were closed to them. Not for one moment could most nineteenth-century missionaries even conceive that an image, a ritual, a scriptural passage could have more than one meaning, or that behind the curtain of initiation teachings might be given which bore practically no relation to the public face of popular religion.

The Theosophists' attitude could not have been more different. It is safe to say that most Theosophists were as little impressed as was the average missionary in India by the forms of expression of popular Hinduism. But they were at least prepared to try to penetrate to a region of 'hidden meanings' behind the facade. Often it seemed that the one interpretation they were never prepared to accept was that which was most obvious and most natural – at any rate they could and did go to extraordinary lengths in quest of the hidden essence behind the manifestations of Hindu religion. This habit of mind ensured that in their reading of the Gita (or any other sacred scripture) the Theosophists would be unaffected by the kind of moral scruple from which the missionary corps was never wholly free.

15. 'The book of the philosophy of the *Logos*'

Much of later Indian history might have been different if in 1879 the leaders (and virtually the only members) of the Theosophical Society, founded in New York four years earlier, had not chosen to settle in India. In making for Bombay these leaders, Madame H.P. Blavatsky and Colonel H.S. Olcott, may have been attempting to distance themselves from an unfriendly America. But once arrived – and particularly after their further move to Adyar, a suburb of Madras, in 1883 – they found themselves in a position to exercise a great deal of influence on the emergent Indian national movement. The extent of that influence has never been properly documented, partly because of the reluctance of later generations of Indian nationalist leaders to admit too great a dependence on foreign ideological aid. Bipinchandra Pal, however, was one who acknowledged that the Theosophists' message, ' ... coming from the representatives of the most advanced peoples of the modern world ... at once raised us in our own estimation and created a self-confidence in us that commenced to find easy expression in a new propaganda ...'; and further that Theosophy had helped to remove the inferiority complex from India's educated classes, a complex produced by modern European culture.[1]

The early leaders of the Theosophical Society were demonstrably not British (Madame Blavatsky indeed being suspected for a time of being a Russian spy); still less were they Christians. The extent of their acceptance of first Buddhist and later Hindu ideas (or what they thought were Buddhist and Hindu ideas) became well known; and in time they were able to do a great deal to convince Hindu India that not all Europeans and Americans were India's natural enemies. Had they arrived in India fifty years earlier or fifty years later, they would not have been able to make anything like the same impression. As it was, their timing, though doubtless accidental, could not have been bettered. Setting up their organisations in India at precisely the moment when the Gita was being added to the armoury of the national movement, they could not but react. And from the 1880s the Theosophists began, cautiously at first and with a great deal of Hindu help, to add their interpretations of the Gita to those of the pandits, the nationalists and the missionaries.

Although some of this Theosophical material was written by Hindus and many of its arguments were not strictly Western at all, the Theosophical Society itself originated in the West and was led by Westerners. There is therefore no reason not to include it in this survey.

*

During the first decade of Theosophical work in India the Society's leaders were wisely reluctant to set themselves up as authorities on Indian religion; and when they did venture into this field it was more often in a Buddhist than a Hindu direction. Their initial focus of interest had been elsewhere, centred on the Kabbala, Hermetic writings and 'the occult' generally. While they were still in America there is no evidence that they had ever given the Gita more than a passing thought; clearly it came to their attention only after their move to India. In an editorial in *The Theosophist* in 1882, we find Blavatsky writing:

> We never set ourselves up as teachers of Aryan philosophy and science … Our great desire has been to foster a school of native students of, and writers upon, those majestic themes, and to arouse into vital

[1] Pal, *Memories of my Life and Times* (Calcutta 1973), pp.344, 401f.

activity the latent talent which abounds in the Indian race especially.
Such will continue to be our endeavour ...[2]

This policy explains why the first Theosophical interpreters of the
Gita were all Indians, to whom the Western leaders were for the
most part content to defer. But there was clearly a growing interest
in the Gita in Theosophical circles. As yet there was no hint of
possible political dimensions, however. Madame Blavatsky's
passionate concern was to uncover 'occult meanings' in scriptures,
and although in the 1880s the Brahmanas seemed to her to be a
more promising quarry of occult doctrine (which indeed they were)
she had begun to take the Gita seriously. In August 1883 she
announced that since the hidden meaning of what she called the
'Aryan shastras' was so important her journal was about to begin to
expound 'the esoteric meaning of the text of the *Bhagavad Gita*'.[3]
'Some of our readers, especially Hindus,' she added, 'will be
doubtless astonished to discover the almost perfect identity between
the concealed sense of the immortal epic [the Gita, not the
Mahābhārata] and the Arhat Tibetan Doctrine ...'[4]

Substantially the same point emerges in a little flurry of words
which took place in the following year, 1884. The cause was the
publication of Sinnett's *Esoteric Buddhism* and a review by W.Q.
Judge. The review in question had referred to some of the doctrines
of esoteric Buddhism as being contained in the Gita. Blavatsky was
led to announce that ' ... positively *all* the doctrines given in *Esoteric
Buddhism*, and far more yet untouched, are to be found in the *Gita*,
and not only there but in a thousand more known and unknown
MSS. of Hindu sacred writings'.[5] This was of course a matter of
principle – that there is one secret doctrine, and that wherever the
illuminated mind has been at work, there it is capable of being
discovered by anyone who possesses the key. The Gita is as yet not a
special case, and although in *The Secret Doctrine* we may read that
there are 'things occult' hidden in 'that great Indian esoteric work',[6]
there is surprisingly little mention made of the Gita, and when it is
mentioned it is on a basis of the work of T. Subba Row.

*

[2] Blavatsky, editorial in *The Theosophist* (August 1882), p.263.
[3] *The Theosophist* (August 1883), p.265.
[4] Cf. Blavatsky, *Collected Writings* (vol.5 (Pasadena 1950), p.68.
[5] Blavatsky, *Collected Writings* vol.6 (Pasadena 1954), p.147.
[6] Blavatsky, *The Secret Doctrine* vol.1 (Pasadena 1952), p.620.

Subba Row was the first of a number of Indian commentators on the Gita to work under Theosophical patronage. We may pass over Damodar K. Mavalankar, who refers occasionally to the Gita in his writings but without breaking any new ground. Subba Row, however, was considerably more influential, and already in 1883 we find him expounding in the pages of *The Theosophist* the 'real meaning of the allegory of the war between the *Pandavas* and the *Kauravas*'. The Pandavas (Arjuna's branch of the family) represent the higher, spiritual part of man, and his enemies, the Kauravas, represent the lower, while Krishna is 'the only manifested deity, the *logos* in each man's heart'.[7]

Aside from the rather curious use of the Greek word *logos* in this context (which must surely have been as a result of Subba Row's association with Madame Blavatsky), one is struck most of all by the relative simplicity of this approach. Allegory as a method was neither exclusively Hindu nor particularly Theosophist. But it did have the advantage of flexibility, as well as being well known to Hindus. As K.P. Mukerji was to put it in 1891, every Hindu knows that the shastras have several meanings, aside from the obvious one, and that the Gita has several occult meanings, one of which is that ' ... it is an allegory in which the trials, sufferings and different stages of progress of an aspirant are given out in detail'.[8]

At all events, for a few years in the 1880s Subba Row was the Theosophical Society's Gita expert. Sometimes he corrected, and provided tart comments on, other people's Gita articles. But in 1885 he delivered a lecture on the Gita to the T.S. Convention, and in December 1886 he lectured again at much greater length on the same subject. It was the text of these 1885 lectures which went to make up his influential book *The Philosophy of the Bhagavad Gita* (1888).

Subba Row's interpretation of the Gita is thoroughly allegorical. This is not to say that he discounts the historical element, though he clearly regards it as of comparatively little importance, at least when compared with the view that the Gita is a discourse about the relationship of body and soul, matter and spirit, or (in his own Theosophical terminology) man, the monad (*ātman*) and the Logos (the ultimately Real). In general terms what the Gita depicts is the struggle between the human spirit and the lower passions in the physical body. Vyasa, he writes (Vyasa being of course the

[7] Subba Row, in *The Theosophist* (October 1883), p.322f.

[8] Mukerji, 'The Bhagavad Geeta as an allegory', in *Lucifer* (March-August 1891), p.110f.

traditional author of the *Mahābhārata*), '... looked upon Arjuna as man, or rather the real monad in man; and upon Krṣna as the Logos, or the spirit that comes to save man'.[9]

The Gita, then, is to be seen as a discourse addressed by a *guru* to a *chela* determined upon renunciation – though some may find it hard actually to see Arjuna's original troubles in this light. 'Krishna is teaching Arjuna what the Logos in the course of initiation will teach the human monad, pointing out that through himself alone is salvation to be obtained.'[10] At this point again we can see the influence of Blavatsky, who viewed the ancient esoteric writings as an interlocked chain of initiatory instructions, to be interpreted in a Gnostic light and with the use of Gnostic terminology. (We may add perhaps that the possible initiatory use of the Gita is an option to which scholars might give much more attention, though initiation into a school of *bhakti* rather than a Gnostic fellowship.) When Subba Row goes on to say that this view 'implies no idea of a personal God', we may also see a combination of Vedantic and Theosophical-Gnostic ideas – Vedantic because the Real is high above the limitations of personality and *nāmarūpa*, Theosophical for similar reasons, though with the added polemical edge of a dispute with accepted Judaeo-Christian theology. In either case, the conventional and obvious *bhakti* interpretation is bypassed, in the implicit belief that it represents an undeveloped an un-Gnostic alternative suitable only to the uninitiated. This same point of view is expanded – though, we are bound to say, somewhat haphazardly – in Subba Row's later lectures. But there is one further point in his introductory presentation which is at least worthy of a mention: namely, his emphasis on the importance of numerology.[11] This is not an unimportant point, and adds a dimension of genuine esotericism, which Western commentators otherwise have totally overlooked.

In his more extended lectures on the Gita, delivered at the eleventh T.S. Convention in December 1886 and first published in *The Theosophist* in 1887 on the basis of shorthand notes, Subba Row adds more details, but these often get lost in a welter of generalisations. For instance, we have to read forty-five pages of the subsequent book before coming to the first mention of the Gita! Again he emphasises the Logos, the monad, and Gnostic (esoteric) initiations:

[9] Subba Row, *Esoteric Writings* (2nd edition Adyar 1931), p.93.
[10] Ibid., p.98.
[11] Ibid., p.100f.

All the initiations that men ever invented were invented for the purpose of giving man a clear idea of the *Logos*, to point out the goal, and to lay down rules by which it is possible to facilitate the approach to the end towards which nature is constantly working.[12]

The Gita, then, is 'the book of the philosophy of the *Logos*'.[13] Krishna actually *is* the Logos, descending to the plane of the soul in order to accomplish some great purpose.[14] And spiritual development and progress actually entitled one to a union with the Logos, and then 'there is, as it were, a sort of reaction emanating from the *Logos* for the good of humanity'[15] – though this does not appear to be central, when compared with personal spiritual culture. Beyond this Subba Row does not go; it is true that he hints at a deeper mystery hidden in the Gita, but since he expressly states that he does not intend to expound it we are left guessing as to what it might have been. All he does is to refer vaguely to H.P. Blavatsky's *The Secret Doctrine* for elucidation – though according to Eek he found the first draft of that book 'both diffuse and chaotic'.[16] And certainly *The Secret Doctrine* as we have it refers to the Gita only in passing, and then by way of Subba Row's lectures. Apparently we have here the classical case of two locked boxes, each of which contains the other's key!

On some occult matters, Subba Row's interpretation of the Gita did not, despite Blavatsky's support, meet with universal approval among Theosophists. I am myself in no way qualified to deal with the details in question, though the main bone of contention appears to have been his espousal (on the basis of the Mandukya Upanishad) of a fourfold, rather than a sevenfold, division of the infinite cosmos. At all events controversy ensued. He was charged by at least one American Theosophist with 'Brahman narrowness', and partly on this account left the Society shortly afterwards.

*

With Damodar and Subba Row the third outstanding Indian Theosophist of the early days was the Bengali Brahmin Mohini Mohun Chatterjee, a descendant of Ram Mohun Roy and also

[12] Subba Row, *The Philosophy of the Bhagavad-Gita* (2nd edition Adyar 1921), p.43.
[13] Ibid., p.60.
[14] Ibid., p.49f.
[15] Ibid., p.63.
[16] Eek, *Damodar and the Pioneers of the Theosophical Movement* (Adyar 1965), p.664.

related to the Tagore family. By profession a lawyer, Mohini lectured widely in Europe and America, and in the 1880s he was regarded as one of the great intellectual forces in the society. At first he was held in high esteem by Madame Blavatsky, but things subsequently went sour (for reasons which I do not propose to enter into) and he too subsequently slipped out of the Society – though not before he had made his contribution to Gita study.

Subba Row, as we have seen, was concerned with the inner meaning of the Gita. At this time, it seems that for those Theosophists who did not read Sanskrit, reference was still made to the century-old translation of Charles Wilkins, though there were others. Mohini set himself to produce a new translation, which appeared in 1887 as *The Bhagavad Gita, or The Lord's Lay.* (A second edition also appeared in 1887, and it was reprinted in New York as recently as in 1960.) It contains little actual interpretation, though it does strongly affirm the transcendent unity of all religion, urges that the Gita ought to be read alongside the Bible, and in all essentials follows Śankara, 'the spiritual chief of modern India'.[17] Its conclusion is that 'human nature is one, God is but one, and the path of salvation, though many in appearance, is really but one'.[18]

Whether or not Mohini's translation was intended to become a standard Theosophical version is not quite clear, but my guess is that it appeared under something of a cloud, at least as far as India was concerned. Therefore it was always more important in America than in India.

*

During the 1880s, then, we have been able to observe among Theosophists a growing interest in the Gita as a 'book of initiations' and a quarry of Gnostic doctrine, which needed to be interpreted not historically but allegorically if its secrets were to be unlocked. We find Theosophical writers (most of them Indians) following a mixture of occult and traditional Hindu lines of interpretation, working out allegories and ocasionally calculating the age and origin of the Gita on the basis of astrological data. The question of the historicity of Krishna was sometimes dealt with in the same way.

In the late 1890s there was a discussion conducted partly in the pages of the *Madras Christian College Magazine* and partly in *The Theosophist* about the relative historicity of Christ and Krishna. At

[17] Chatterjee, *The Bhagavad Gita* (New York 1887), p.xi.
[18] Ibid., p.276.

this time it was not uncommon for Christians to compare the historicity of the two, not altogether to Krishna's advantage, and to assert that the New Testament belongs to the area of fact, the Gita to the realm of fiction. Why Hindu (and Theosophical) writers should have risen to this bait at all is not clear, since on their view absolute Reality does not belong within the realm of historical cause and effect at all. But a challenge is sometimes very hard to resist, particularly if an opponent is felt to be gaining some advantage from it. This particular controversy was an excellent example of two parties arguing at cross purposes, using completely different methods and arriving at opposite conclusions. P.C. Mukherji, the main Theosophical spokesman, spent a fair amount of time being rude to his Christian antagonists but finally used astrological data to show ' ... the date of his [Krishna's] incarnation to have been at least about 1400 B.C., if not 3102 B.C., which is our record still in vogue in our almanacs'.[19] One is tempted to comment that a method which can get a variability of 1700 years over the matter of an individual's birth cannot really be called precise. But that is not the point. The point is that Theosophists (and other Hindus) were becoming aware that there are historical problems connected with the Gita – problems concerning date of composition, the actual personality of Krishna, Arjuna and the other heroes, and the actual context in which the work was first written (or composed). This, as we have seen, was the type of question that had come to fascinate Western scholars. But most Theosophists at this time were either unaware that these questions were being asked, or were prepared to accept some improbable answers. In this case the astrological 'data' amounted to little more than a single incidental reference in X:35, in which Krishna says: 'Mārgaśirṣa am I of months.' The procedure then was to calculate how long it had been since that particular constellation had coincided with the vernal equinox. The arguments are set out in full in a series of articles published in *The Theosophist* in 1908, though Mukherji's article of 1897 rests on the same assumptions. Since these were more a matter of mythical than of actual time, they convinced only the faithful.

*

The first generation of Indian Theosophists seem not to have been particularly interested in possible political implications of the Gita,

---

[19] Mukherji, in *The Theosophist* (November 1897), p.109.

though Subba Row had concluded his 1886 lectures by asserting
that in the light of the Gita much of popular Hinduism had not served
to 'promote the welfare of the Hindu nation' but had demoralised it
and sapped it of its spiritual strength ' … and have led to the present
state of things, which, I believe, is not entirely due to political
degeneration'.[20] There were echoes here of Ram Mohun Roy and
Dayānanda Sarasvatī, both of whom had seen that moral and
national renewal for India's part needed to be preceded by religious
renewal.

16. 'A clear-tongued prophecy of Christ'

Orientalism and Christian missions have generally approached India
from different, if not altogether opposite, angles. The one has sought
knowledge and understanding, the other persuasion and, wherever
possible, conquest. And yet the difference has never been absolute.
Among Orientalists previously mentioned in these pages some of the
best-informed were also warm supporters of Christian missions: Max
Müller lectured on missions in Westminster Abbey, and Monier
Monier-Williams, as we have noted, was a staunch Evangelical.
Among active missionaries in India, however, there were relatively
few who had the training or the capacity to qualify as Orientalists.
Before 1900 there were practically none. Even if they had had the
inclination most were simply too busy to acquire the necessary
specialist knowledge. And always there was the problem of religious
presuppositions and prejudice; by 1900 there had been a certain
relaxation in attitudes previously hard and inflexible, but liberal
missionaries were still few and unrepresentative.

The first British Protestant missionary in India to qualify as an
Orientalist in his own right was likewise the first to attempt an
independent interpretation of the Gita since Griffith in the 1850s. His
name was John Nicol Farquhar (1861-1929).[1] In 1903 and 1904
Farquhar published three separate essays on the Gita, *Gita and Gospel*
(1903), *Permanent Lessons of the Gita* (1903) and *The Age and Origin of
the Gita* (1904), at which time he was a YMCA Secretary working in
Calcutta. He had entered missionary service in 1891 and had taught
for a decade at the London Missionary Society's school at
Bhowanipur, Calcutta, before joining the YMCA in 1902. He had

[20] Subba Row, *The Philosophy* … , p.126f.

[1] On Farquhar, see Sharpe, *J.N. Farquhar: a memoir* (Calcutta 1962), *Not to Destroy
but to Fulfil* (Uppsala 1965).

been a Scholar of Christ Church, Oxford, and was proficient in Sanskrit and Bengali; time and time again he urged on his missionary colleagues the necessity of acquiring linguistic proficiency, of deep study of the phenomena of Hinduism, and of Christian centrality in their interpretation. Later he was to write three outstandingly important books, *The Crown of Hinduism* (1913), *Modern Religious Movements in India* (1915) and *An Outline of the Religious Literature of India* (1920). On this occasion, however, we shall concentrate on his 75-page book *Gita and Gospel*, which comprises five short chapters and an appendix.

The appendix is in some ways the most important part of the book, since in it Farquhar gives a brief account, based mainly on Bengali sources, of the rise of the literary 'Neo-Krishna' movement. The first essays he lists are those published by Bankim Chandra Chatterji in 1884, after which he provides publishing details of twenty-six books and poems which appeared between 1886 and 1903. He does not claim that Krishna and the Gita were previously an insignificant component in Bengali religious life; merely that the Gita 'leaped into greater prominence than ever'[2] as a result of impulses coming ultimately from Ramakrishna and Keshab Chandra Sen and inspired on the literary level chiefly by Bankim Chandra. But he also sees clearly that the 'Krishna renaissance' is part of a larger whole:

> This period has witnessed the appearance of the whole Neo-Hindu movement, with its literature, lectures, societies and missionary propaganda, the rise of the Indian National Congress and of the social reform movement, the advance of native journalism to its present extraordinary influence, and the establishment of the native unaided colleges, which have so seriously changed the balance of influence in Higher Education. Neo-Krishnaism, then, is one result of the operation of that potent spirit whereby India has become conscious of her unity, and her sons have been roused to a vigorous defence of all that they have inherited from the past.[3]

Concerning the Bengali literature itself, Farquhar places it in two classes, *historical* and *traditional*. Only two works, he says, treat the historical question with any seriousness at all. Tattvabhusan's *Hindu Theism* (1898) and Jogindranath Mukherji's *The Young Men's Gītā* (1900) both assign to the Gita a fairly late date. 'All the rest of the books on the list fall into the second class; for they hold the

---

[2] Farquhar (under pseudonym: Neil Alexander), *Gita and Gospel* (Calcutta 1903), p.67.
[3] Ibid., p.70.

traditional position about Krishna.'[4]

It is at this point that Farquhar's chief criticism, less of the Gita itself than of its devotees, becomes evident (as it had done in the first chapter of the book): that there *are* criteria by which the age of the Gita can be determined, at least approximately; but that that age in no way coincides with the period of the historical event to which it is claimed to relate, namely, the battle of Kurukshetra. The traditionalists he sees as being forced to resort to desperate arguments in support of the traditional origins of the Gita. For instance, to argue, as Bankim Chandra had done, that the grammarian Pānini belonged to the tenth or eleventh century B.C., when his celebrated grammar related chiefly to a much later form of Sanskrit, 'is much the same as proposing to push Johnson's Dictionary back before Chaucer'.[5]

> Bankim Babu's date for Pānini being thus altogether untenable, his whole argument for the historicity of the *Pāndava Mahābhārata* and Krishna's character as therein portrayed tumbles in ruins, and brings down with it all the rest of this Krishna literature.[6]

The whole point of this argument about dating is that the Gita, its excellence notwithstanding, is a work of imagination and not of history. Farquhar clearly had deep respect and admiration for the Gita. He calls it 'the loveliest flower in the garden of Sanskrit literature', and goes on:

> For the Western mind also the poem has many attractions. The lofty sublimity to which it so often rises, the practical character of so much of its teaching, the enthusiastic devotion to the one Lord which breathes through it, and the numerous resemblances it shows to the words of Christ, fill it with unusual interest for men of the West.[7]

On the matter of 'resemblances ... to the words of Christ', it may be worth noting that Farquhar was uninterested in Lorinser's theory of New Testament influence on the Gita: this attempt, he noted tersely, 'must be pronounced a failure'.[8]

Poetry, however, is not a substitute for history as a source of religious truth, and it was the historical approach to the Gita which

---

[4] Ibid., p.71.
[5] Ibid., p.74.
[6] Ibid., p.75.
[7] Farquhar, *Permanent Lessons of the Gita* (Madras 1903), p.1.
[8] Ibid., p.2, n.1.

revealed, in Farquhar's view, its weakness as the source and support of a nation's faith. After a review of the evidence for the origin and date of the Gita, Farquhar is forced to conclude that the story 'that Krishna uttered the Song on the battlefield, is a pious imagination'.[9] It is an extremely effective piece of imaginative writing, certainly, but literary skill is no substitute for historical accuracy, and the fact remains that Krishna is a mythical figure, skilfully drawn but the product of a human mind.

What then is the missionary (and perhaps also the Hindu inquirer) to make of the Gita? First, he must approach it with reverence, not as the record of a new revelation, but as the summing-up of centuries of earlier religious development. The Gita ' ... is the concentrated essence of Hinduism. It is the expression of all the highest hopes, aspirations and ideals of the best Indians that have ever lived ... It is the revelation of the Indian people.'[10] In it we see 'the Hindu people ... reaching out after God'. This the crux of the matter for the missionary. The creation of the Krishna myth proves that the Hindu people felt the need of a Saviour; the missionary, however, is forced to answer that this need cannot be satisfied on the level of the imagination. Only in the *historical* figure of Jesus Christ can this need be satisfied.

> On the one hand ... we have the imaginative portrait of Krishna, surrounded by millions of adoring worshippers ... on the other stands the historical Jesus of Nazareth, Son of Man and Son of God ... Rightly read, the *Gītā* is a clear-tongued prophecy of Christ, and the hearts that bow down to the idea of Krishna are really seeking the incarnate Son of God.[11]

Thus there are two separate sides to Farquhar's argument in this series of monographs and pamphlets. One concerns the dating of the Gita and the historicity of Krishna. On this point he was following all the best Western Orientalists of the turn of the century, and at no point does he indulge in either special pleading or in the convenient polemical device of introducing the Krishna of the *Purāṇas* in an attempt to discredit the Krishna of the Gita. The other is strictly a matter of Christian (or more properly Liberal Protestant) argument. A further brief word about this may not be out of place here.

In the later part of the nineteenth century Christianity, having

---

[9] Ibid., p.15.
[10] Farquhar, *The Age and Origin of the Gita* (Madras 1904), p.23.
[11] *Gita and Gospel*, p.59. Cf. *Permanent Lessons* (2nd ed. Madras 1912), p.31.

suffered somewhat at the hands of radical critics of the Bible and of miscellaneous companies of 'scientists', had come to the conclusion that God had revealed himself, not in the infallible words of the Bible, but in the process of history itself. After a long and arduous period of preparation in the history of Israel, the decisive revelation had come in and through the life, death and resurrection of Jesus of Nazareth, the 'Christ' (anointed one) of God. Historical study, it was held, had been unable to shake the authenticity of the New Testament record in its essentials. Further, it was considered that the core of the teaching of Jesus had been 'the kingdom of God', partially realisable here on earth in terms of righteousness, peace and joy, but to be fully manifested only at the end of human history. History therefore became the central category of this type of Christianity. Certainly other nations had their history too, but this might equally be taken to be a varied *praeparatio evangelica*, a preparation for the Gospel of Jesus Christ and the kingdom of God. The argument was not about the existence of God (which all the great religions acknowledge, in one way or another), but about salvation. In India's case, there was the further argument that only Christianity (not so much the organised forms as the 'essential' message) could provide an emergent nation with the ethical motive power to move confidently into the future. Thus Hindu 'quests' were to find their fulfilment and goal in the one incontrovertible (from the Christian point of view) historical revelation, that of Jesus Christ. Other purported revelations – for instance those through the Hindu *avatāras*, of whom Krishna was the chief – posed questions, but did not answer them. For the Hindu answers took the devotee outside the historical process altogether, into the regions of the irrational and 'theosophical' make-believe, and generally did nothing to create a consistent pattern of ethics. Wherever they might lead, it would not be in the direction of the kingdom of God.

Given these complex presuppositions (and there were perhaps others, of a more explicitly political nature, involved somewhere along the way), one may begin to understand Farquhar's insistence on the *historical* nature of 'true' revelation, and his rejection of the testimony of the Gita as beautiful, but unhistorical.

It was perhaps a sign of the pressure exerted on India by the West at that period in her history that some Hindus should have attempted to answer this objection by affirming the strict historical trustworthiness of the Krishna tradition. The more authentic Hindu position was perhaps that metaphysical truth is in no way dependent on the changes and chances of history, which belong to a lower order of being altogether. That this attempt led them into difficulties was perhaps not surprising, all things considered. Theosophists, as we have seen, fell into similar tangles when they attempted to meet the historical argument by recourse to tradition and astrology – neither of them accurate as means of measuring time.

Farquhar's little books represent (whether or not one is able to accept their arguments) at least a respectable level of inquiry and intelligent use of Orientalist sources. Other missionary literature on the Gita from this period is often shallow and disappointing. For instance in 1903 there also appeared J.P. Jones' book *India's Problem: Krishna or Christ* – originally delivered as lectures in America in 1902. Oddly enough, Krishna and the Gita rate scarcely a mention in its pages. The tone of Jones' book may be gauged from this paragraph, which comes immediately after a rhapsody on the 'divine origin' of the Christian Bible:

> Nor can any one fail to appreciate the beauty and sublimity of some of the Vedic hymns of the Hindus or the profound depth of the philosophic reach of the Upanishads, those sublime 'guesses at truth', or the great excellence of the Bhagavad-Gita which is the gem of all Hindu literature. And yet the puerilities of many and the obscenity of others of the Vedic songs and prayers are well-known. So are the strange vagaries and the rambling character of many of the Upanishads. And as for the Bhagavad-Gita it is simply a dialogue whose gist is the argument of Krishna – 'the Supreme God' – to urge the tender-hearted and the conscience-smitten Arjuna to slay his relatives in war. Its argument is that no evil which one man may do to another is of any moment, since he cannot touch his soul which is eternal and beyond the reach of any human power! In the destiny of a soul what can the destruction of one of its bodies signify? This is an argument which is subversive of morality and of social order.[12]

The *Purāṇas* and *Tantras*, however, are even worse, communicating an atmosphere which is 'morally pestilential and spiritually degrading'. To exchange the study of the Bible for the study of these scriptures is 'to exchange the pure air of heaven for the charnel house'.[13]

Three years later, in 1906, George Howells, the principal of Serampore College, wrote in the Baptist *Missionary Herald* a series of short essays on 'The Bhagavad Gita and the Christian Gospel'. He was respectful, but in the end lukewarm about the Gita and its contents:

[12] Jones, *India's Problem: Krishna or Christ* (New York 1903), p.104.
[13] Ibid., p.105.

> The Gita contains much that is true and beautiful and good, but in comparison with the New Testament, it is, and I say it with deliberate conviction, but as a candle in the presence of the sun.[14]

The Gita received surprisingly little mention at the Edinburgh World Missionary Conference of 1910, but one comment made in discussion is worth a mention. Speaking of the beginnings of a reformed Hinduism, Brother (later Bishop) F.J. Western drew attention to 'the widespread use of the Bhagavad-Gita as a book of theology and devotion. The book has been, one might almost say, re-discovered by English educated Hindus, and many are learning from it not only quietism, but to borrow words of Professor [A.G.] Hogg, quoted in the Report – the strenuous mood, and the consecration of life to service.'[15] This was a significant observation. Even though many Christian missionaries in India might still have believed the Gita's message to be 'quietist', the revolutionary years before 1910 had made the view practically impossible to sustain further. Might this use of the Gita then not be a positive sign of the turning of the mind of young India in the direction of an ideal man – a quest that missionaries for their part had no doubt would find its fulfilment in Christ?

[14] Howells, in *Missionary Herald* (1906), p.182.
[15] World Missionary Conference, 1910, *Report of Commission IV: the missionary message in relation to non-Christian religions* (Edinburgh and London 1910), p.313f.

6

Gandhi's Gita

17. 'Understand in order that you may act'

Madame Blavatsky, the co-founder of the Theosophical Society, died on 8 May 1891. Previously we have seen how the first generation of Theosophists, over which she exercised an almost dictatorial leadership, had begun to interpret the Gita in terms of their own interests and concerns. Most of these early interpreters had been Hindu by birth, and although all had to some extent been influenced by Blavatsky their work continued to be fairly closely related to Hindu tradition.

This is not the place to give an account of the struggle for the leadership of the Society which followed Blavatsky's death. We may note merely that within a very few years the movement had split in two. On the one hand there were the majority of the Americans, led by William Q. Judge, who sought to free the society of bondage to the shade of Blavatsky and the Buddhistic enthusiasms of her collaborator Olcott. On the other there was the international majority, led by a comparative newcomer to the movement, Annie Besant, from the society's headquarters in Adyar, Madras. Judge had no very high opinion of Mrs Besant. Both however were more interested in the Hindu than in the Buddhist tradition (what little they knew of it); where they differed was that Mrs Besant was actually living in India and was very much more interested in the practicalities of the emergent political situation than was Judge, for whom Hindu scripture remained a quarry of esoteric teaching on the purely individual level.

As we have seen, there had been a flurry of Theosophical publication on the Gita during the 1880s, undertaken chiefly by

Hindu members of the Society. At the turn of the century both the new leaders undertook to provide new, 'theosophical' versions of, and commentaries on, the text of the Gita for the instruction of the faithful. As Judge noted in the preface to his version (dated October 1890), thus pre-dating Besant by fourteen years), the Gita ' ... is being read to-day by hundreds of sincere Theosophists in every part of the world'.[1] He therefore offered them a new translation to replace the Theosophical reprint of Wilkins – still the only one easily available in India, after over a hundred years. Annie Besant's translation did not see the light until 1904 (more than a decade after she had first set foot on Indian soil). Doubtless it was meant in part as an alternative to Judge. Neither, however, was a Sanskritist. What help Judge had in preparing his version it is a little hard to say, but Annie Besant acknowledged the assistance of four Benares friends, Pramada Das Mitra, Ganganath Jha, Kali Charan Mitra and Upendranath Basu, and, for the third and fourth editions, Bhagavan Das. Her role therefore was limited to that of presiding over the final form of the English text.

To accompany the text both Judge and Besant delivered lectures and wrote articles, and it is these which will concern us here. Again the Judge commentaries are earlier, dating from between 1887 and 1895. Annie Besant's parallel effort comprised a series of lectures delivered at Adyar in 1905 and published in 1906 as *Hints on the Study of the Bhagavad Gita.*

Judge began by drawing what was already becoming a normal and natural contrast between Indian wisdom and 'the materialising influence of western culture'.[2] The Indian approach to matters of the spirit rests on a unique 'psychological system' (psychology being then a very new and indistinct science, let it be remembered: 'spiritual method' would have done just as well), and this 'system' can only be found out by reading between the lines of the poem. Linguistic methods as such are of no manner of use, and in any case Judge was totally unqualified to use them. Pure history is irrelevant. But within every sacred text there is an inner, true meaning, related to the outward form of the text as the soul is related to the body:

> This valuable privilege of looking for the inner sense, while not straining after impossible meanings in the text, is permitted to all sincere students of any holy scriptures, Christian or Pagan.[3]

[1] Judge, *The Bhagavad-Gita: The Book of Devotion* (4th ed. Los Angeles 1928), p.xvii.
[2] Judge, *Notes on the Bhagavad Gita* (Los Angeles 1918), p.3.
[3] Ibid., p.6.

Therefore it is necessary to look for 'that *undisclosed* Veda' between the lines of the Gita.[4] The Brahmins generally appear not to know it, priestcraft being, in the Theosophical view, as pernicious in the Hindu as in the Christian setting. But what does that matter? The inner meaning emerges by insight and intuition, not by professional training or as a result of scholarship. Orientalists, Judge claimed, always look for the lowest, rather than the highest meanings of words. But inner meanings cannot emerge in that way. In Christianity and Hinduism alike 'priests and churches' have wilfully misinterpreted everything they have touched, succeeding only because 'a weak humanity ... needs a support beyond itself on which to lean'.

The root of the matter is that the Aryans recognised that 'man in his essence *is God*' and therefore 'naturally looked up to Him and referred everything to Him'.[5] From this point on everything falls into place: the Gita is of course an allegory of the struggle going on in human nature. Dhritarashtra is 'that part of man, which, containing the principle of thirst for existence, holds material life'. The Ganges 'typifies the sacred stream of spiritual life incarnated here'.[6] The generals and commanders lined up on the field of battle 'must be a catalogue of all the lower and higher faculties in man'.[7] Arjuna is Everyman, fighting a battle 'raging on the sacred plane of our body'.[8] Krishna is 'the charioteer of the body with its horses – the mind'.[9] He is also 'the higher self' and 'the inner guide',[10] and when we read the Gita 'we are face to face with ourselves'.[11]

What the Gita teaches, therefore, according to Judge, is how we are to be at peace with ourselves: how we are to be strong and calm, and how we are to gain that philosophical knowledge which underpins all these virtues. The apparatus may be – indeed it is – symbolically convoluted, but the underlying 'truths' are startling in their simplicity. Being a Theosophist, Judge could not forbear to introduce a good deal of occultist furniture, involving Adepts, Hierophants, Messengers and Elder Ones (alas, ' ... no body of Hierophants has taken up its actual residence in Europe or America as yet'),[12] from time to time losing touch with the Gita along the

---

[4] Ibid., p.7.
[5] Ibid., p.12.
[6] Ibid., p.15.
[7] Ibid., p.16.
[8] Ibid., p.17.
[9] Ibid., p.20.
[10] Ibid., p.26f.
[11] Ibid., p.28.
[12] Ibid., p.49f.

way. Judge was somewhat prone to digress on such matters. But he was also honest enough to admit that at various points he was unable to expound the full meaning of the Gita's text. One such point concerned the meaning of sacrifice, which he claimed to be reluctant to tackle on the grounds that he would only expose himself to 'a charge of madness, superstition, or ignorance'.[13] He tackled it nevertheless, allegorising as best he could, though missing the normal and natural meaning of sacrifice (*do ut des*, 'Give to the gods that they may give to you') in the process.

There is no need to proceed further with Judge's comments on the Gita. They were to achieve considerable popularity among Theosophists, partly because they made absolutely no demands in respect of knowledge of things Indian and so neatly slotted the 'inner meaning' of the Gita into the universal Theosophical system of secret, if somewhat banal, knowledge. Above all his articles removed the Gita altogether from the regions of living Hindu piety. Being conceived and written in America, they related more to an imaginary India than to any Indian reality, whether ancient or modern. Such was perhaps the inevitable consequence of the allegorical method.

The 'Antecedent Words' prefaced to Judge's own translation (or re-working) of the text of the Gita – dated October 1890 – sounded the same note of indistinct moralism. One quotation will suffice:

> The *Bhagavad-Gîtâ* tends to impress upon the individual two things: first, selflessness, and second, action; the studying of and living by it will arouse the belief that there is but one Spirit and not several; that we cannot live for ourselves alone, but must come to realise that there is no such thing as separateness, and no possibility of escaping from the collective Karma of the race to which one belongs, and then, that we must think and act in accordance with such belief.[14]

*

In her early days in India Annie Besant had refused to become directly involved in politics, though at what cost to her habitually political consciousness we can only imagine. That she understood well enough the political implications of the Hindu renaissance is very clear; also that in the long run she wished to play a part in it.

---

[13] Ibid., p.86.
[14] Judge, *The Bhagavad-Gita*, p.xvii.

And how better to do so than by entering into the interpretation of the Gita, the national scripture *par excellence?*

Her contribution in this area was slightly delayed, but at the thirtieth anniversary meeting of the Theosophical Society in Adyar she did what Subba Row had done twenty years before and delivered four lectures on the Gita, which were published in the following year as *Hints on the Study of the Bhagavad Gita* (1906).

These lectures retain much of the homiletical style of her rejected past, whether Anglican or Fabian Socialist. Krishna has replaced Jesus Christ, it is true, but the terms remain much the same. There is still faith, doubt, understanding, action, revelation, submission. She sees the message of the Gita as universal, after the style of the Christian Gospel, addressing itself not to Hindus, or even to those Gnostics who are able to unravel its allegories, but to humanity as a whole. To speak of the Gita, she announces, ' ... is to speak of the history of the world, of its vast complexity, of that web of desires, thoughts, and actions which makes up the evolution of humanity'.[15] If the Gita appears at first sight complex, this is only because of the complexity of the world – a world in which ' ... the author of the *Gita* is the upholding and the sustaining life'.[16] The 'author' is of course Krishna, not Vyasa or an anonymous editorial committee: Mrs Besant has accepted a theory of direct personal inspiration closely akin to that of the Christian fundamentalist. Some intermediate hand there may have been; but the authority of the Gita could not be sustained by any less support than that of Krishna himself. And Krishna *is* God.

To God one can do nothing save submit in faith and trust – to do the *sādhana* of the Gita. To 'understand' the Gita one must live it – and only to those who actually *do* live it will the final mystery be revealed.[17] For although the subject-matter and message of the Gita are universal, Annie Besant would not have been Annie Besant (and certainly she would not have been a Theosophist) if she had not believed in a final core of mystery and secrecy, revealed only to an inner circle of initiates. But each initiate is henceforth able to instruct others, on a cosmic plan: 'Each true reading marks a stage of human evolution, marks a point in human progress.'[18] Again this sounds very like Sri Aurobindo, and again one is left wondering about the possibility of mutual influence somewhere along the way.

[15] Besant, *Hints on the Study of the Bhagavad-Gita* (Benares and London 1906), p.1.
[16] Ibid., p.2.
[17] Ibid., p.4f.
[18] Ibid., p.6.

There are, she says, two 'quite obvious' meanings of the Gita, which in effect represent macrocosm and microcosm – the world and the individual, history and allegory. The first of these is a plain statement of *wie es eigentlich gewesen ist* ('what really happened') which anyone can learn simply by reading and believing.

> The inner meaning, as it is sometimes called, that which comes home to the hearts of you and me, that which is called the allegory, is the perennial meaning, repeated over and over again in each individual, and is really the same in miniature.[19]

The one is not 'truer' than the other: 'just as history is true, so is allegory true.' Krishna is God. God would not and cannot deceive us. So what he says about the course of events must be so. To the question 'How do you know that any of these things are so?' only one answer is possible: namely, 'If Krishna is God, then they must be so.' And to Annie Besant, Krishna was clearly God – for India.

She had of course not the slightest doubt that Krishna was what the Gita and the *Purāṇas* say he was – an *avatāra*, come to turn India into a world-saviour.[20] In arguing this case she made much incidental use of Christian imagery, speaking of humiliation, crucifixion and resurrection, though never other than in an Indian context. But now the drama was not that of the *avatāra* of nationalism, come to expel the foreign *daityas* and *asuras*, but the drama of universal human history. The *avatāra* of Krishna had come down for the benefit of mankind as a whole, and not just for Indians, and hence there was in process of emerging from India's humiliation a universal gospel.[21]

But the message still had clearly political overtones. In a period of political and cultural upheaval it was necessary to take Krishna at his word in all things. It was Arjuna's duty (and by implication, the duty of the new India) to fight, and despite Arjuna's initial doubt Krishna had manifested himself to teach wiser and, above all, more effective counsels. 'Doubt saps virility, vampirizes the mind ... Understand in order that you may act.'[22] Such was the unveiling of history which she found in the Gita, and which she assiduously taught to revolutionary India, while reserving the right to point her inner circle toward higher things.

[19] Ibid., p.7.
[20] Ibid., p.12f.
[21] Ibid., p.15f.
[22] Ibid., p.27.

The Gita is, then, history: ' ... the Great Unveiling, the drawing away of the veil that covers the real scheme which history works out on the physical plane ... '[23] But the Gita is also allegory.

Here Annie Besant breaks with the Gnostic terminology of Madame Blavatsky and Subba Row, and turns to some more or less equivalent Hindu expressions. The Gita reveals a conflict between the lower *manas*, the mind unfolding, symbolised by Arjuna; and *kāma*, the ties of the past, symbolised by Arjuna's relatives. The story of the Gita is then the story of the gradual unfolding of the *manas* to wisdom and decisive action. Arjuna is the hero, almost the Nietzschean superman, who is the captain of his fate, the master of his soul: 'Into the battle he must plunge alone; by his strong right arm, by his own unflinching will, by his own unwavering courage, that battle must be fought to the bitter end.'[24] For only thus is the self formed.

In its essence, the Gita is a Yoga Shastra, a manual of disciplined action directed to a particular purpose; and only in so far as we are able to learn Yoga from it can it be said to have succeeded in its purpose. 'The eleventh *adhyaya* is the very heart of the Gita, its essence.' And she sums up:

> Right activity, then, is the lesson of the *Gita*, and right activity is acting in harmony with the divine will. That is the only true definition of right activity; not for fruit, not for desire for movement, not from attachment to any object, or to any results of activity, but, wholly in harmony with the Will that works for universal good.[25]

Of course, Mrs Besant was to have a great deal more to say about the Gita. In 1904 she had published her own version of the text, assisted by a number of Hindu pandits, and often in succeeding years she was to urge Hindus to contemplate Krishna as the ideal leader of men, the 'active' and 'gracious' one, in whom one could discern 'half-heard melody' and 'elusive fleeting grace, scarce seen but sensed', but also 'human greatness as a politician, as statesman, as a guide of nations'.[26] At all events Krishna had a much wider appeal than Shivaji, though perhaps a less purely human appeal than Gandhi was ultimately to demonstrate. But that is another, later story. It is worth suggesting, however, that the allegorical interpretation in which the early Theosophists excelled was to

[23] Ibid., p.9.
[24] Ibid., p.31.
[25] Ibid., p.46.
[26] Quoted by Sarma, *Studies in the Renaissance of Hinduism* (Benares 1944), p.202f.

exercise an unacknowledged influence on the way in which Gandhi read the Gita.

18. 'The real facts'

We must now turn briefly away from the Indian political situation and return to Europe. In India the Gita was fast becoming a symbol of Hindu resistance to British rule, a widely-read scripture for the whole of politically-minded India. But in Europe it was still permissible to regard it as belonging less to the present than to the remote past, as a useful text for beginners in Sanskrit poetry, and on the matter of composition, as still something of a puzzle.[1]

Given that the Gita contained elements belonging to a number of different schools of Hindu thought – *Sāṁkhya, Yoga, Vedānta* and *Bhakti*, at the very least – there were two obvious possibilities. The first was that it was the product of a single eclectic mind, who was bent on reconciling the differences between the schools while drawing on those schools for whatever material he needed. Most Western Indologists broadly accepted this view. But the second was that it was a composite work, put together in stages as each successive view was superimposed on the others. The Gita, for instance, could not be both theistic and pantheistic: to the Western mind the one ruled out the other. And yet both traits were found in the Gita. If they really were separate and distinct approaches, then again the question might be asked: which of them came first?

In his massive work *Das Mahābhārata und seine Theile* ('The *Mahābhārata* and its Parts') (1895), Adolf Holtzmann of Freiburg had argued that the 'pantheistic' element in the Gita had been the older, being later modified in the direction of a theistic belief in Vishnu-Krishna as the supreme God. This was in line with the more general theory among students of religion at the time, that monotheism had been a late development and ethical monotheism the latest development of all in the world of religion. The theism of the Gita was perhaps imperfect, but it was at least a move onward and upward in evolutionary terms, and therefore must have emerged at a relatively late stage in the formation of the Epic.[2]

---

[1] Lamotte, *Notes sur la Bhagavadgītā* (Paris 1929), p.viif.: 'Aussi longtemps que la chronologie de la Gītā et des Darśanas sera flottante, et que la genèse du culte de Kṛṣṇa sera mystérieuse, aussi longtemps serons nous *in the dark* sur la préhistoire de la Gita.'

[2] Holtzmann, *Das Mahābhārata und seine Theile* (Kiel 1895, repr. Osnabrück 1971), vol.4, p.165ff.

Arguing against Holtzmann, Richard Garbe of Tübingen took precisely the opposite point of view. In 1905 he published in Leipzig a new translation and commentary, *Die Bhagavadgītā*, in which he argued that the apparent irregularities in the Gita were best explained on the hypothesis that it had originally been composed (in the second century B.C. or thereabouts) on the basis of the *Sāmkhya-Yoga* philosophy, but as a strictly theistic tract in glorification of Krishna. The 'pantheism' of the Upanishads had subsequently been superimposed upon this original composition, perhaps by Brahmins bent on furthering their own priestly concerns. This, however, was only part of Garbe's theory, though it was the part which was most debated in subsequent years.

Fortunately for the English-speaking world Garbe was asked to write the article on the Gita in James Hastings' *Encyclopaedia of Religion and Ethics* (Volume II, 1909)[3] and took the opportunity to summarise his findings. These were textual only in part.

First, Garbe believed Krishna to have been a historical figure, the leader of a warrior and pastoral non-Brāhman tribe long before the time of the Buddha. He was also the founder of the religion of his race, which was non-Vedic, but monotheistic and strongly ethical. The adherents of this 'religion' were called (or called themselves) *Bhāgavatas*. Subsequently the Brahmins took over the god of the sect, transforming him (as they were later to do with Buddha) into an incarnation of Vishnu. The Gita was originally the scripture of the sect, the 'pantheistic' elements of which are therefore to be explained in terms of this brahminical take-over, as an attempt to camouflage its alien origins. Garbe's theory was thus 'Euhemeristic' (gods and goddesses are great men and women of the past, revered while living amd worshipped after death) – a point of view which is sometimes true, but which on this occasion lacked any real support from external evidence.

Garbe's theory was however entirely consistent, given the premises on which he was working. The trouble was that neither he nor anyone else could demonstrate the existence of a pre-Buddhist 'Bhāgavata religion'. The earliest date to which the worship of Krishna could be traced in India was between the fourth and third centuries B.C., and even that date rests on some fairly shaky evidence, involving the identification of Krishna with the Greek Herakles. This is not to say that there could not have been a 'Krishna of history', merely that Garbe had no way of proving his

[3] Garbe, 'Bhagavad-Gita', in Hastings (ed.), *Encyclopaedia of Religion and Ethics* (Edinburgh 1909) vol.2, pp.535-8.

existence. This did not prevent him from asserting, with Teutonic over-confidence,

> Briefly stated, then, the real facts are that in the ancient poem a Kṛṣnaism based upon the Sāṅkhya-Yoga philosophy is set forth; in the additions of the recension the Vedānta philosophy is taught.[4]

These 'real facts' had actually not been arrived at by analysis of the text, but by the superimposition of the text upon a historical hypothesis.

In a parallel article, 'Bhakti-Marga', in the *Encyclopaedia of Religion and Ethics*, a retired Indian civil servant, George A. Grierson, restated the Garbe theory of the origins of Indian monotheism in equally categorical terms:

> Under any circumstances ... the following facts may be taken as accepted by most students of the subject:- The founder of the religion was one Kṛṣna (Krishna) Vāsudava, a Kṣatriya ... He called the object of his worship the *Bhagavat*, or the 'Adorable', and his followers called themselves Bhāgavatas, or 'Worshippers of the Adorable'. The religion was first adopted by the people of his own tribe, and gradually spread over the greater part of the Outland ...[5]

Grierson also outlined the 'stages' through which this 'religion' had developed – plausibly but unconvincingly – down to its latest manifestations in 'modern Bhagavatism', otherwise *bhakti*.

Garbe's last word on the subject of the origins of the Gita and the 'Bhagavata religion' was found in a collection of essays published in 1914 and entitled *Indien und das Christentum* ('India and Christianity'). While allowing that there might be a measure of Christian influence on later Krishna literature, and for that matter much more probably on some Buddhist literature, he was unwilling to allow any substantial Christian influence on any part of the *Mahābhārata*. The only possible exception he felt might be in the legend of the land of Śvetadvīpa in Book XI, but that need not concern us. Garbe was particularly harsh in his criticism of the American scholar E.W. Hopkins, who had indicated in his book *India Old and New* (1901) that there might be something to say for Lorinser's almost-discarded theory.

Garbe did not in so many words accuse Hopkins of dishonesty, but he came very close to it, claiming that even when Hopkins had shown

[4] Ibid., p.536b.
[5] Ibid., p.540b.

restraint in his claims, this had been no more than a cunning tactic to convince the laity that Christian influence had to be taken seriously.[6] This Garbe denied categorically, on the simple grounds that there was no Christianity in India at the time of the Gita's composition. Hopkins had in any case spoken out of both sides of his mouth, claiming in his book *Religions of India* (1898) that ' ... the teaching of Christianity certainly may be suspected, but it cannot be shown to exist in the Divine Song',[7] and in *India Old and New* that the evidence is ' ... almost conclusive in favour of one of the religions having borrowed from the other'.[8] Poor Hopkins had also shown some uncertainty as to whether Krishna had originally been a human chieftain or an anthropomorphised mythical figure. On this matter Garbe could accept only one view – his own.

It was very strange, he thought, that so many scholars (among them Tiele, Senart, A. Barth, Kennedy and Keith) could imagine Krishna to have been a sun-god or a vegetation-deity, when all the evidence pointed in the other direction: 'Krishna is not an anthropomorphised god, but a deified man ...'[9] If Euhemerism is involved, then so be it: the theory is by no means always false, and has been proved to be common in India. Why then should there be any doubt as to the facts of the case?

Garbe may well have been right about 'the Krishna of history', except that his historical Krishna existed, if he existed at all, beyond the reach of historical evidence. Concerning Garbe's technique of dividing up the Gita into earlier and later strains, with priestly *Vedānta* superimposed upon an earlier level of non-priestly *Sāmkhya-Yoga*, again this might have been a possibility, but it was desperately difficult to prove, one way or the other. In any case, it was unlikely to convince the faithful in India or scholars in other parts of the Western world. In 1905, when Garbe's theories were first launched, Bengal was partitioned and national sentiment passed beyond the range of rational discourse, pulling with it most questions connected with the age and origin of the Gita.

19. 'That interpretation is not true which conflicts with Truth'

Between 1920 and India's independence in 1947 a great many people

---

[6] Garbe, *Indien und das Christentum* (Tübingen 914), p.200f.
[7] Hopkins, *The Religions of India* (New York 1898), p.429.
[8] Hopkins, *India Old and New* (New York 1901), p.155.
[9] Garbe, *Indien und das Christentum*, p.214.

in the West came to view India, Hinduism and the message of the Gita in the light of their impression of one man, Mohandas Karamchand Gandhi. To those who judged sanctity on a scale of moral strenuousness he was a saint. To those who had to negotiate with him he was an enigma. The secular wing in the West regarded him as a fanatic, either deluded or supremely cunning, who had in some mysterious way shown himself capable of achieving political results by religious means (or vice versa). To India he was a holy man, whose holiness rested fairly and squarely on his devotion to the Gita and had been sealed not by what he had achieved but what he had rejected.

Unlike many of the interpreters of the Gita whom we have passed in review in these pages, the outlines of Gandhi's life and career are well known – the more so since the *Gandhi* film. His love for the Gita is likewise known to all and mentioned in (it is safe to say) every one of the innumerable Gandhi studies. Repeatedly throughout his life he bore testimony to that love, never more intimately than at an assembly of Christian missionaries in Calcutta in 1925:

> ... when doubt haunts me, when disappointments stare me in the face, and when I see not one ray of light on the horizon, I turn to the Bhagavad Gita, and find a verse to comfort me; and I immediately begin to smile in the midst of overwhelming sorrow. My life has been full of external tragedies, and if they have not left any visible and indelible effect on me, I owe it to the teachings of the Bhagavad Gita.[1]

Gandhi, however, was not a man of the West, and his contacts with Westerners did little to modify his essentially Hindu cast of mind – which was that of the Hindu merchant rather than the Hindu philosopher, and the Gujerati rather than the Bengali. George Woodcock has written that Gandhi was the one ' ... who alone among the colonial revolutionaries went to the west and came back unconverted'.[2] But unconverted to what? Arguably he went to the West in the 1880s determined to attempt to become a lawyer and a Westerner; in the first he succeeded, in the latter he failed miserably. Rather he became what previously he had not been: consciously and religiously Hindu. And part of this process had to do with his discovery of the Gita. But he did not rediscover the Gita as he might have rediscovered it in India, under the guidance of a *guru* and within the intellectual framework of one or other orthodox tradition

---

[1] Andrews, *Mahatma Gandhi's Ideas* (London 1929), p.73.
[2] Woodcock, *Gandhi* (London 1972), p.15.

of interpretation. The Gita was initially mediated to him by Westerners, in an English translation, and by members of a society who had their own special conventions of interpretation. This is the first of several reasons for his inclusion in this survey.

Gandhi in fact provides yet another case of the ongoing two-way traffic of religious ideas between India and the West during the modern period. Without a Max Müller India would not have had a definitive text of the *Rig Veda* as soon as she did, and perhaps not at all. Without a Vivekānanda the West's impressions of Hinduism might have remained at the level of the uncomprehended and the curious. And without the Theosophical Society much that we now take for granted about the religion of South Asia – Buddhist as well as Hindu – would not have shaped itself in the way it did, and Gandhi's introduction to his beloved Gita would not have been effected.

As we have seen, from the time of its establishment in India in the 1880s, the Theosophical Society had set itself up as a champion of Hindu values in almost complete opposition to those of the Christian West and had lent the emergent Indian national movement a good deal of moral and practical support. It contributed to the systematisation of both Hindu and Buddhist doctrine, to Hindu and Buddhist education and to the publication and popularisation of Eastern scriptures. To some extent it also helped to give Hindus a new and workable terminology – a term like 'the law of *karma*' was a Theosophical invention, for instance.[3] On the level of personal contacts, Theosophists were often able to inspire in Hindus a level of confidence which otherwise was uncommon among Indians and Europeans (except in the case of missionaries, who generally worked either with the very young or the very poor, and had little contact with intellectuals). During the early years of the national movement Theosophical influence was felt throughout the upper levels of Hindu society. After 1919 this level was not maintained, partly due to intensifying anti-Western feeling, which led to a reluctance on the part of Hindu nationalists to accept outside assistance, and partly to the eccentricities of the Theosophists themselves. That, however, is not a story we can tell further on this occasion.

In 1889 the Theosophical Society was still very much a 'new religious movement', small and not in any way powerful, but represented in the London to which Gandhi had come two years

---

[3] Very possibly the first statement of *karma* in terms of natural law was in the anonymous work (though written largely by Annie Besant), *Sanatâna Dharma: an advanced text book of Hindu religion and ethics* (Benares 1903), p.108ff.

earlier as a law student. Up to this time Gandhi was, on his own admission, virtually illiterate in religious terms. But the Theosophists were not to know that, and two brothers, members of the Society, who had been reading Sir Edwin Arnold's *The Song Celestial*, asked him to read the original with them. This he knew that he was unable to do. He hoped, however, that he might be able to give them some slight help along the way, and so it was that he read with them the Gita in Arnold's version.

> The book struck me as one of priceless worth. The impression has ever since been growing on me with the result that I regard it today as the book *par excellence* for the knowledge of Truth. It has afforded me invaluable help in my moments of gloom. I have read almost all the English translations of it, and I regard Sir Edwin Arnold's as the best. He has been faithful to the text, and yet it does not read like a translation. Though I read the *Gita* with these friends, I cannot pretend to have studied it then. It was only after some years that it became a book of daily reading.[4]

The same two brothers also persuaded Gandhi to read Madame Blavatsky's *Key to Theosophy*, and in March 1891 he was indeed to become an associate member (though he never became a full member) of the Theosophical Society.[5] His other reading at this time included Carlyle's *On Heroes and Hero-Worship*, Arnold's *The Light of Asia* and Annie Besant's *How I Became a Theosophist*. He also had a fleeting encounter with Evangelical Christianity, but neither then nor later did it make the slightest impression upon him.

Gandhi's initial encounter with Hindu ideas was thus mediated by Theosophists. At this stage he had no Hindu orthodoxy to fall back upon, whether in respect of the interpretation of the Gita or anything else. He shared with the Theosophists an aversion to the cruder kind of missionary Christianity – Theosophy in its earliest phase being passionately anti-Christian – though in Gandhi's case, actual first-hand contact with missionaries in India had been slight. In one important respect, therefore, he was entirely open to Theosophical influence: namely, in respect of the allegorical interpretation of the Gita.

It is clear from everything Gandhi ever wrote or said about the Gita that he read it as a normal allegory of man's condition in the world, rather than as history in any strict sense. Western readers of

---

[4] Gandhi, *The Story of my Experiments with Truth* (Allahabad 1969), p.50.
[5] Polak *et al.*, *Mahatma Gandhi* (London 1949), p.17ff.

Gandhi have sometimes been tempted to suppose that this was Gandhi's own invention (or rather his own insight), and that it set him apart in some way from the mainstream of Hindu orthodoxy. Louis Fischer, for instance, wrote that

> The orthodox Hindu interpretation of the *Gita* as a divine summons to caste obligation and killing was repugnant to Gandhi and even when he read the book in London in 1888-9 he called it an allegory in which the battlefield is the soul and Arjuna man's higher impulses struggling against evil.[6]

But the matter cannot be stated so simply. Quite apart from the fact that it is hardly possible to speak so baldly of an 'orthodox' Hindu interpretation on these lines, on his own admission Gandhi's *study* (as opposed to the mere reading) of the Gita was not really begun at this time but developed only gradually over a number of years. Certainly the allegorical method was well known within Hinduism and is amply documented; but again at this stage in his life Gandhi would have known little of it and almost certainly did not derive his approach from any of the existing 'schools'.

It is clearly stated, however, that Gandhi's first introduction to the Gita was effected by Theosophists; and, as we have seen, the Theosophists knew of no other approach to the text than along the lines of allegory. Subba Row, Judge, Besant – all had made extensive use of the allegorical method in their quest for esoteric content and hidden meanings. And the simplest of those meanings was that the battlefield of the Gita represents the struggle between higher and lower impulses in man. This was, one might say, a Theosophical commonplace by the late 1880s and must have arisen again and again in Gandhi's early contacts with the Gita. This being so, we need look no further for the immediate source of Gandhi's insistence that the Gita is to be read allegorically and not literally, that it does not justify the use of violence and that the battlefield of the Gita is to be understood as the battlefield of human nature, with higher and lower impulses contending for supremacy.

On many occasions in later years Gandhi was to bear testimony to the long-term impact which his continued reading of the Gita had had on him. Looking back in 1931, he recorded that even on his first acquaintance he had felt intuitively

> ... that it was not a historical work, but that under the guise of physical warfare, it described the duel that perpetually went on in the

[6] Fischer, *Gandhi: His Life and Message for the World* (New York 1954), p.17.

hearts of mankind, and the physical warfare was brought in merely to make the description of the internal duel more alluring.[7]

The struggle which the Gita described in terms of *dharma* appeared to Gandhi in the light of a struggle for Truth, and it was his conception of Truth which determined his reading, not only of the Gita, but of the whole of the remainder of his sacred library.

To Gandhi Truth was far more an ethical than a metaphysical concept and might indeed be said to have summed up practically the whole of his religion.[8] Clearly this is not the place to try to expound Gandhi's religion as a whole, but a little more must be said on the subject. 'I have come to the conclusion,' he wrote in 1931, 'that the definition, "Truth is God", gives me the greatest satisfaction. And when you want to find Truth as God the only inevitable means is Love, i.e. non-violence, and since I believe that the means and the end are convertible terms, I should not hesitate to say that God is Love.'[9]

Truth – Love – Non-violence – God: the terms are virtually interchangeable. Love certainly rules out violence, and thus non-violence (*ahimsā*) was Gandhi's key to the understanding, not only of the Gita, but of every other sacred scripture and ultimately of the nature of God himself. The equation 'God is love is non-violence is Truth' was Gandhi's own law of life – in sharp contrast, it should be noted, to the convictions of the more extreme nationalists of the period. In terms of at least one line of Hindu tradition the nationalists had *dharma* on their side: namely, in the belief that force used in the protection of one's person, family or property is not violence (*himsā*) at all. But did the conditions of the Kurukshetra battlefield give rise to *himsā*? Could the Gita be interpreted on the traditional grounds of a threat posed by an *ātatāyin* to one's interests? In which case force might be used but would not be *himsā*? Gandhi, like the Theosophists, seemed scarcely to have thought in these terms at all.

To Gandhi the only person on whom a measure of force might be exercised was oneself, in the form of self-discipline. And for Gandhi self-discipline, self-restraint, renunciation was the only way to that Truth which is God. 'Renunciation of the flesh is essential for realising Truth.'[10] Previously he had said:

---

[7] Gandhi, *Hindu Dharma* (Allahabad 1950), p.140.
[8] Also, according to the Freudian school of psychoanalysis, Gandhi's psychological makeup. See Erikson, *Gandhi's Truth* (New York 1969), passim.
[9] *Hindu Dharma*, p.60.
[10] Ibid., p.136.

That interpretation [of the Gita, or any other scripture] is not true which conflicts with Truth. To one who doubts even Truth, the scriptures have no meaning. No one can contend with him. There is danger for the man who has failed to find *ahimsa* in the scriptures, but he is not doomed. Truth – *Sat* – is positive; non-violence is negative. Truth stands for the fact, non-violence negatives the fact. And yet non-violence is the highest religion. Truth is self-evident; non-violence is its maturest fruit. It is contained in Truth, but as it is not self-evident a man may seek to interpret the *shastras* without accepting it. But his acceptance of Truth is sure to lead him to the acceptance of non-violence.[11]

The epic tradition located the Gita within a framework of violence. But *himsā* in the technical sense presupposes anger, hatred and 'attachment'; and Gandhi saw the purpose of the Gita as being to carry its readers 'to the state beyond *sattwa, rajas* and *tamas* [to] a state that excludes anger, hatred etc.'.[12] Perhaps those on a lower level of spiritual attainment, those who have not yet realised their *dharma*, may still find that they have to fight actual physical battles; and cowardice is to be shunned – 'Better far than cowardice is killing and being killed in battle.'[13] But to those who understand, and who are prepared to put their understanding into practice, the Gita provides a more excellent way than the way of *himsā* – the way of Truth. 'This is the unmistakable teaching of the *Gita*. He who gives up action falls. He who gives up only the reward rises.'[14]

*

There were good reasons why Gandhi's interpretation of the Gita should have left a deep mark on the mind of the West during the inter-war years. The chief of these was undoubtedly connected with the West's war-weariness after the traumatic experience of 1914-1919, and the desire during the chaotic 1920s to find, not only the pragmatic, but also the metaphysical and moral foundations of a lasting peace. The West failed in both, though it was not for want of

[11] Ibid., p.135f.
[12] Ibid., p.137.
[13] Ibid., p.138.
[14] Ibid., p.143.

trying.[15] At one extreme there were the total pacifists; at the other those who sought power at whatever cost; in the middle the disenchanted and scared majority who wished to build up rather than destroy, to conciliate rather than confront and if possible to be left in peace to pursue their own interests. Struggle there would clearly always be – on the economic and political levels if nowhere else (and there were those who saw in Gandhi's campaigns a level of psychological pressure which might in the long term prove even more destructive than a measure of honest warfare). The kingdom of God of which the New Testament had spoken was longed for more intensively than ever, as a reign of righteousness, love, justice and peace – but mostly peace. Gandhi for his part had his own idiosyncratic way of dealing with the words of the Bible, claiming on one occasion to live according to the 'passage', 'Make this world the Kingdom of God and His righteousness and everything will be added unto you'.[16] His intention was clear enough, however, and, what was more important, he showed every sign of actually being capable of living according to his precepts and his high ideals. References to the kingdom of God and the Sermon on the Mount reinforced the conviction on the part of the liberal wing of the Christian West that Gandhi himself was not far from that kingdom. The ease with which he brought together the Sermon on the Mount and the Gita under the canopy of an ethically conceived divine Truth was compelling and convincing.

Although Gandhi claimed to be 'an orthodox conservative Hindu',[17] his Hinduism was scarcely that of the textbooks. His conservatism was not to be found at the level of traditional scriptural interpretation, but at the level of spiritual discipline. It was this, his vision of Truth and the demands of Truth upon his own life and conduct, which gave him his unique authority in India and ensured that even the West, though it hardly understood him, could not ignore him. And taking note of Gandhi, the West was compelled to take fresh note of his reading of the Gita. Whatever impression the Gita may have made on the mind of the West before the 1920s, after that date the fact could not be escaped, that it was an inspiration to a

---

[15] Europeans in India during the inter-war period were often acutely aware of this. Typical was the judgment of the novelist Edward Thompson that by the late 1930s the Englishman in India had been 'manoeuvred into a position where everything he did was wrong'. And again: 'The days of our pride are nearly finished and our race is about to come to judgment.' Quoted by Greenberger, *The British Image of India* (London 1969), p.100.

[16] Gandhi (ed. Hingorani), *The Message of Jesus Christ* (Bombay 1963), p.43.

[17] Andrews, *Mahatma Gandhi's Ideas* (London 1929), p.167.

man like Gandhi – and millions of his close or distant followers. It had to be recognised, therefore, as the scripture of a *karmayogin* – a manual of devotion and action in the modern world, and not merely a relic out of India's remote past.

Even so Gandhi's own temperament prevented him from attempting to impose the discipline of the Gita on others, even within India. 'The *Gita* will never be universal by compulsion from without,' he wrote in connection with the teaching of the Gita in India's schools. 'It will be so if its admirers will not seek to force it down the throats of others and if they will illustrate its teachings in their own lives.'[18]

This was precisely what Gandhi had done to the utmost of his capability. His was not the only interpretation of the Gita to leave a mark on the West in the 1920s and 1930s, nor can it seriously be suggested that the West rushed to read the Gita as a result of the impression made by the 'naked fakir'. But at least from this time on the West was generally persuaded that the Gita (read or not) was a scripture which taught that non-violence which seemed to be the genuine Hindu view of conflict in the world. In many ways, this opinion of both the Gita and Hinduism is one which has persisted at the popular level to this day. Gandhi would surely not have been dissatisfied with that result.

*

Where sacred scriptures are concerned, it is sadly inevitable that the scholar and the devotee will read them in different ways, approaching them with different presuppositions, asking of them different questions and finding in them different answers. Each will suspect the motives of the other and out of these suspicions will fuel the furnaces of 'fundamentalist versus modernist' controversy. The Gandhian period, as it happened, was one such period in Christianity – though Gandhi himself can hardly have given the matter a thought. In passing now to an attempt to apply the methods of modern biblical criticism to the text of the Gita we are moving into a world remote from that of *satyāgraha* and Gandhi's Truth. And yet the attempt was made by a man who was a sincere lover of India, and a believer in inter-religious dialogue many years before the term became common. Rudolf Otto was to have met Gandhi on a visit to India in the late 1920s but was prevented from doing so by ill health.

---

[18] *Hindu Dharma*, p.260.

At this time he had not written the Gita commentary which we shall discuss next. Had he done so, it is unlikely that Gandhi would have understood the intention behind it.[19]

[19] On Otto's travels and negotiations in India, see Forell, *Från Ceylon till Himalaya* (Stockholm 1929), especially p.310f.

7

Rudolf Otto, J.W. Hauer and T.S. Eliot

20. 'The original Gita'

It is always dangerous for a scholar who has established a reputation
in one branch of learning to venture unbidden into another. This
general principle is very evident in the field of Oriental studies, both
because of the great demands which must be made in respect of
philological competence and because of the danger of imposing the
methods and presuppositions of one field upon the material of
another. It has been rightly said that philology is the needle's eye
through which the scholarly camel has to pass on its way to sure and
certain knowledge; philology is not all there is to the business of
scholarship, but without it dangers lurk at every turn. Methods must
be appropriate and illuminating in respect of the material under
consideration, and if they have been worked out in another field
altogether the transplantation may be a highly risky operation.

Perhaps in a sense every Western Orientalist is an amateur. Most,
however, have submitted to a long and arduous course of training
before venturing to express themselves publicly on matters of
controversy. But occasionally an individual has ventured into the
field without adequate preparation. One such was Lorinser, whose
theories about the influence of the New Testament on the Gita we
have mentioned from time to time already. Another was Rudolf Otto
(1869-1937), a German philosopher-theologian who in 1933
published in German a book which when translated into English
carried the title *The Original Gita* (1939).

This is not the place to write at length about Otto's career before
he became involved in the interpretation of the Gita.[1] His

[1] See Almond, 'Rudolf Otto: Life and Work', in *Journal of Religious History* 12/3
(June 1983), pp. 305-21.

best-known book was, and is, *Das Heilige* (1917; Eng. tr. *The Idea of the Holy*, 1923), in which he had appealed to the intuitive and the non-rational as the fundamental religious attitude, and had started a debate which still shows no sign of abating, half a century and more later. But since 1911, when he paid his first visit to India, he had also been deeply concerned with the problem of the relationship between Eastern and Western forms of religion, and particularly with the question of the nature of 'mysticism'. He had undertaken the study of Sanskrit and had been for some years attracted to the varying forms of Hindu devotion, especially *bhakti*. His books *West-Östliche Mystik* (1926; Eng. tr. *Mysticism East and West*, 1932) and *Indiens Gnadenreligion und das Christentum* (1930; Eng. tr. *India's Religion of Grace*, 1932) had been widely acclaimed. These were of course essays in comparative theology and should be judged as such.

The Original Gita was another matter altogether. It was, as its title indicates, an attempt to account for the apparently composite character of the Gita and to establish its 'original' form by recourse to the methods of critical biblical scholarship, linguistic and textual. Otto was of course not the first Western scholar to attempt to distinguish between different 'layers' in the text of the Gita. The most notable of the previous attempts in this direction had been made by Garbe (see above), who had distinguished between an older, *Sāṃkhya*, and a newer, *Vedānta*, layer. But Garbe's attempt, successful or not (most Indologists were not happy with the method), had been relatively cautious and modest. Otto's book, though dedicated to Garbe, threw all caution to the winds. Instead of two layers, Otto distinguished an 'original' Gita, to which had subsequently been added no less than eight separate and distinct 'treatises' and a very large number of 'interpolations' – a category dear to the hearts of the more extreme biblical scholars of the late nineteenth and early twentieth centuries.

It was perhaps a little too easy for other scholars to pour scorn on Otto's 'patchwork quilt' view of the Gita, Franklin Edgerton going so far as to call his effort 'the *reductio ad absurdum* of the Garbe school'.[2]

But on one point at least Otto was surely correct: that the Gita was less likely to have been an original Upanishad than 'a fragment of most magnificent epic narrative'.[3] It began, in other words, not as a philosophical treatise but as a dramatic episode in the *Mahābhārata*, and the interpreter simply has to begin at that point. In this sense the Gita has much in common with the *Iliad* and the *Odyssey*, or even

---

[2] *Review of Religion* (May 1940), p.448.
[3] Otto, *The Original Gita* (Eng. tr. 1939), p.10.

with the *Nibelungenlied,* differing only to the extent to which speculative material has been introduced into the fabric of the narrative.

As to the various groups of verses which Otto identified as 'treatises', he has this to say:

> No one, I believe, can doubt that these actually are interpolations that have gradually been added from time to time and which, still further, exhibit many mutual discordances as well as (in my opinion) occasional traces of attempts to correct, outdo or render innocuous earlier declarations, advanced from another viewpoint opposed to the writer's own dogmas.[4]

The trouble was that in his analytical zeal Otto allowed himself to be carried away and produced a final 'version' of the Gita which appeared to be the product of a committee rather than a single work of a single creative mind. If he had been less enthusiastic doubtless he would have been more convincing.

With few exceptions, Hindus reading Otto's book were totally unimpressed by his method. As for the Orientalists, typical was the reaction of Franklin Edgerton, that Otto '... constantly, though no doubt unconsciously, distorts the text to make it seem favourable to his theories'.[5] And further, Otto

> ... lacked Garbe's profound knowledge of Sanskrit, and probably did not realise how he manhandled the language. No really good philologist, no one who knew Sanskrit well, and whose first interest was an unprejudiced interpretation of the text, could, I think, have been guilty of so many distortions, suppressions of the true, and suggestions of the false, as abound in his pages.[6]

Lastly, the same critic pointed out that the English translation was 'very bad', the translator obviously knowing no Sanskrit and making a 'sad hash' of Otto's German to boot.

Paul Hubert, on the other hand, in his *Histoire de la Bhagavad-Gîtâ* (1949), contented himself with a brief résumé of Otto's argument, taking the view that any study which prompted others to examine the text more closely was to be welcomed.[7]

Hindu scholars have seldom deigned to comment on the

4 Ibid., p.132.
5 Edgerton, op.cit., p.448.
6 Ibid., p.448f.
7 Hubert, op.cit., p.48.

Garbe-Otto method of analysis. For practically all it has been axiomatic that the Gita is and always has been a divinely-inspired unity, and that any attempt to prove otherwise is ill-informed, malicious or both.[8] Entirely typical is S.C. Roy's assertion that the Gita ' ... represents in the best and the most beautiful manner the spirit of India, the spirit of synthesis and reconciliation ...',[9] and his stated intention ' ... to discover the fundamental unity of the Poem ...'[10]

To this one can only respond that the 'fundamental unity' of the Gita has never really been in question and that even Otto, in trying to distinguish the component parts out of which the final version has been assembled, was saying nothing about its later *function* in the Hindu life of devotion. But it so easily seemed that his dissections were in the nature of vivisections. He may well have been less well equipped philologically than some 'professional' Orientalists – though he was hardly so ill-equipped as Edgerton supposed. Perhaps his real trouble was that in a period of intense national feeling in India, he appeared to be calling in question the authenticity of India's holy scripture *par excellence*. He was asking important questions, but questions for which the literary material did not provide the answers. The more cautious Orientalists felt that even Garbe had gone beyond the range of the available evidence in attempting to reconstruct the origins of the Gita's text. His pupil had gone even further – but by the time his book appeared in English (and hence was available to be read in India) Otto himself was dead and had no opportunity to answer his critics. In this field of scholarship he had no disciples.

21. 'Dem kämpfende Geschlechte'

During the second, violent, phase of the Indian national movement, there were, as we have seen, many in India who were prepared to make of the Gita a symbol of violent resistance to foreign rule. In the

---

[8] But see G.S. Khair, *Quest for the Original Gita* (Bombay 1969), which argues that the Gita was written by three different philosopher-poets between the sixth and third centuries B.C.

[9] Roy, *The Bhagavad Gita and Modern Scholarship* (London 1941), p.3 – a book written as a polemic against Garbe and Otto.

[10] Ibid., p.7f.

West, generally speaking, most of those who read the Gita were entirely lacking in sympathy for interpretations of this order. Their insights being set on questions of metaphysics on the one hand, and on the problems of ancient literary history on the other, they found it distasteful to be reminded that the *karma* (works) of which the Gita spoke was a matter of immediate human action in the world. The dialogue of Krishna and Arjuna had taken place on the battlefield, after all; and nowhere had Krishna been taught the lesson of pacifism. Certainly in the 1920s Gandhi had insisted that the Gita was to be interpreted throughout in a non-violent sense, under the canopy of *ahimsā* in which he so passionately believed; but he could arrive at this conclusion only through the free exercise of an allegorical method which side-stepped questions of history altogether. There remained throughout the uncomfortable fact that Krishna had exhorted Arjuna to fight, provided only that he did not do so for personal gain. Pacifism (or at least non-violence) could be read into the Gita; it could scarcely be read out of it, except by a resolute ignoring of its *Sitz im Leben*.

However, not all Westerners who read the Gita were idealists, nor were they all pacifists. Those who were not – those for whom military matters and the pursuit of heroism were part of the serious business of life – were rather liable to read the Gita as a treatise on the exercise of duty, even when that duty involved the shedding of blood. If there were to be salvation, it would certainly not be found by turning one's back on one's duty to the nation, but on the far side of the faithful exercise of loyalty and obedience to duly constituted authority. When duty had been performed, then and only then would it be time to seek for the ultimate realities which lay beyond the shadow-play of human affairs. This may have been the way in which Warren Hastings had read the Gita. Over the next century and a half, however, it was to become uncommon among Western interpreters. Broadly speaking the Western military mind had all the 'religious' prototypes it needed in the historical records of ancient Israel. India was taken to be the source of something antithetical – calm indifference in face of the passing show and of the convolutions of politics. The actualities of Indian life had been far different – though again most Western readers of the Gita were unprepared to view it in the light of Indian politics. The Gita was not obviously a treatise on statecraft, nor was it easily fitted into the broad category of 'Germanic legend', with its grandiose stories of the heroes of old time, who had won their battles for so long as the fates permitted, only to submit to *wyrd* (fate) in the end. Arjuna, in short, was not

Beowulf or Siegfried; nor was Krishna the precise equivalent of Thor.

It is perhaps a little strange that these connections were not made more frequently, since the broad Indo-European connections had been well enough documented for a century or more. The *Mahābhārata* obviously had many points in comon with the Homeric epics, the *Nibelungenlied* and the world of the Norse gods and heroes. And the Gita was a part of the *Mahābhārata*, placed within its action and related to the broad sweep of its story. Might the message of the Gita, then, not have had more in common with the heroic ethos than the idealists had noticed?

If the connections were to be made at all, they would have to be recognised by those for whom the Aryan (= Indo-European) ideals were a living reality: that is, among the German nationalists. And so indeed they were, cautiously at first, but stated finally with considerable force by the German Indologist J.W. Hauer, in a little book on the Gita entitled *Eine indo-arische Metaphysik des Kampfes und der Tat* ('An Indo-Aryan metaphysic of battle and action', 1934).

A year earlier, in July 1933, Hauer, who had been a missionary in India under the liberal Basel Missionary Society and was an accomplished Indologist, had founded the *Deutsche Glaubensbewegung* (The German Faith Movement), the object of which was to unite German nationalists in a form of religion which would be thoroughly Aryan and thoroughly German. It might remain Christian in some respects, provided that the Jewish element was purged from Christianity. Above all, it would be faithful to the great Nazi principles of 'blood, race and homeland'.

In terms of the race theories of the day the Germans might be the most Aryan of Aryans; but there was no 'scientific' way in which Hindu India could be excluded from the Aryan category. The very word *ārya* (= noble) was Sanskrit, after all. And during the 1930s there developed a high degree of mutual respect between conservative elements in Germany and Hindu India. The name of the prince of German Indologists, Max Müller, was 'transphonemized' into *mokṣa mula*, 'root of salvation'; some Hindus believed that the German army had been able to build its terrifying weapons of war on the basis of 'recipes' found in the Vedas; some even believed Hitler to be an *avatāra*, or at least a *mahātma*, on the grounds that he did not eat meat, he did not have intercourse with women, he never even married, and he was 'the visual incarnation of Aryan polity'.[1]

---

[1] Agehananda Bharati, 'Hindu scholars, Germany, and the Third Reich', in *Update: a quarterly journal on new religious movements* (September 1982), p.44-52.

Even German Indologists remained largely ignorant of rhapsodies of this order. They were not, on the other hand, ignorant of the affinity between the Hindu *kshatriya* (= warrior) ideal and that which inspired the armies of the Third Reich.

Hauer's little book on the Gita was dedicated 'to those who do battle' (*Dem kämpfende Geschlechte*). It began by saying that the Gita ought not to be regarded as a kind of Bible; it belongs on the other hand to 'one of the most important phases in the history of Indo-Germanic faith'.[2] And although other elements have been blended into it, its core is sound and pure. India, Hauer emphasised, is not only a land of meditating recluses but also a land of action, due principally to the influence of immigrant 'Nordic' blood – the 'Aryans' of racial mythology.[3] These Aryans were and are to be found all the way from the Scandinavian and Baltic countries to South Asia.

The Aryan outlook on life, said Hauer, is bipolar. It has its introspective side, turned to the creative depths of the soul and inquiry into the nature of human experience; but it has a desire also to turn outward, in action and struggle. The question is, how these are to be brought into 'creative tension'. Between ideals and action there is seemingly a gulf fixed, and failure to reconcile them is the root of all tragedy. In Arjuna's case Hauer speaks of 'the tragedy of war between brothers' (*Die Tragik des Bruderkampfes*),[4] a tragedy which strikes the whole of life, but which actually creates the hero.

> The warrior who must kill, becomes not a destroyer of men, but merely the instrument of events in the world-process. *Ahiṃsā*, 'non-killing' [*Nicht-töten*], is an ancient demand made of Indo-Aryans, arising out of their profound respect for life. Here in the Bhagavadgītā the commandment and its root, respect for life, penetrated to its depths. *Ahiṃsā* is practised by the one who is truly enlightened, even when duty compels him to kill. For it is revealed to him that his actions do not extinguish life itself. In this way the frightful becomes tolerable. The guilt which, bound by fate, he lays upon himself, is not guilt which is eternal and cannot be atoned for, but belongs to the temporal order. It is merely a part of earthly and human necessity.[5]

In this way Hauer states the *kshatriya* ideal of traditional Hindu society in terms clearly attractive to, and to a large extent identical

---

[2] Hauer, *Eine indo-arische Metaphysik des Kampfes und der Tat* (Stuttgart 1934), p.vi.
[3] Ibid., p.1.
[4] Ibid., p.7.
[5] Ibid., p.10 (my translation).

with, those of the German military establishment of the Prussian-dominated period (1870-1945). He quotes one of the great German Indologists of the earlier part of the century, Winternitz: 'Today, ye warriors, the great door to heaven stands wide open! ... It is wrong for the warrior to die at home: to die in battle, that is the warrior's eternal duty.'[6]

Hauer was not uninterested in the Gita's metaphysics, though he clearly regarded these as secondary, compared to the tragic theme announced in the Gita's first two books – 'Honour and the warrior's duty on the one side, blood relationships on the other. Both demands penetrate to the depths of the heart and will of Indo-Aryan man.'[7] And further: 'To live is to act. And to act is tragic.'[8]

In interpreting the Gita in the light, not of the metaphysics of *Vedānta* and *Sāṁkhya-Yoga*, but of its dramatic setting as part of India's great epic tradition, Hauer was doing something not altogether new (Garbe and Otto in their various ways had drawn attention to the evident fact that the epic narrative provided the setting for the Gita's teachings) but in terms of Western priorities, something highly unfamiliar. The West had generally drawn back from placing undue emphasis on the Gita's 'heroic' setting, preferring instead to puzzle over its metaphysics. But in the Germany of the 1930s there were political and ideological reasons why this element should have come to the fore. Outside Germany – where Hauer was probably little read – it was easy to dismiss this approach as mere militaristic rubbish, and at a much later date, Gerald James Larson was to mention Hauer's monograph (in a footnote) only for the sake of its 'incredible title'.[9] But Hauer had a point nevertheless.

Whether or not Hauer's application of the Gita's teachings carried any weight depended entirely on the extent to which the Gita could be regarded as still an essential part of the *Mahābhārata*. Most Western interpreters had simply taken it for granted that the Gita had a life and an essential message of its own, wholly independent of its setting in the context of the Epic. But in Germany and the German-influenced world of the period between Bismarck and Hitler there was a powerful and persistent interest in epic and heroic poetry on the one hand and its ideological implications on the other. It was least of all populist: rather it emphasised the duties and privileges of a

---

[6] Ibid., p.11.
[7] Ibid., p.13f.
[8] Ibid., p.17.
[9] Larson, in *Journal of the American Academy of Religion* (December 1975), p.666 note 45.

chosen military caste, which it took to be representative of 'Aryan' qualities generally. Although its chief historical prototype was the Roman Empire, other Indo-European (= Aryan) epics were also subjected to a fresh examination, from *Heliand* and the *Nibelungenlied* to the *Mahābhārata*. Everywhere the same qualities were found: an initial unwillingness on the warrior's part to enter into battle but, once convinced of his duty, a total commitment to war and an exhibiting of the qualities of courage, resourcefulness and trustworthiness. On this view the 'Aryan' warrior never entered into battle casually, or for personal gain, but in the line of duty, to protect his family, tribe, nation or race (*Rasse, Art*). That the Germans regarded themselves as the most Aryan of all the Aryans perhaps goes without saying.[10] But even lesser Aryans might have made their contribution to the total ideology.

Seen from this angle, the Gita was not a detached devotional discourse but a justification of action in the world, a teaching addressed to a warrior in the midst of the battlefield, which did not dissuade him from fighting, but which supplied metaphysical reasons for his total personal involvement in the battle. Bal Gangadhar Tilak would surely have approved, since he and Hauer both shared the desire to find in the Gita justification for energetic action in the world.

The Germany of the 1930s might have found this interpretation appealing – at least for the time being. Elsewhere in the West, however, Gandhi was a far more persuasive interpreter than Hauer could possibly be. Gandhi had refused to admit that the Gita could possibly contain any overt element of the justification of violence and had insisted that it should be read, not historically but allegorically, for its true message to emerge. There were compelling reasons in a war-weary world why the Gandhian approach should have won the day. The stars in their courses were fighting against Hauer and his kind, though on the right wing of Hindu opinion in India, where even Hitler was admired as a champion of Aryan values, other views were possible. The Gita which the greater part of the West was reading in the 1930s was not the Gita of remote Indo-European history, but a

---

[10] This attitude was fairly constant during the latter part of the nineteenth and the early twentieth centuries, not least on the part of certain German Indologists. One was Leopold von Schroeder, who wrote in a volume sent to German troops in the First World War field: 'Unter allen Ariern sind die Deutschen die echtesten, die am meisten arischen Arier. Den edelsten Grundzug dieser vornehmsten Völkerfamilie zeigen sie am reinsten und kräftigsten.' von Schroeder, 'Deutsche Art', in *Deutsche Weihnacht* (Cassel 1914), p.31.

Gita shaped and reshaped by generations of metaphysics and allegory. Yet the warriors of Kurukshetra might have seen things differently.

22. 'Fare forward, travellers!'

Among twentieth-century English writers, the spontaneous reading of Indian literature has been somewhat uncommon, at least in comparison with European authors of a century earlier. But there have been exceptions, of whom the most outstanding was T.S. Eliot (1888-1965).

Born in America and educated at Harvard, close to the geographical heart of the Transcendentalism of the 1830s, Eliot came to Europe on study tours just before the First World War, settling permanently in England on its outbreak. His earliest poetry began to appear in print shortly after the war and in the early 1920s, and was conceived and written in the dismal spirit of post-war economic and mental depression. After 1927, when Eliot became a British citizen and a member of the Church of England, he emerged as a champion of traditional values, basically conservative though still radical in approach and style. His reading was always vast and eclectic, and he delighted in building abstruse references, allusions and quotations into his poetry – his prose remaining austere in comparison. His acknowledged poetic masterpiece was his *Four Quartets* (written between 1936 and 1942, and first published in its entirety in 1943), in the course of which he revealed that the Gita had been one of his innumerable sources.

The theme of the *Four Quartets* was 'time and eternity' and the relationship of past, present and future in the human apprehension of life. The poems therefore fall into place as part of a protracted debate being conducted among Western intellectuals in the wake of the First World War around the theme of the meaning of time and history. A brief word about this debate may not be out of place here.

Before 1914, the West had been convinced of the inevitability and irreversibility of progress in all matters involving human life and the life of man in society. Taught first by the philosophers of the Enlightenment and reinforced by the biological theories of Darwin, a synthesis was attempted by Herbert Spencer and in large measure achieved. Between about 1900 and 1914 it was almost universally believed that human affairs were subject to the same comprehensive laws of development and evolution: everything concerning humanity was moving towards higher and fuller insights and achievements.

After 1918, however, the West lost its faith in the inevitability of progress (for what could be the value of a system which had led to the four-year slaughter of the war?) and discarded the idealistic philosophies which appeared to support it. But alternatives were hard to find and harder still to sustain. The Christian world began once more to affirm that the final solution to the riddle of human history lay entirely in the hand of God, but that it would emerge, not out of the processes of human history, but as a catastrophic end to human history, in the 'eschatological' (from the Greek, *ta eschata*, 'the last things') event of the coming of the kingdom of God. The more optimistic continued to believe in the gradual emergence of a kingdom of God on earth, but as the 1920s and 1930s continued this view (which was a chastened version of the pre-war idealism) proved harder and harder to affirm with any conviction. Many retreated into 'existentialism', which was less a philosophy than a declaration of the bankruptcy of every philosophical system. Here it was exhorted that one could do nothing save concentrate on, and find meaning in, each moment as it came. If there should be any final 'meaning' to the human encounter with Time, that meaning is certainly hidden from human eyes. Time may or may not be moving in any particular direction; the only thing of which we can be certain is the imperative of the present moment.

Eliot's *Four Quartets* should be seen in part against this background, as a series of reflections on the nature of time and history. In common with most of his contemporaries, Eliot had turned his back on an over-simplified notion of development,

> ... a partial fallacy
> Encouraged by superficial notions of evolution,
> Which becomes, in the popular mind, a means of disowning
>   the past.[1]

Time is not dismissed so easily, however. Our past is built into our present experience, and even prehistory has left its mysterious mark:

> The backward look behind the assurance
> Of recorded history, the backward half-look
> Over the shoulder, towards the primitive terror.[2]

And in a word certainly derived from the Hindu view of life:

---

[1] Eliot, *Four Quartets* (London 1944), p.28.
[2] Ibid., p.29.

Time the destroyer is time the preserver ...[3]

It is at this point, in the poem 'The Dry Salvages', that the Gita enters the picture. In the Gita, Krishna had of course revealed himself to Arjuna as an apotheosis of Time, the sustainer but ultimately the destroyer of all things. Eliot reflects on Krishna's meaning:

> I sometimes wonder if that is what Krishna meant –
> Among other things – or one way of putting the same thing:
> That the future is a faded song, a Royal Rose or a
>   lavender spray
> Of wistful regret for those who are not yet here to regret,
> Pressed between yellow leaves of a book that has never
>   been opened.[4]

From one moment to the next no human being is the same, since even in the moment of reflection consciousness and self-understanding change. And since to Eliot as a Christian the possibility of reincarnation was ruled out, there remains only the journey which reshapes the instants of one life in sequence:

> Fare forward, travellers! not escaping from the past
> Into different lives, or into any future ...[5]

One must regard the future and the past 'with an equal mind'.
    In the future, there is only one individual certainty, the certainty of death:

> Though you forget the way to the Temple,
> There is one who remembers the way to your door:
> Life you may evade, but Death you shall not.
> You shall not deny the Stranger.[6]

In 'The Dry Salvages', Eliot refers, finally, to the Gita's central doctrine of *nishkāma karma*, 'selfless endeavour', as perhaps the solution of the riddle. Striving after the illusory and the imaginary – which is after all what the future chiefly consists of – is destructive. One may go forward, indeed one must go forward, but with a mind

[3] Ibid.
[4] Ibid., p.29f.
[5] Ibid., p.30.
[6] Eliot, *Selected Poems* (Harmondsworth 1951), p.115.

fixed on that which is presently alive and vital. These are some of the words which Eliot imagines as having been intended, though not spoken, by Krishna himself:

> 'At the moment which is not of action or inaction
> You can receive this: "on whatever sphere of being
> The mind of a man may be intent
> At the time of death" – that is the one action
> (And the time of death is every moment)
> Which shall fructify the lives of others:
> And do not think of the fruit of action.
> Fare forward.
>   O voyagers, O seamen,
> You who come to port, and you whose bodies
> Will suffer the trial and judgement of the sea,
> Or whatever event, this is your real destination.'
> So Krishna, as when he admonished Arjuna
> On the field of battle.
>   Not fare well,
> But fare forward, voyagers.[7]

---

[7] *Four Quartets*, p.31.

8

The Gita and the Counter-Culture

23. 'The interchange of vibration'

The caustic American writer H.L. Mencken died in 1956 and therefore did not live to see the onset of the frantic 1960s. This was in many ways rather a pity, since one would have welcomed his reaction to the emergent phenomenon of the 'counter-culture', and particularly to its bizarre notions of religion and spirituality. He had no very high opinion of religion generally and was a persistent critic of what he disliked about it – which was admittedly practically everything. On one occasion he drew a distinction between two types of human being:

> ... those who are what [William] James called tough-minded, and demand proofs before they will believe, and those who are what he called tender-minded, and are willing to believe anything that seems to be pleasant. It is the tender-minded who keep quacks of all sorts well-fed and active, and hence vastly augment the charm of this world. They find it wholly impossible to distinguish between what is subjectively agreeable and what is objectively true ...[1]

It is perhaps best not to reflect too deeply on the likelihood of establishing 'what is objectively true' in matters of religion; but it is arguable that during the 1960s almost a whole younger generation attempted to reconstruct the world on a basis of what they considered 'subjectively agreeable'. At least all were of one mind about what was subjectively *dis*agreeable – power, authority, war, pollution, industrialisation, constraints, once-for-all monogamy and

---

[1] Mencken, *Prejudices: sixth series* (London n.d.), p.101.

all the works and ways of 'the establishment'. Against this catalogue of aversions those same young people set up an 'alternative' scale of values of their own – a scale in which at least the image of India, Indian culture and Indian religion played a well-known and important role.

The key concept in all this was probably 'self-realisation'. Believing that that religion favoured by the establishment existed only to tell them how bad they were, and to attempt to prevent them from doing what they found enjoyable, they gravitated to any philosophy of life which told them that they were basically good, that they had access to latent powers within themselves and that those powers could be tapped by means of simple techniques (usually one or another form of meditation). Even in the West this approach was by no means new. It had been used by the Christian Scientists since the 1880s, and in 1893 Swami Vivekānanda had enthused the delegates to the World Parliament of Religions in Chicago by telling them that they were not 'sinners' but 'divinities on earth'. But Vivekānanda's was only one voice. By the 1960s (and leaving aside what had happened in the meantime) there were many hundreds – gurus and their disciples – offering self-realisation against discipline and (usually) payment.

It was only to be expected that repeated appeals should be made to the Gita in support of these new movements and their techniques. It is probably true to say that only in one case (that of the International Society for Krishna Consciousness) did the Gita assume the dimensions of a genuinely holy scripture. But it would not be too much of an exaggeration to say that the Gita was one of the commonest books on the counter-culture bookshelf. In a manner strongly reminiscent of the Transcendental wave of the mid-nineteenth century, it was read assiduously if shallowly, being skimmed for every shred of meaning it might possess on the spiritual level, the tough historical and textual questions meanwhile being wholly ignored by a generation which knew no language save its own and had no sense of history whatsoever.

In the neo-Hindu counter-culture movements of the time the delivery of lectures and the writing of books about the Gita was more or less expected of every guru. But such was the nature of these movements that although there was a considerable transfer of disciples from one to another each individual guru tended to preside over his own conventicle in isolation from the others. Generally their stock of ideas was small, and impressions were conveyed more by means of constant repetition than by gradual deepening (though this was a characteristic of most religion in the 1960s, Christianity having also fallen into the same style). But the disciples, many of whom had little or no knowledge of religion before joining up, found these few ideas exotic and sweeping, and accepted what they were told as so much pure gold. Human nature being what it is, most gurus clearly enjoyed their success, and modesty was a rare attribute. Their role was to instruct the faithful from a position of authority, and this at least was done in traditional style.

The contents of Gita commentaries and lectures produced for the new readership were similar and in many cases virtually identical in import. The Gita is proclaimed as transcendental truth, to be absorbed unquestioningly as a condition of discipleship. Each commentary is assumed to be revealing the Gita's full meaning for the first time. An example will illustrate this.

Paramahansa Yogananda, having completed his commentary (by dictation) announced:

> A new Scripture has been born! Millions will find God through this book. Not just thousands. Millions! I *know*. I have seen it.[2]

The disciple who recorded this extravagant statement – the new Scripture was not the Gita but the commentary on it – was allowed to read the manuscript, and added his testimony:

> I found the experience almost overwhelming. Never before had I read anything so deep, and at the same time so beautiful and uplifting … His book was filled with the deepest wisdom I had ever encountered. Unlike most philosophical works, however, it was fresh and alive, each page a sparkling rill of original insights.[3]

A disciple of Sri Chinmoy, for some years resident guru of the United Nations, sounded precisely the same note of immoderate adulation in respect of his master's product:

> To the transcendental perception of the eternal truths presented in the Gita he has added the magnificently beautiful touch of the poet. The beauty of his expression is so fascinating that one is tempted to glide through the text enraptured by its poetry without trying to grasp its true depth.[4]

Yogananda's disciple also related in some wonderment what kind of

---

[2] Kriyananda, *The Path* (Nevada City, Calif. 1977), p.403.
[3] Ibid., p.403f.
[4] Chinmoy, *A Commentary on the Bhagavad Gita* (Blauvelt, N.Y. 1973), p.viif.

work had gone into the preparation of his guru's commentary. Yogananda had read no other commentaries (though he knew enough of Shankara to be critical of his one-sidedness). Instead he had 'tuned in to Byasa's [Vyasa's] consciousness' before beginning his dictation. In that way he could be sure that everything he said was what Vyasa intended (Vyasa, it will be remembered, was the traditional author of the Gita). Oddly enough, though, this same disciple also recorded that, in preparing the commentary, ' ... Master invited our suggestions, and seemed content to pursue much of his work on a basis of them'.[5] This was perhaps not unconnected with the further recorded teaching that 'once the devotee sincerely longs for freedom it is only a matter of time before that desire is fulfilled ... the sincere longing for liberation is hardly a step away from freedom itself'.[6] Was the Master, then, only giving the disciples what he knew the disciples wanted?

In the 1960s the 'will to believe' was strong – so strong, that a revered guru could teach and even command without the slightest fear of contradiction. The disciple would accept any statement of a 'spiritual' nature, however improbable, without requiring any evidence. Again an example from Yogananda:

> 'Yesterday I wanted to know about the life of Sri Ramakrishna. I was meditating on my bed, and he materialised right beside me. We sat side by side, holding hands, for a long time.'
> 'Did he tell you about his life?' I inquired.
> 'Well, in the interchange of vibration I got the whole picture.'[7]

Evidently much the same 'technique' had been used in the interpretation of the Gita – a process of 'tuning in', followed by improvisation on whatever theme the text suggested. Naturally only those were convinced who were prepared to be convinced. Outside the immediate circle of disciples, no one was listening.

Among other discourses on the Gita compiled by Hindu teachers in the West during the 1960s and 1970s there is little to distinguish one from another in point of content. But some at least reach devotional heights which others do not. One of the less flamboyant and more successful of the new generation of international *gurus* was Sri Chinmoy, who gained an entry into the United Nations, thanks to his contact with the then Secretary General of that organisation,

---

[5] Kriyananda, op.cit., p.407.
[6] Ibid., p.410.
[7] Ibid., p.416.

the Burmese U Thant. In 1973 he published a *Commentary on the Bhagavad Gita: the song of the transcendental soul* (oddly enough, it appeared under the imprint of the Anthroposophical 'Rudolf Steiner Publications'). But it was not a commentary in any real sense: rather it was a series of short discourses on selected Gita themes, clearly aimed at the young and the inexperienced. It contains the usual transcendental rhetoric:

> Is the Gita a mere word? No. A speech? No. A concept? No. A kind of concentration? No. A form of meditation? No. What is it, then? It is *The Realisation*. The Gita is God's Heart and man's breath, God's assurance and man's promise.[8]

It quotes from authorities ranging all the way from Jesus to Sri Aurobindo, William Q. Judge and George Bernard Shaw. And yet in the last resort there is only the supreme authority of the Gita itself; and this at least generates a certain respect, even though the tone of Sri Chinmoy's teaching sometimes contains overtones of an oriental version of the Sunday-school.

The 'commentary' over, the same book ends with a sequence of aphorisms, which sound the genuine note of *bhakti*, even in translation:

> The Gita is Sri Krishna's Heart, his Vision-in-Fulfilment. The Gita is Humanity's Breath, its Journey towards Immortality.

> Sri Krishna's Flute stirs the Universal Consciousness. Sri Krishna's Gita enchants the Transcendental Consciousness.
> Sri Krishna plays on His Flute. We hear. We do something more. We barter our body's dust with His Soul's plenitude.

> If the Avatar Sri Krishna is the most complicated Door, then the Gita, His Song, is the most effective Key.[9]

At least on this occasion the Gita was allowed to remain on the level of *bhakti*, without evangelistic diatribes, and one has no reason to doubt the sincerity of Chinmoy's proposed exchange:

> The West says that she has something special to offer to the East: The New Testament. The East accepts the offer with deepest gratitude and offers her greatest pride, the Bhagavad Gita, in return.[10]

[8] Chinmoy, op.cit., p.xv.
[9] Ibid., p.124.
[10] Ibid., p.xv.

24. 'Krishna with his Magic Mantra'

In the English-speaking world the first century of Gita interpretation was dominated by one translation, that of Wilkins, while during most of the second century there were innumerable translations and commentaries jostling one another on the bookshelves and in the minds of would-be readers. Since 1968, however, one version has risen head and shoulders above all the others in respect of numbers sold or otherwise distributed. Impressively entitled *The Bhagavad Gita As It Is* – implying a total rejection of all its competitors – it was the work of an elderly Bengali *swami*, born in 1896. He was at first content to be described as Swami A.C. Bhaktivedanta, but later acquired the resonant title of His Divine Grace A.C. Bhaktivedanta Swami Prabhupāda, Founder-Acārya of the International Society of Krishna Consciousness (ISKCON, better known as the 'Hare Krishna' movement). *The Bhagavad Gita As It Is* first appeared under the international commercial imprint of Collier-Macmillan in the great year of student revolt, 1968, but since then has been reprinted innumerable times by ISKCON's own publishing house, the Bhaktivedanta Book Trust, established in 1972. It may or may not have been read more widely than its competitors, but at least it has been more easily accessible than any other.

In many ways this version was not, and is not, a 'Western' product at all. Its character, tone, illustrations – all exhibit almost an aggressive Indianness. But it was produced initially for a Western market, and its first American edition contains material (or rather endorsements) by three Americans – material omitted from all subsequent editions, incidentally.

The remote origins of the Krishna Consciousness movement have been much discussed since the late 1960s, and here we may simply recapitulate some of its more outstanding features. Its founder, Krishna Chaitanya (originally Viśvambhara Miśra, 1485-1533) was a Bengali, deeply devoted to Krishna and his consort Radha, whom he celebrated by means of dancing, singing and processions. The style of the movement which he founded was ecstatic through and through, and its chief scripture was the *Bhagavata Purāṇa*, together with various devotional lyrics. Interestingly enough, the Gita appears to have played little or no part in the formation of the Chaitanya movement: where it celebrated Krishna, the Krishna in question was the youthful demigod of the *Purāṇas*, not the philosophical teacher of the Gita.[1] However, the rise to prominence of the Gita at the turn of the century directed the movement toward the shorter and more philosophical scripture, while not directing it away from the *Bhāgavata Purāṇa*. Nevertheless it maintained strongly that its own succession of teachers was unbroken and that that succession had begun with Krishna himself, who took precedence even over Brahma. In the 'disciplic succession', Sri Bhaktivedanta, Swami was named as Number Thirty-two, 'Lord Chaitanya' being Number Twenty-two.

Bhaktivedanta arrived in New York in 1965, practically penniless, to proclaim the message of the sole lordship of Krishna and to teach the youth of America 'Krishna Consciousness'. He succeeded beyond the range of any reasonable expectation, and in a more worldly-wise man his very success might have come as a great surprise. But Bhaktivedanta simply accepted success as the divine seal of approval set on his mission. He knew little or nothing of the country or the people to whom he had been sent and appears never to have reflected on the sociological or psychological reasons behind his triumph. His International Society for Krishna Consciousness was founded in July 1966, attracting a motley company of alienated and confused young Christians and (notably) Jews, seeking the voice of wisdom and authority in an unwise and divided world, and prepared to accept India as its ultimate source. Unlike some other jet-age gurus, Bhaktivedanta made no conscious concessions to the West, other than the use of English. He admitted no compromises where scriptures were concerned (nor in respect of dress, food or life-style). As a swami he talked down to his followers, he did not discuss with them. His position was simple. Krishna is God. The *Purāṇa* is about Krishna, but the Gita is the Word of Krishna and therefore infallible. What emerged was therefore a species of Hindu fundamentalism, which some Western observers found almost as distasteful as its Evangelical Christian variant – though the conventions of the 'age of dialogue' made it harder to say so.

The many volumes of the *Bhāgavata Purāṇa*, though expensively produced and sold to libraries and a few individuals, clearly could not serve as a pocket guide to Krishna Consciousness. The Gita could, on the other hand, and did.

ISKCON has always recognised the value of what the advertising world calls 'endorsements' – expressions of approval produced by celebrities in various walks of life. So it was that the first edition of

---

[1] On Chaitanya, see e.g. Farquhar, *An Outline of the Religious Literature of India* (Oxford 1920), p.307ff.

The Bhagavad Gita As It Is appeared accompanied by three such statements, two by well-known American poets, Allen Ginsberg and Denise Levertov, and the third by a Roman Catholic monk and popular theologian, Thomas Merton. (These have not appeared in any later edition, incidentally.) Ginsberg, already known as the archetypal poet of the counter-culture, produced a stream of impressions, of 'Krishna with his Magic Mantra', of the Krishna movement as 'an ancient perfectly preserved piece of street India' and of the chanting of the 'Hare Krishna' *mantra* as ' ... a universal pleasure: a tranquillity at realisation of the *community* of tender hearts; a vibration which inevitably affects all men, naked or in uniform'.[2] But that he thought that this was perhaps going to help produce – in the neurotic depths of the Vietnam war – 'our own true America' was abundantly clear. Denise Levertov was much more restrained and ventured to criticise the early devotees for their fundamentalism and for the apparent lack of concern for issues of war and social justice. Still, she thought that the study of the Gita might be valuable, at least to judge from 'the changed lives of those who do study it', provided that it could be taken 'symbolically, not literally'.[3] Thomas Merton was just moving into his final spiritual phase, as a distant devotee of Eastern wisdom. The Second Vatican Council had just exhorted the Catholic faithful to enter wherever possible into dialogue with other religions and cultures, and Merton was evidently bent on doing just that. Western culture he felt (like practically everyone else in the late 1960s) to be spiritually bankrupt and destructive, lacking as it did (or appeared to do) 'the inner depth of an authentic metaphysical consciousness'. This India might be able to provide. There were, however, problems attached to the reading of the Gita, most notably its apparent endorsement of war. That was hardly a point in its favour, though it might be read differently by 'a few sensitive and well-meaning souls', and since these were the kind of people most likely to read the Gita anyway the danger might not be too great. Merton clearly knew nothing of the use to which the Gita had been put in the Indian national movement! Otherwise Father Merton was more impressionistic than precise, but welcomed Krishna consciousness as an antidote to 'an affirmation of our own individual self as ultimate and supreme'.[4] This was however

[2] *The Bhagavad Gita As It Is: with introduction, translation and authorized purport* by A.C. Bhaktivedanta Swami, Acharya, International Society for Krishna Consciousness (New York 1968), p.14f. (Allen Ginsberg).
[3] Ibid., p.16f. (Denise Levertov).
[4] Ibid., p.18-22 (Thomas Merton).

fairly typical of the well-meaning niceness of post-Vatican II writers on inter-religious dialogue.

To pass from the endorsements to the text proper is to exchange impressionism for an almost clinical precision. Swami Bhaktivedanta was uninterested in anything save hammering his message home, and this he did in an utterly uncompromising manner. There are no problems of dating and authorship. 'The Speaker is Lord Krishna.'[5] Therefore, 'One who wants to understand The Bhagavad Gita should accept Krishna as the Supreme Personality of Godhead.'[6] Reading the Gita absolves one of the necessity of reading any other Vedic literature[7] – though historically speaking, the Gita is not, and never has been, part of Vedic literature at all. But to the eye of faith, the matter is quite simple: 'The Bhagavad Gita is the essence of all Vedic knowledge. It is said that one who drinks the water of the Ganges will be freed from sin. Similarly, one who studies The Bhagavad Gita has no need of any other literature whatever.'[8]

But it is not enough simply to read the Gita in any convenient version. One must read it as interpreted in the line of 'disciplic succession, without motivated [i.e. unauthorised] interpretation'.[9] Over and over again the point is made that the Gita can be understood only by devotees, that the wrong commentary is worse than no commentary at all and that in the last resort the authority of the Gita is dependent on the authority of Krishna himself: 'Krishna cannot be subject to Illusion.'[10] Devotion implies discipline; that is, the acceptance of 'the Vedic rules and regulations'. One should give up half one's earnings to 'a good cause, such as the advancement of Krishna consciousness', and the absence of devotion of this order is 'infamy'.[11] Those who take any other line of approach are dismissed as 'unscrupulous commentators' who 'hide Krishna' either out of ignorance or malice.[12]

What is chiefly impressive about this interpretation of the Gita is its utter and complete singlemindedness. Alternatives are not even considered. There are no problems, no ambiguities. Every type of work can and should be done for the sake of Krishna. 'No work should be done by any man, except in relationship to Krishna ... If

[5] Ibid., p.23.
[6] Ibid., p.25.
[7] Ibid., p.40.
[8] Ibid., loc.cit.
[9] Ibid., p.45.
[10] Ibid., p.68.
[11] Ibid., p.211.
[12] Ibid., p.206f.

Krishna is the Proprietor of the business, then Krishna should enjoy the profit of the business.'[13] And the Gita as a whole is meant to show ' ... how one can understand his spiritual existence, and his eternal relationship with the Supreme Spiritual personality; and to teach one how to go back Home, back to Godhead'.[14] These last three words, incidentally, make up the title of the ISKCON glossy magazine, *Back to Godhead*.

Denise Levertov was right to see in this movement an 'alternative fundamentalism'. The Bible has been exchanged for the Gita, but otherwise the movement is a perfect parallel. Critical questions are excluded as irrelevant, since the Gita, like the Bible in Christian Fundamentalism, is not of human origin. It inspires action, but paralyses the critical faculties. Criticism is faithless and destructive, if it is acknowledged at all. And being strictly supernatural in its origins it communicates a kind of energy, even to those whose understanding is rudimentary – hence the frenetic distribution of *The Bhagavad Gita As It Is* to friend and critic alike. In this enterprise, some slight measure of deception is perhaps to be expected.

The world-famous film version of the life of Gandhi appeared in 1982, several years after Swami Bhaktivedanta had died. But at least no one could fail to notice that Gandhi had been an avid reader of the Gita (see above, pp. 113-21). By ISKCON standards, therefore, Gandhi was in touch with the Word of Krishna, and might well serve as an unconscious advertising agent for the Gita. Accordingly there appeared advertisements in various newspapers (my example appeared in the *Sydney Morning Herald* on 22 December 1983), offering free copies of 'Gandhi's Book of Truth' and calling the Gita 'India's most famous spiritual work'. It went on:

> Gandhi was never without a copy. He daily studied the Gita's profound wisdom, finding timeless knowledge to awaken the greatest attributes of the human spirit.
> In Gandhi's own words: 'The Gita shall unravel all our spiritual tangles. Those who meditate on the Gita will derive fresh joy and new meaning from it every day.'

The object of the exercise was also stated as being 'to promote world peace' – the most easily acceptable cause of the early 1980s.

Now quite apart from the fact that Gandhi and Swami Bhaktivedanta had absolutely nothing in common there is one

---

[13] Ibid., p.237.
[14] Ibid., loc.cit.

interesting omission from this advertisement – the title 'Mahatma'. Why might this be? Reference to *The Bhagavad Gita As It Is* supplies the answer. According to the Swami,

> A Mahatma is always engaged in chanting the glories of the Supreme Lord Krishna, the Personality of Godhead. He has no other business. When the question of glorification is there, that means one has to glorify the Supreme Lord, praising His Holy Name, His Eternal Form, His Transcendental Qualities, His Uncommon Pastimes (!). One has to describe all these things.[15]

By these standards, Gandhi was anything but a Mahatma, since he did absolutely none of these things. In a word, he did not belong to the Chaitanya sect in any of its various branches. But he did read the Gita. A Catholic might well advertise the New Testament on the grounds that it was read by the Reverend Ian Paisley, with equal (but no more) justification. But where the stakes are so high, what the Buddhist world calls 'skilful means' are presumably justified.

As between the first and subsequent editions of *The Bhagavad Gita As It Is* one important change had come over its appearance, apart from its use of popular bazaar-type religious art. This was its tidying up of Sanskrit words. 'Krishna' was no longer acceptable: it had to be 'Kṛṣṇa'. There was an epidemic of diacritical marks on every word of Sanskrit origin, as though this European scholarly device of the nineteenth and twentieth centuries somehow lent authority and credence to the content of the text. One senses the reasoning behind this manoeuvre, and had the ISKCON members been more practically proficient at Indian languages the impression might have been more convincing. As it is, in the whole of 'Hare Krishna' literature this remains no more than a curiosity and an irritant.

In short *The Bhagavad Gita As It Is* remains substantially an impression of what a particular corner of the Hindu world *imagines* that it is. But because of the great energy and enterprise which went into the furtherance of the Krishna cause in the 1960s and 1970s it created an impression which was altogether more concentrated than that emerging from any other branch of the neo-Hindu movement in the West. A body of devotees was created, prepared to treat the Gita precisely as the Christian revivalist world of a century earlier had treated the Bible, with no greater or lesser justification. Swami Bhaktivedanta was a devoted man with a mission. He loved the Gita. Probably, however, he understood little of the forces which had

---

[15] Ibid., p.201.

shaped the movement over which he came to preside. In comparison other Indian gurus of the same period were less effective and far more capable of compromise. In 'the age of approximation' compromise was of the essence.

9

Ethical Monotheism and Social Caste

25. 'Growing acquaintance with the Spiritual East'

The Western interpreters of the Gita whom we have passed in review in this book almost all had one thing in common: namely, that their own dominant religious tradition (whether or not they actually followed it closely) was Christian. The Gita therefore came in the majority of cases to be set up against one or other branch of the Christian tradition, or one or other individual understanding of Christianity. In some cases it served as a corrective, supplying the Western mind with something which appeared to be missing from its own tradition. In others it posed both a problem and a threat, communicating as it did an alternative Saviour, Krishna, and an alternative way of salvation, the way of *bhakti yoga*. Those parts of the Christian West who found their own religion narrow, rigid or unsatisfying often turned to the Gita for that which they had failed to find in Christianity. Those whose confidence in the Christian Gospel remained firm turned to the Gita in order to read the secret of (and if possible, to counteract) its appeal to the heart and mind of India. For a third group, the Western Orientalists, the Gita posed strictly intellectual and historical problems: when and why had it been written, and what independent elements had contributed to its final composite form? At almost any time since the appearance of Wilkins' translation, and certainly throughout the past century, all three concerns have been operative simultaneously, sometimes independent of one another and sometimes overlapping.

One thing must, however, have emerged from our study thus far: that the Gita is first and foremost a living sacred scripture to Hindus. It follows that insight into the way in which Hindus read and interpret their own Gita must provide a valuable insight into Hindu devotion and Hindu religion generally. The opposite also applies, of course: that a misreading of the Gita, or the subjecting of it to inappropriate categories, though it may satisfy the reader, may communicate no understanding of what it means to Hindus.

Many of the writers with whom we have been concerned in these pages had only an incidental interest in the real India, preferring an idealised or visionary India which in matters of the spirit was all those things which the West was not. This India of the imagination was calm where the West was frantic, spiritual where the West was materialist, intuitive where the West was logical and rational. In reading the Gita, therefore, they sought for what they believed Western religion and culture had lost – chiefly a sense of cosmic oneness, a 'cosmic consciousness' in which diversity was swallowed up in unity, appearance in reality. They also sought relief from their own sense of powerlessness in face of Western impersonality, clothing their longings in the language of geography, the East standing for intuition and instinct, the West for logic and pragmatism. After the First World War, the language of depth-psychology was added: now the West stood for the conscious, problem-solving mind, bent on establishing mastery over the world; the East for the subconscious or unconscious, equally capable of ecstasy or violence, but uncontrollable because inaccessible and largely unrecognised. Some had seen that these were simply two sides to each and every human psyche, Romain Rolland for example writing in 1929 that he desired

> ... to reconcile, if it is possible, the two antithetical forms of spirit for which the West and the East are wrongly supposed to stand – reason and faith – or perhaps it would be more accurate to say, the diverse forms of reason and of faith; for the West and the East share them both almost equally though few suspect it.[1]

Carl Gustav Jung – often in later years wrongly assumed to be the champion of the intuitive over against the pragmatic – had written in the same year, 1929, that although encounter with the East (in this case China) had taught the West 'another, wider, more profound, and higher understanding' nevertheless:

> Growing acquaintance with the spiritual East should be no more than the symbolical expression of the fact that *we are entering into connection with the elements in ourselves which are still strange to us* [my italics].[2]

[1] Rolland, *The Life of Ramakrishna* (Eng. tr. Almora 1944), p.4.
[2] Wilhelm and Jung, *The Secret of the Golden Flower* (New York 1962), p.82.

But at the same time, 'we' are doing so as Westerners:

> Denial of our own historical premises would be sheer folly and would be the best way to bring about another deracination. Only by standing firmly on our own soil can we assimilate the spirit of the East.[3]

The trouble was that then as later, whatever assimilation process there was, took place in a thoroughly haphazard fashion. At one extreme, alienation from the values of Western culture and religion resulted in an emotional desire always to give the East preferential treatment in matters involving the spiritual life. For many years practically monopolised in the West by the Theosophical Society and its various offshoots, since the 1960s this tendency has settled down to become an omnipresent feature of 'alternative spirituality', where the reading of the Gita, and the production of commentaries and superficially edifying discourses on the oneness of all truth, became extremely common. At the other extreme the East and Eastern forms of religion posed too much of a threat to conservative and conventional Christianity to be regarded other than with alarm. One might have expected that even here, the very magnitude of the threat would have inspired a certain desire to come to grips with its presuppositions and its source material. This, however, hardly happened – though for reasons too complex to discuss further on this occasion.

In between these two extremes, however, there was an indistinct ground occupied by various types of liberals – in Christian terms, still loyal to their churches and the traditions they represented, but increasingly prepared to undertake voyages of exploration into foreign territorial waters. Here too the reading of the Gita assumed a certain importance, after the 1960s under the rubric of 'inter-religious dialogue'.

As we have seen, the Gita had been read by Christians since it first became available in English. Warren Hastings had seen in it real assonances with the Christian message, though without specifying what they might be. In the nineteenth century unsuccessful attempts had been made to establish some degrees of historical dependence between the New Testament and the Gita. Liberal Christians in the late nineteenth and early twentieth centuries had seized upon the theory of evolution as a device to justify their paying respectful attention to the Gita, while still maintaining the superiority and

[3] Ibid., p.128.

finality of the Christian revelation. On this view the Gita represented a high point of Hindu religion but had been overtaken by the evolutionary process along the separate Judaeo-Christian line. And whatever inconsistencies and apparent uncertainties the Western mind could find in the Gita could be explained – less as wilful misrepresentation or the workings of an unbridled imagination than as the products of an intermediate stage in the evolution of religion from lower to higher forms, from polytheism to monotheism, from fear to love. This attitude to the Gita came to particularly clear expression in a book by Nicol Macnicol, *Indian Theism*, published in 1915.

In the Gita, wrote Macnicol, we find 'the nearest approach that it was possible for India unaided to make to ethical monotheism'.[4] (Ethical monotheism was at the time regarded as the highest point capable of being reached by religious evolution.) The Gita strives to unite two conceptions, *jñāna* (knowledge) and *bhakti* (loving devotion), and although it does not quite succeed the fact of the attempt being made has given the Gita its unique position in the heart and mind of India. And bearing in mind the modern theistic movements in India, and their appeal to many Hindu minds, it is possible for Macnicol to place the Gita within this modern process:

> The inconsistencies of its teaching are obvious [he wrote], but the direction in which a solution for them may be sought is indicated, and there loom before us the outlines of a Theism that is characteristically Indian in its presuppositions and that has purged itself sufficiently of superstition to be acceptable to thoughtful men.[5]

There still remained a problem to the Western Christian interpreter, however – the problem of ethics. In the early years of this century one might say that, however much the Christian interpreters might have admired some features of Hindu belief and practice, in the last analysis there was almost always a sticking-point. That point came as a result of the apparent absence of any necessary connection between the Hindu conception of God and the question of moral and ethical endeavour. 'The most crucial test of any religion is concerned with its ethical character,' wrote Nicol Macnicol. 'Is it, or is it not, an instrument for producing righteousness?'[6] And again, leaving the *Purāṇas* on one side, even the Gita seemed (particularly to

---

[4] Macnicol, *Indian Theism* (Oxford 1915), p.75.
[5] Ibid., p.202.
[6] Ibid., p.248.

missionaries) to be less than convincing on this particular point. After all had not some fairly extreme nationalists been able to enlist the support of the Gita for acts of violence? This whole question of the nature of Hindu ethics is of course a very complex one, and one which we cannot go into more fully; but it seemed for a time as though to Western minds, as long as the ethical question remained uppermost, appreciation of the Gita would remain at best partial, at worst slightly hollow and motivated less by genuine feeling for its values than by a nervous desire not to offend Hindus.

Here and there, genuine attempts were made to overcome this difficulty. The American psychologist J.B. Pratt, for instance, writing on *India and its Faiths* in 1916, observed that in the Gita's own terms the whole religious question is psychological, being removed altogether to the 'inner sphere'.[7] But Christians continued to stress the moral issue. Edgar Thompson in 1933 reflected that 'one of the chief defects of Hinduism is that it has so uncertain a hold on morality', and asserted that the Gita, bearing 'a very uncertain testimony to a Personal God, who is the treasury of all good qualities', whatever it may be, is not a prophetic book, 'which summons men to leave the lower and obey the highest only'.[8] A similar, though less baldly stated, view is found in Sydney Cave's book *Hinduism or Christianity?* which appeared in 1939. Toward the end of the book, Cave has this to say:

> The issue between Hinduism and Christianity will not be solved by the academic discussion of two world-views. Interesting and illuminating as such discussion can be, it can never be decisive, for the values by which men judge are dependent on their ideals, and these ideals are created in part by the doctrines they already hold.[9]

To this one might add that it was when Western scholars began comparing and contrasting the Gita with their own religious and ethical ideals that the quality of genuine understanding began to prove very elusive indeed. The purely historical questions – of authorship, dating, provenance and redaction history – could be (and were) dealt with calmly; but once the Gita began to be re-established in India as a popular source of spiritual comfort and sustenance, and to be interpreted for the most part allegorically, even these questions began to be coloured by partisanship. Whether their

[7] Pratt, *India and its Faiths* (London 1916), p.101.
[8] Thompson, *The Word of the Cross to Hindus* (London 1933), pp. 148, 309.
[9] Cave, *Hinduism or Christianity?* (London 1939), p.236.

answers appear convincing is bound to depend, therefore, on one's prior convictions in areas only incidentally related to the interpretation of a particular scripture.

*

Over the past few decades Gita interpretation on a comparative basis has become much less common than it once was, and many of the closely-argued issues of the past appear to have been popularly discarded, being replaced by a general acceptance of the Hindu view of the Gita as a comprehensive and unified synthesis of the *Sanātana Dharma* in its entirety. Still in the 1930s attempts were being made here and there to come to terms with the old question of the Gita's origins. As we have seen, Rudolf Otto had published in 1933 in German and in 1939 in English a treatise on *The Original Gita*, in which, following Garbe, he had attempted to apply some of the methods of modern biblical criticism to the text of the Gita, starting from the conviction that the Gita was originally neither an Upanishad nor a *bhakti* treatise, but 'simply a fragment of most magnificent epic narrative'.[10] It may be argued that Otto went to work far too enthusiastically in trying to isolate this interpolation and that from the totality; and yet Otto's instincts were surely right on one point, that 'in the beginning was the drama' -- the epic – and that the literary critical enterprise simply has to begin at this point.

At the opposite critical extreme, so to speak, there stands such works as S.C. Roy's *The Bhagavad-Gita and Modern Scholarship* (1941), which is mainly a defence of the Gita's integrity over against the claims of a few Western scholars, principally Garbe and Otto: the Gita, writes Roy,

> is both a product and monument of [the] reconciling, all-absorbing spirit of the Indian civilisation, and viewed in this light, all its contradictions can be easily removed, and all its difficulties satisfactorily resolved.[11]

The identical point is made by Heinrich Zimmer (or possibly by Joseph Campbell) in *Philosophies of India* (1951):

---

[10] Otto, *The Original Gita* (Eng. tr. 1939), p.10.
[11] Roy, *The Bhagavad-Gita and Modern Scholarship* (London 1941), p.5.

Numerous contradictions have been pointed out by Western critics, yet to the Indian mind these contradictions are precisely the value. For they represent the beginning of the great *rapprochement* and, besides, are readily resolved by a realisation of the One in all.[12]

Similar statements are to be found in practically every work of more recent Hindu philosophy and religion: according to Radhakrishnan, for instance, 'It [the Gita] represents not any sect of Hinduism but Hinduism as a whole, nor merely Hinduism but religion as such, in its universality, without limit of time or space ...'[13] And S.C. Chatterjee sums up: 'The synthetic outlook and the catholic spirit of Hinduism are seen at their best in the religion of the Bhagavad Gītā.'[14] Perhaps then it is not surprising that the modern Hindu should reckon the fundamental unity and the transcendental value of the Gita among the necessary presuppositions of his faith, for which he sees absolutely no reason to argue in detail. On questions of interpretation he will as a rule be convinced that the Gita is to be treated, not historically, but allegorically.

What is perhaps a little more surprising is that some modern Western interpreters have themselves moved so far in the same direction. Often, however, they seem not so much to have transcended the older critical questions as to be content to ignore them. In fact the post-war emphasis on what has come to be called 'inter-religious dialogue' has led in some cases to a degree of superficiality in treatment of this and similar sources.

It may be invidious to single out one example of a recent writer in order to emphasise this general point, but since it is through the writings of Geoffrey Parrinder that many present-day Western readers in the English-speaking world have been introduced to the Gita, a brief comment on Parrinder's work may not be out of place. The comment cannot be other than brief, for although he has produced a verse translation of the Gita, and has written about it in a number of books and papers, including *Upanishads, Gītā and Bible* (2nd ed. 1975), *The Significance of the Bhagavad-Gītā for Christian Theology* (1968) and *Avatar and Incarnation* (1970), he has done little more than tell his wide readership more or less what the poem contains. He appears to have no very firm views on any major critical question, and seems almost always to lean heavily on the work of such writers

---

[12] Zimmer (ed. Campbell), *Philosophies of India* (New York 1951), p.381.
[13] Radhakrishnan, *The Bhagavadgītā* (London 1967), p.12.
[14] Chatterjee, 'The basic beliefs of Hinduism', in Morgan (ed.), *The Religion of the Hindus* (New York 1953), p.201f.

as S. Dasgupta. He asserts that 'the Gita has inconsistencies that are remarkable even among religious books,'[15] but makes little attempt to account for them, except to say that 'it is a work of religion, and it naturally has the paradoxes of theology'.[16] He quotes Otto's *The Original Gita* without appreciation; and his reflections on the theism of the Gita echo those made by Nicol Macnicol more than forty years earlier. In the last analysis his purpose is to show to a Christian readership that Christian theologians might profitably study the Gita, since 'whatever there is of good in this poem comes from "the Light that lighteth every man" '.[17] He approaches a deeper view in his chapter on 'Theophany' in *Avatar and Incarnation*, and yet seems curiously unwilling to commit himself too far on any question involving comparison and contrast. Of a kind, this may perhaps be called an essay in phenomenological *epoché*; the final result, however, can scarcely be said to advance phenomenological understanding (*Verstehen*), except on a fairly superficial factual level.

Rather more successful is the well-known Gita edition published by R.C. Zaehner in 1969. Zaehner admits himself to be a convinced believer in 'the essential unity of the Gītā' and accordingly aligns himself with the dominant tradition of Hindu exposition and commentary. But again he leaves the old critical questions of origin and dating almost entirely to take care of themselves. His exegesis is thematic, but hardly historical; once more an influential Western interpreter is doing his utmost to avoid asking the traditional Western critical questions and to take instead a functional view of the Gita. On matters of dating he assigns the Gita (without saying why) to a period 'some time between the fifth and second centuries B.C.', and on questions of interpretation he appears for the most part to follow Rāmānuja, who (he says) 'probably comes nearest to the mind of the author of the Gita'. Otherwise, Zaehner's chief intention was to produce a readable text, and to interpret that text theistically, critical questions meanwhile being dismissed as of no particular importance.[18]

[15] Parrinder, *The Significance of the Bhagavad-Gītā for Christian Theology* (London 1968), p.8.

[16] Ibid., p.8.

[17] Ibid., p.10.

[18] Zaehner, *The Bhagavad-Gītā* (London 1973), pp.5-8. Zaehner also mentioned the Gita repeatedly in other contexts. See e.g. *At Sundry Times* (London 1958), pp.117-33; and many references in *Concordant Discord* (London 1970). Always he was concerned mainly with the Gita's 'mystical' dimension.

26. 'The tactics of the author of the Gita can no longer succeed'

The greater part of this study of Western images of the Gita has been concerned with impressions made on the minds of individuals. The argument has moved chiefly on the level of beliefs and theories concerning the nature of reality, the 'over-soul' and God. Most of the recipients of those impressions have had very little inclination to discuss the *social* implications of the Gita's teachings, the sole partial exception being provided by those Protestant missionaries in India who in the earlier part of this century saw the Gita's teachings as deficient in respect of progress and moral seriousness. But as the twentieth century proceeded, and particularly following India's independence in 1947, social issues came to bulk large in both the Indian and the international discussion concerning India's long-term future. Increasingly the religious and philosophical question of the motives for action in the world came to be replaced by the pragmatic question of goals, methods and strategies for development. As the India which had been the Romantics' refuge from the corrosion of modern Western society became no more than a peculiarly problematical part of the 'third world', so the emphasis shifted away from spirituality and in the direction of economics, particularly where the socialist wing of world opinion was concerned.

Mostly the Gita has entered this debate only incidentally, however. But the Gita's place in twentieth-century consciousness being what it was, it could not be excluded altogether. The explicit focus of social concern was to a very large extent the institution of caste, while the indirect question was whether the Gita did, or did not, sanction its maintenance.

*

In Madras in 1969 I happened to hear a lecture delivered by a prominent Indian civil servant on the subject of 'The Raja, the Monk and the Mahatma' – Ram Mohun Roy, Swami Vivekānanda and Mahatma Gandhi respectively. The burden of the lecture was that all three, despite their reforming zeal, had been prevented from fulfilling their intentions by their reluctance even to attempt a root-and-branch abolition of the institution of caste. Certainly all three had attempted to bypass some of its cruder features. In the end, though, none had made much impression on the massive edifice as a whole. This the lecturer thought had been unfortunate for the future of India.

The caste system of course stratifies Hindu society, while Hindu doctrine provides caste with a religious foundation, by locating caste in the order of creation (*Rig Veda* 10:90), and by claiming that individual caste status in any one of the immortal soul's 'incarnations' on earth is dependent in large measure on spiritual, ritual and ethical conduct in previous existences. The nub of the customary caste argument is of course that in each successive rebirth every individual receives precisely his or her 'just deserts' on a basis of conduct in previous existences; that there is no such thing as *unmerited* well-being or suffering; and that no one is at liberty to opt for any caste status other than that which previous, though unremembered, deeds (*karma*) have made inevitable. The inequalities of human life on earth are therefore explained away at a stroke, as normal, natural and indeed inevitable, while attempts to improve the lot of the poor, the dispossessed and the suffering may be seen as an impertinent interference with the processes of cosmic law. At the same time, though, it should also be pointed out that since the knowledge of previous existences on earth is withheld from all save the ultimately enlightened, the *karma* theory is neither provable nor falsifiable, and the mitigation of suffering brought about by outside agencies may equally be seen as a consequence of accumulated *karma*. Generally speaking, though, caste status cannot be changed by the individual as an expression of a mere will to social advancement. At any given point in the world's history, the social structure is what *karma* has made it. Hindu social structure therefore is nothing if not hierarchical.

Caste and socialism are totally incompatible. Caste knows no equality of human status, no *liberté, egalité, fraternité* such as has increasingly dominated Western political and religious thought since the end of the eighteenth century. *Liberté* can be gained only by breaking free from the phenomenal world altogether. *Égalité* may obtain among men within a caste, but otherwise every caste group – even among 'untouchables' – gains its identity partly by relating to its 'natural' superiors and inferiors. *Fraternité* likewise exists within the individual caste, as within the family, but not between castes on different rungs of the social ladder. Small wonder then that the injection of radical socialist and semi-socialist ideas into India during the nineteenth and twentieth centuries placed the theory at the heart of Hindu society under severe strain. Those Hindus who felt the pressure – in practice those educated in English-language schools, colleges and universities on 'democratic' principles – were forced either to rethink or to retreat into a half-world of custom unsupported by any convincing theory.

This however was only one of the tensions brought about by the introduction of Western ideas into the mind of Hindu India. The most trying was perhaps the learning of democratic principles in a country governed through an authoritarian bureaucracy. But the belief in progress and development in a country dominated by the ancient notion of *karma* was another. Inevitably some Hindus were pulled in one direction, some in another. The ultra-orthodox were unimpressed by the Western argument and contradicted it at every turn. The ultra-radical took up the line of Karl Marx as far as they could – though even then often with concessions in private to tradition. In between an assorted collection of liberals attempted as best they could to 'restate' Hindu doctrine in line with social ideals which they could neither fully accept nor fully reject. The institution of caste and the arguments which supported it could therefore be affirmed as a divine ordinance; rejected out of hand as a throw-back to a discredited past; or rendered innocuous by being restated in, for instance, 'division of labour' terms.

The Gita had a place in all three arguments, though it is with the socialist argument that we shall be chiefly concerned here. The heirs of Tom Paine, Benjamin Franklin, Comte, Marx and Engels simply could not accept any social order which was prepared to acquiesce in divinely-ordained human inequality. Time and time again during the past two centuries the socialist West has put forward the argument that such a 'system' could not possibly be in India's best interests. Indians educated in the West or in India in accordance with Western patterns followed suit. Some fairly recent examples will illustrate the point.

Jawaharlal Nehru was often scathing in his criticism of religion and urged his countrymen to turn from religion and towards science as a necessary condition of progress. Caste in particular he regarded as a prison for the mind of the Indian people, a 'weakening factor' in the national consciousness: 'along with the growth of rigidity in the caste system,' he wrote, 'grew rigidity of mind.'[1] But caste was in Nehru's view in spite of everything an aspect of Hindu religion, and Hindu religion an aspect of religion in general. Nehru could perhaps countenance the private practice of religion; but for its organised forms he had no time at all, writing in *The Discovery of India* that organised religion

---

[1] Nehru, *The Discovery of India* (Bombay 1961), p.84.

... encourages a temper which is the very opposite to that of science. It produces narrowness and intolerance, credulity and superstition, emotionalism and irrationalism. It tends to close and limit the mind of man, and to produce a temper of a dependent, unfree person.[2]

And where else should one look for the quintessence of 'unfreedom' than to caste, which Nehru saw as the supreme symbol of exclusiveness among Hindus: ' ... in the social organisation of to-day it [caste] has no place left.'[3]

Thus to the extent to which the Gita advocates the practice of caste duty, it falls under the blanket condemnation of religion.

Critics more recent than Nehru have made precisely this equation. The Indian socialist has waged untiring war against caste:

... the caste system practised in the past and as it is still in practice is indefensible ... On such a view of the human situation, Indian culture cannot command respect. There is room in it neither for dignity nor for freedom of man.[4]

Distinctions have been drawn between 'the brahmanical culture' – traditional, caste-oriented, hierarchical, authoritarian, based on agriculture and the village – and 'modernity' – scientific, rational and achievement-oriented. To the sociological-socialist mind there can be no doubt on which side of this divide the Gita is to be located. Certainly attempts may be made to interpret it as being supportive of 'modernity', but these cannot shake it free of the 'brahmanical' matrix. The question here is not whether the Gita, or parts of the Gita, can be allegorised, spiritualised or theosophised in order to become acceptable to individual seekers after spiritual insight; it has to do rather with its teachings as a whole and with the social group which has had the interpretation of them in the Hindu setting. The Gita maintains that one's caste duty should be performed without thought of the fruits accruing thereby. Both elements are unacceptable to the socialist critic: caste duty as such, for reasons already stated; and non-attachment to the fruits of action, since this is bound to militate against progress. A.D. Moddie writes, on this second point, that

[2] Ibid., p.545f. Nehru was not however without respect for the Gita's vision of 'the ideal man'. On this subject, see Narasimha Char, *Profile of Nehru* (Bombay, n.d.), ch.12, and especially p.160f. Char adds that ' ... the metaphysical part of it [the Gita] did not appeal to him' (p.161).

[3] Ibid., p.553.

[4] Nigam, 'Science and Indian culture', in Shah and Rao (eds.), *Tradition and Modernity in India* (Bombay 1965), p.31.

The Gita's philosophy of 'Nishkam Karma' or labour without attachment to its fruits may be a very noble metaphysical concept, but it hardly promotes a keen desire to count the fruits and measure results.[5]

Indeed it does not. Put somewhat crudely, *nishāma karma* cannot really coexist with five-year plans for economic and social development. In these circumstances the Gita may continue to be revered in the abstract for its role in the shaping of India's Hindu culture, but hardly be followed in detail – if one's basic convictions are socialist, that is.

*

Examples of western socialist evaluations and denunciations of religion are plentiful, though very few exhibit any really close acquaintance with that which is being criticised. Usually a few generalisations suffice, before the argument shifts to the 'real' problems of economics and politics. The Swedish sociologist Gunnar Myrdal's massive book *Asian Drama*, for instance, bypasses religion almost entirely, save for a few incidental references. Religion, he writes, is always the enemy of progress and development, 'a tremendous force for social inertia'. The reason, in Myrdal's mind, is patently obvious: it is 'the permeation of religion ... by irrational views and illogical thinking' which renders it 'inimical to the spread of the modernisation ideals and to their realisation'. For India's part, caste is the social quintessence of this irrationality:

> In a national setting of extreme poverty, it [caste] tends to make the existing inequalities particularly rigid and unyielding.[6]

Caste also 'stultifies ordinary human feelings of brotherhood and compassion' throughout Hindu society.[7] Myrdal does not mention the Gita explicitly, it is true. But to the extent that the Western reader of the Gita actually pays attention to what is said and implied

---

[5] Moddie, *The Brahmanical Culture and Modernity* (New York 1968), p.25. Precisely the opposite point may however also be made: that the Gita's message has been India's chief source of spiritual inspiration and political fulfilment. This has been stated by K.M. Panikkar, and also by Malhotra: 'The role of the Bhagavadgita in Indian politics', in *the Research Bulletin (Arts) of the University of the Panjab* 36 (1962), p.3.

[6] Myrdal, *Asian Drama* (Harmondsworth 1968), p.103ff.

[7] Ibid., p.745f.

in it about *varṇāśramadharma*, the lesson must be obvious: that the Gita not only sanctions caste law and warns most severely against its neglect but may also be seen as a powerful instrument in the perpetuation of caste sentiment and caste practice.

The Westerner reading the Gita as a 'spiritual pilgrim', however, will not necessarily notice that there is any social aspect of any kind to the Gita. The quest for the 'over-soul' and the widespread tendency to allegorise the Gita's message have certainly had this consequence among many: that absolutely nothing in the Gita need be taken at its face value. What is stated in the Gita in terms of *varṇa* will be interpreted as though it referred to levels of spiritual enlightenment and awareness, and nothing more.

This may perhaps go some way toward explaining why, during the most recent period of Gita *Schwärmerei* in the West, the 1960s, Western Gita enthusiasts appear to have failed altogether to pay any attention at all to the caste question, or indeed to any question concerning the religious aspect of social stratification in India. Still less did they draw any connection between the words of the Gita and their deeply-felt concern for social justice. The social philosophy of Western youth in the 1960s might well be described as 'soft Marxism' – a Marxism stopping short of actual revolution. India it saw as problematical, certainly; but possessed at the same time of vast reservoirs of spiritual power and energy, unrelated to such mundane factors as culture and society. The Gita it read as a gateway to a deeper self-realisation and not as an analytical tool – criticism and hard analysis being reserved for the works and ways of the West. The Indian radical mind, however, had other perceptions, as we shall see in a moment.

But first we may pause to record that the extreme political left could occasionally pay attention to the details, as opposed to only the blurred outlines, of religion in the world. In 1969 a Swedish Marxist, Anna Törngren, published what she called 'a critique of the history of religion' under the revealing title of *Opium för folket* ('Opium for the people'). Here the political ideology is at least consistent: religion is seen as something entirely human ('Religion is not about gods and supernatural beings, but about people'),[8] and as something always devised either by the upper, priest-dominated classes to keep the lower classes under subjection, or emerging from the desire of the oppressed poor to create for themselves a better – though of course imaginary – world beyond the range of the jackboot. Törngren devotes a number of pages to the triad of Jainism, Buddhism and

[8] Törngren, *Opium för folket* (Lund 1969), p.10.

bhakti under the rubric of 'The religious offensive of the warrior caste'.[9] All three, she claims, were the products of a bygone class war. First came Buddhism and Jainism to challenge the Brahmins and their authority but creating a new and separate network of communities and monastic hierarchies in the process. From the Hindu side the response was *bhakti*, which was a further protest on the part of the kshatriyas against the brahmin monopoly. The result was the great epic the *Mahābhārata*, of which the Gita is of course part. The brahmins, however, had their own way of coping with this threat, neutralising it by absorption. She writes:

> One of the explanations of this has to do with the bhakti duty ethic (*pliktmoral*) which not merely accepts, but also actively supports, the caste system. The duty which Krishna praises [in the Gita] is that of the caste laws, which in this instance means those of the warrior caste ...[10]

Once again, therefore, a socialist critique returns to the sore point of caste – so obviously unegalitarian and discriminatory to the Western socialist mind. One has the impression that having arrived at the point of determining that the Gita is in favour of caste – a Bad Thing *a priori* – nothing else which the Gita might perchance contain could be taken seriously by the writer of the political Left. In this case Anna Törngren's analysis ceases at that fairly remote historical and sociological point. To her the Gita is *only* a historical document and of value only in so far as it provides evidence of the post-Buddhist period in Indian history.

The point is however not irrelevant. There are passages in the Gita which speak as clearly as one can imagine of the necessity of observing one's own specific caste duty. It is better to perform the duty of one's own caste badly than another's duty well. To confuse castes leads to the most horrendous consequences, even to the extent of women being debauched and the ancestors toppling out of heaven, deprived of their offerings of food and drink. Arjuna is virtually commanded to place his duty as a *kshatriya* over his duty to his family. Certainly there are verses elsewhere in the Gita which stress that devotion to Krishna overrides the devotee's caste or sex. But to the reader whose sights are set on the questions of social stratification there can be no two opinions: the Gita does indeed advocate caste and uphold the notion of caste law. Therefore it is at the very least not on the side of revolution, or even of political

[9] Ibid., p.254ff.
[10] Ibid., p.261.

mobility. To that extent we can understand the socialist reaction. We can understand too how little the socialist mind would be likely to be impressed by any purely 'spiritual' reading of the Gita.

*

One could no doubt assemble a considerable catalogue of indictments of Hindu traditionalism from India's radical press during the post-independence period. This however would carry us far beyond the bounds of this study. One further example may on the other hand be instructive, less for the ideas it contains than for its unhesitating identification of the Gita and its teachings as the most virulent enemy of India's progress.

Prem Nath Bazaz, like Nehru a Kashmiri Brahmin by birth, published in 1975 his massive (over 700-page) book *The Role of Bhagavad Gita in Indian History*. His argument is based on the juxtaposition of two 'facts': first that the Gita has been the Hindus' 'most venerated scripture' at least since the fourth century A.D.; and secondly that India's 'dark age' covers precisely the same period, down to 1947.[11] Bazaz is convinced that the two are related as cause and effect, and that ' ... on the whole, its teachings can help (and have helped) only to subvert human progress and nourish social evils', the Gita being no more than 'a philosophy of the upper classes', deliberately contrived to keep the lower classes in subjection. Even Gandhi was no exception, since he 'used its teachings to annihilate the rising tide of secular democracy'.[12]

Bazaz' book is however less a detailed consideration of the Gita than a personal review of Indian history, in its sweep and angle of approach not unlike Nehru's *Discovery of India* and containing a consistent polemical point directed against Brahmins and their devices. Also reminiscent of Nehru is Bazaz' belief in a total acceptance of 'science' as the only guarantee of a bright future for India and her masses:

Real knowledge based on discoveries of science is within the grasp of everyone. India, like any other country, has become a part of the world in the sense it was never before. The tactics of the author of the Gita can no longer succeed in keeping the Indians in the thraldom of Brahminism. One after another the cherished theories of the hoary creed are being demolished by science based on reason.[13]

[11] Bazaz, *The Role of Bhagavad Gita in Indian History* (New Delhi 1975), p.vii.
[12] Ibid., p.ix.
[13] Ibid., p.700.

And finally:

> ... anyone who desires the welfare of impoverished and brutalised millions of this vast land will choose science and technology in place of the Gita and Gandhism. By doing so he will no doubt disturb a hornet's nest but, undaunted and undeterred, let him go forward ...[14]

Bazaz' extended diatribe against the Brahmins and 'their' Gita is in reality little more than the customary socialist attack on religion, brought to a sharp focus. In assuming that the symbolical position occupied by the Gita in the post-1880s national movement had been occupied since the Gita first took shape – whenever that may have been – he is in error. That, however, is not the point. The point is surely that to the extent that 'neo-Hinduism' adopted the Gita as its all-sufficient scripture it was inviting the foisting on the Gita of all that is negative, as well as all that is positive, in Indian religion and culture. Bazaz should not be seen as an uncritical disciple of Nehru, whom he on one occasion calls 'a weak-minded person'.[15] And yet his approach is similar to Nehru's in many ways, though pressed to populist extremes never reached, and scarcely even contemplated, by Nehru himself. His enemy is Brahmanism.

The Gita is Brahmanism's scripture. In comparison with the baneful influence of Brahmanism, even the nationalists' traditional bogeyman, Lord Curzon, receives from Bazaz high marks as 'a pioneer-founder of modern India'.[16] The period of British rule in the nineteenth century is praised as having been 'a golden age in Indian history ... the most secure, must fruitful and the happiest [years] for the people in the British territories'.[17] A firm believer in basic rationality and the power of education to create it, Bazaz is however temperamentally less a twentieth-century socialist than a nineteenth-century radical.

*

The evidence presented briefly here may perhaps serve as a warning to those in the West who may still persist in assuming that the whole

---

[14] Ibid., p.702f.
[15] Ibid., p.526.
[16] Ibid., p.409.
[17] Ibid., p.411.

of Hindu India is directed by the purest of spiritual values and in believing that the secular alternative is of no consequence. The reality is far different. The secular voice of India has been growing more and more powerful throughout the century, though it has seldom spoken out against the Gita as Bazaz has done. This has of course been due in large measure to impulses coming from the West, though expressed in terms of Indian priorities. It might indeed be argued that there exists a higher degree of consonance (or perhaps dialogue) between Indian and Euro-American secularists than between religionists in East and West. The same concepts are used, and the same targets are attacked – even, in this case, the otherwise revered Gita itself – both for what they support and for the attitudes to which they give rise. It is salutary to be reminded of this towards the end of a survey from which 'hard' sociological fact has been largely absent.

At least, though, the Gita and its teachings are considered worth attacking, and this may serve as an oblique testimony to the influence of both, in East and West alike, during the 'modern' period. India is after all a secular state, and a few years ago was happy to circulate a film titled 'Temples of Tomorrow': its subject – hydro-electric power stations!

27. Conclusion

The writers with whom we have been concerned in this study were in many cases innocent of all but the most superficial knowledge of Sanskrit. Sometimes they had no Sanskrit at all and made no pretensions to be able to evaluate the Gita in its original form, or in its native setting. Not in every case, however. Some were Orientalists of outstanding ability, but even these were concerned to interpret the Gita to non-Sanskritists, in the evident belief that the enterprise was a worthwhile one and that either the text or its central message would have something to say to non-Hindu readers. Precisely what they supposed that message to be was a variable quantity, however, ranging all the way from a supremely valuable insight into the conditions governing man's place in the universe to a dire warning of the depths to which the human mind might sink when deprived of the light of 'true' revelation; that is to say, that their presuppositions were of the most diverse kinds. Faced with this single text, or with what others had written about it, they incorporated what they believed it to contain each into his own particular map of the universe. Often they would have been hard pressed to say precisely why they reacted to the Gita in the way they did, since maps of the universe are not always consciously drawn.

One option was to try, using the tools of critical historical scholarship (greatly refined during the course of the nineteenth and early twentieth centuries), to discover what the Gita might *originally* have meant and what its compilation might have been intended to achieve. But even this, straightforward as it might seem in point of methodology, was never quite the simple option it sometimes appeared to be. A parallel example may serve to illustrate the point.

David Daiches, in his essay on 'translating the Hebrew Bible',[1] points out that the Hebrew Old Testament conveys a totally different impression when translated into Latin, German, French or English from what it conveys in its original Hebrew, since each translation assumes the literary conventions of its own period and country. The Hebrew Bible, he says, 'has been a different book to different readers and different generations';[2] and he concludes:

> The Bible is not only what modern scholarship holds the text to mean; it is also what the text has meant to generations of devout readers. Modern scholarship, after all, is concerned to reconstruct the meaning originally intended by the first writers or compilers of the text, but that meaning cannot have been constant even for those early writers. The simplest lyric poem, as every modern critic knows, takes on new meanings with each sensitive reading, and how much more so must a work like the Bible![3]

The Bible (Hebrew and Greek) has of course been revered and read in the West for centuries. The Gita, from the moment of its first appearance on the Western scene at the end of the eighteenth century, was novel and exotic. Nevertheless it had had 'generations of devout readers' away in India; it had helped to inspire devotion, and it had produced a long tradition of commentary. And if we take Daiches' other point seriously we may safely assume either that it had never had a single, consistent 'meaning' or that that 'meaning' was so remote as to have become irrecoverable. This did not of course prevent its latter-day readers, whether Hindu or non-Hindu, from asserting categorically that the 'essence' of the Gita is to be found in this, that or the other element of doctrine or piety. That is not the point at issue: the point is merely that there are, potentially at

---

[1] Daiches, *Literary Essays* (2nd ed. Edinburgh and London 1966), pp.191-205.
[2] Ibid., p.201.
[3] Ibid., p.204.

least, many such 'essences', depending on the presuppositions of a particular reader in a particular time and place, and that the question of 'original' meaning is subject to these same conditions.

A second option, however, is to take the text of the Gita and build it into a *Weltanschauung* which the reader already holds, while remaining indifferent to questions of date and provenance. Since not all Western readers of the Gita were (or are) Orientalists, a great deal of the material of this study has fallen into this category. Perhaps not all those concerned were as categorical as a Thoreau in proclaiming his absolute unconcern with 'critical' questions; but, whether stated or not, a similar unconcern has often been present in Western readers of the Gita (and, for that matter, of the *Tao Te Ching*, the *Zohar* or the *Corpus Hermeticum*). If 'the truth' is universal, then what does it matter where or under what conditions it manifests itself? All that is needful is that the universal message should be recognised, translated and interpreted – in the process becoming progressively freed from its non-essential elements.

There remains a third option. In his essay 'The Study of Religion and the Study of the Bible',[4] Wilfred Cantwell Smith discusses the *function* of Holy Scripture in the life of religious communities. 'For religious life,' he writes, 'the story of formative centuries is logically subordinate to that of subsequent ages'[5]: that is to say, that, to the extent to which a scripture has remained a focus of practical piety, it has continued to fill a diversified function in the lives of individuals and groups, a function which may be related only incidentally to whatever conditions may have existed at the time of its origin. The Qur'an for instance, is not only a seventh-century, but equally an eighth- twelfth- and twentieth-century document; and however interesting may be its origin in the seventh century, equally interesting is 'its role as an organiser of ideas, images, and emotions, as an activating symbol'[6]. Smith is writing mainly about the role of the Bible; however, the Qur'an – and for that matter the Gita – have filled a certain function in Western society as what he here calls 'an activating symbol'. Subordinate to that of the Bible, perhaps: but not for that reason to be ignored or treated as altogether insignificant.

This is not to say that questions of the first two kinds – concerning historical origins on the one hand and individual speculation on the

---

[4] Smith, 'The study of religion and the study of the Bible', originally in *Journal of the American Academy of Religion* (1971), reprinted with minor alterations in Oxtoby (ed.), *Religious Diversity: essays by Wilfred Cantwell Smith* (New York 1976), p.41-56.

[5] Ibid., p.46.

[6] Ibid., p.47.

other – are unimportant. It is however surely the case that to treat these as the only two available hermeneutical options is to ignore the functional alternative. To be sure, the Gita does not play, nor has it ever played, a role in the Western world at all comparable to that of the Bible, save perhaps in certain Hindu-inspired expressions of 'alternative religion', of which we have taken the International Society for Krishna Consciousness as the most obvious example. Nevertheless the Gita has, within certain limits, served to help organise (even when it did not actually create) worlds of values and their attendant symbols, and is fully capable of being discussed in these terms. In the technical sense of the word the Gita has for two centuries been a source for one of the Western world's alternative mythologies and has been subjected to precisely the same range of critical and speculative thought, as well as being focus of the same range of personal devotion, as the scriptures of the Old and New Testaments.

*

In an essay published in 1975 the American scholar Gerald James Larson asked a number of questions about the hermeneutics of the Gita.[7] Some were related strictly to its Indian context and need not concern us. Others are central to what has been attempted in these pages. What has been the impact of the Gita on Western consciousness and history? Why should the modern Western student be interested in the Gita at all? How has the image of the Gita and its message been transmitted to that student? And what presuppositions does he or she bring to the study of the Gita?

Obviously we should be unwise to assume that for two hundred years the Gita has been present to the mind of the West as a whole. It has not. It has been read by only a small number of Westerners and written about by even fewer. Even then it has generally been judged on a basis, not of its contents as a whole, but what it has been imagined to contain – though this canon of popular interpretation would apply equally to the Bible, even in some cases among those who are prepared to assert its total infallibility. Leaving aside the professional Orientalists, for whom the Gita was seen chiefly as a historical riddle to be unravelled, each Western interpreter has approached the Gita having already decided, consciously or

---

[7] Larson, 'the *Bhagavad Gītā* as cross-cultural process', in *Journal of the American Academy of Religion* (December 1975), pp.651-69.

unconsciously, what it might be expected to contain.

The interpretative process has been complicated by the Gita's extreme mobility during the past two centuries. Originating in post-Buddhist India, for a millennium and a half the Gita lived and moved and had its being purely in Hindu India. Then it was translated and injected into the Europe of first the Enlightenment and subsequently the Romantic movement, where it served as a key to an idealised spiritual landscape and a refuge from the corrosive influences of a beginning process of secularisation. Fed back into India by the Theosophists and their sympathisers, it came in the heyday of British imperialism to assume the role of a national symbol over against the unfair pressures of politics, economics and Christian mission. Identified as the spiritual charter and declaration of independence of the Indian people, its reading became compulsory for all those who wished to drink from Indian sources, especially in a West torn apart by the ferocity of the twentieth century's two-act world war. In the pause between the two acts the West was easily persuaded of the Gita's pacifist message, as proclaimed by Gandhi (who had been first introduced to the Gita by Theosophists, and had first read it in an English translation) and later by Vinoba Bhave.[8] Since the 1960s the West's newest forms of 'alternative religion', especially those of Hindu origin, have brought the Gita once more to the fore – still in English and other European languages, and still against a dark background of neurosis, alienation and Western religious indecision.

By the end of this process, however, no one really knew why the Gita should have assumed its position of pre-eminence in the first place. The missing historical link was of course the Indian national movement in the years around the turn of the century, which even post-Gandhian India had largely forgotten. Larson writes that the Gita

> ... became a primary symbol for the Indian freedom movement and for a new cultural identity for modern India only after having passed through a radical cross-culture mediation and transformation.[9]

But the process did not stop there. Having been 'a kind of nationalistic tract' before the First World War – in which capacity it could not appeal very greatly to the mind of the West – in later years

---

[8] Vinoba Bhave, who was Gandhi's perhaps most faithful disciple and followed his example most closely, wrote in similar terms about the Gita in *Talks on the Gita* (London 1960).

[9] Larson, op.cit., p.665.

it reassumed the role it had held in the days of Emerson and Thoreau, as 'a symbol of universal spirituality'.[10]

But appearances can be deceptive. The second of these positions by no means implied the abandonment of the first. In affirming the universality of Hindu spirituality Vivekānanda, Aurobindo and those who came after them were making a quite explicit claim for the superiority of the Hindu tradition over all other religious traditions, on the simple grounds that all religions are relative but that since only Hinduism (post-Ramakrishna Hinduism, it should be added) was prepared to acknowledge that relativity, *ergo* Hindu insights are superior to those of Hinduism's competitors. Hinduism is particularly superior to Christianity in this regard, since Christians habitually insist on the uniqueness of their own revelation. India had little need to be belaboured by this message, though Christian missionaries in India (before independence, a quite considerable number) perhaps did. Otherwise the message was formulated, from the 1893 World's Parliament of Religions on, with the West in mind. It was expressed in English, adapted to Western modes of thought, formulated in answer to Western questions, and backed up by a growing network of Hindu missionary organisations. The 'bible' of most was of course the Gita.

It is simply absurd, in the light of this long development, to continue to speak of Hinduism not being a 'missionary religion'. Shortly before his retirement from public life in 1910, Aurobindo Ghosh wrote:

> Our own belief is that the motions of the world are travelling towards a signal refutation of the atheistic and agnostic attitudes and that India is the place selected for the revelation ... A new religion summing up and correcting the old, a religion based not on dogma but on direct knowledge and experience, is the need of the age, and it is only India that can give it to the world.[11]

A few months previously he had located the Gita in this enterprise:

> The teaching of the Gita is the teaching for life, and not a teaching for the life of a closet. It is a teaching which means perfection of action. It makes man great. It gives him utter strength, the utter bliss which is the goal of life in the world.[12]

[10] Ibid., loc.cit.
[11] Aurobindo, *Karmayogin: Early Political Writings* vol.2 (Sri Aurobindo Birth Centenary Library II, Pondicherry 1972), p.408.
[12] Ibid., p.430.

The Hindu mission to the world, from this point down to the International Society for Krishna Consciousness and the *Vishva Hindu Parishad* (the closest thing which Hinduism possesses to a coordinating missionary society), has never wavered in respect of these convictions. The essential teachings of Hinduism, as enshrined for all time in the Gita, are for the world and not for India only. The message therefore has to be transmitted, translated, interpreted in terms of the world's – and especially the West's – manifest needs.

Universal claims of this order are of course a species of apologetics, and quite specific in their universality. The message proceeds from a definite centre, from the point at which the revelation was first granted and its import first understood. The Gita has become the written summary of India's religious and cultural message to the world as a whole, in theoretical terms the fulfilment of all other such revelations, though in practice complete and all-sufficient, as in the Gita-centred ISKCON.

The West has reacted to all this only to the extent to which it has been prepared to pay attention; that is, in a thoroughly haphazard fashion. Here and there in the West there has been an imprecise sense that the Gita ought to be taken to be what India claims. This, however, has been seriously compromised in practice by lack of awareness of the presuppositions which Hindu India has brought to the reading of the Gita.

On this point, it must be recognised that the Gita this century has been, as K.M. Panikkar expressed it, 'the scripture of modern educated India'[13] – within which description may perhaps be included 'the scripture against which modern secular India has been forced to react'. To the West, on the other hand, the Gita has been either a historical source illustrative of India's remote past or one among many sources out of which timeless wisdom might be distilled. In neither case has a great deal of notice been taken of the Gita's symbolical role in the life of modern Hindu India.

In the absence of an authoritative Western tradition which lays down that the Gita is to be read in one way and not another and locates the Gita in a liturgical or disciplinary framework, the West has had to rely on a mixture of impulse and unwritten convention in forming its Gita images. Not unnaturally in this process the Gita's synthetic character has generally taken the upper hand of its Krishna-centredness, the 'Hare Krishna' interpretation being the one outstanding exception. The Gita therefore might be seen as the ideal scripture of universal human consciousness, being located, as

[13] Panikkar, *Common Sense about India* (London 1960), p.26.

Larson puts it, in ' … a context that is neither ancient nor modern, neither Christian nor Hindu, neither humanistic nor social-scientific, but which is in some significant sense profoundly human'.[14] This however would require the deliberate setting aside of the Gita's explicit character as a work of Krishna-bhakti and the systematic ignoring of much of its explicit detail. It would also depend on whether such a purely 'human' consciousness is considered to be worth striving after.

Those periods during which the Gita has appealed most strongly to individual minds in the West have been periods of disillusion with dominant Western religious and social orthodoxies, post-Napoleon, post-Kaiser, post-Hitler, perhaps even post-Kennedy. But such periods have never lasted long, and today's tendencies are far more in the direction of the specific and the authoritarian than the synthetic and instinctive – which may be one reason why in the 1980s *The Bhagavad Gita As It Is* occupies such a strong position among the translations and commentaries. Compared with the 1960s, the level of popular interest today in the Gita and its message is low among Westerners. Seemingly in today's climate holy scripture is to be taken literally or not taken at all.

To return finally to Larson's questions – the Gita's impact on Western consciousness has on its own not been very great, though it has exercised a great deal of influence on a small number of seekers. But when combined with other aspects of the West's interest in the East – commercial, political, imperial, missionary – the image of the Gita has supplied many impulses and impressions. Because of its compact size and its character as a reconciliation of differing views under the canopy of Krishna-bhakti, it has served the West well as a brief compendium of Hindu doctrine, sometimes to the exclusion of all else. Equally it has served as a refuge from secularisation and an affirmation of values and attitudes lost or forgotten by the post-enlightenment West. Arguably, though, those values would never have been recognised at all had they not already been present in the Western consciousness in some form, however attenuated. To the West the Gita's India was chiefly an imaginary India, just as the Enlightenment's China was an imaginary China and the Theosophists' Tibet an imaginary Tibet. The Gita spoke to what the West believed itself to be in process of losing among the smokestacks – immediacy and wholeness. But to Westerners of a different cast of mind it spoke of *Mystizismus*, quietism and lack of moral purpose in the world, and was located in the real India of the emergent

---

[14] Larson, op.cit., p.669.

twentieth century. That the Gita should have been seized upon by the Hindu national movement as a symbol of *Hindutva* was entirely appropriate to the first of these classes of Western readers, while remaining an enigma to the second – the enigma growing still deeper during the Gandhian period. Since Gandhi the Gita has in a manner of speaking settled down in Western consciousness, while remaining relatively little read. (I have been struck on more than one occasion that Western students of comparative religion almost all claim some familiarity with the Gita, but that almost none has actually read it.)

Larson's second question was: why should the Western student be interested in the Gita? To this there are several answers possible. Any of the following might serve: as an element in the understanding of the historical development of Hindu religion; as a key to the intellectual aspect of religion in modern India; as a source of esoteric wisdom (though this presupposes a 'student' of rather a special kind); or as an outstanding example of that process which is technically known as hermeneutics, or scriptural interpretation. In this the Gita is by no means a special case, since a similar range of options is open in respect of the Bible, the Talmud or the Qur'an. To my mind, the most valuable of these approaches is along the path of hermeneutics.

Over forty years ago, Betty Heimann confessed to the sense of dismay she felt on being asked to read and recommend yet another book on the Gita, on the grounds that almost everything that could be said about it had already been said many times.[15] But she was not thinking of the Gita's hermeneutical tradition; that is, of the role its interpretation had played in the development of Indian, or for that matter Western, thought. In this perspective there is much untrodden ground, and much to observe and record. There is another point which may be made. In the Preface of his book *The Buddhist Nirvāṇa and its Western Interpreters* (1968) Guy Richard Welbon wrote that 'problems in intercultural hermeneutics can be approached most satisfactorily *sub specie particularis*'.[16] In other words if the student of the encounter of East and West were to concentrate on a single identifiable issue, such as in Welbon's case the concept of *Nirvāṇa*, attempting to find out what a significant group of Western scholars had thought it to mean, more would be achieved than would have been possible by choosing a shapeless subject like 'Western attitudes to Buddhism'. I had begun this study before having read Welbon's book, but I am happy to acknowledge his

---

[15] Heimann, Preface to Roy, *The Bhagavad-Gita and Modern Scholarship* (London 1941), p.vii.
[16] Welbon, *The Buddhist Nirvāṇa and its Western Interpreters* (Chicago 1968), p.viii.

example: like his, my study has been directed to a specific issue, while intended as 'a footnote to the comprehensive understanding of European [and in my case, also American] intellectual history in the nineteenth and twentieth centuries'.[17] In the process it has been possible to note the kind of question which the West has thought it proper to ask when confronted by an unfamiliar sacred scripture; from both questions and answers it ought to be possible to deduce a certain amount about Western states of mind *vis-à-vis* India and Hinduism during the past two centuries. One might also claim to have obtained some impression of how the image of the Gita has been transmitted to the West during the period in question.

What presuppositions, lastly among Larson's questions, does the Western student bring to the study of the Gita? Here it is extremely difficult to generalise, since no two students will have precisely the same combination of presuppositions – interest, curiosity, idealism, alienation, linguistic ability (or the lack of it), coupled with past or present religious commitment (including the commitment to no-religion). But what none can escape is the impression that the Gita is important in its own right. And what none can do is to approach the Gita in a state of total freedom from presuppositions. Of those which I have mentioned the most destructive is alienation, that fashionable attitude which decries what belongs to one's own intellectual heritage and lauds to the skies the exotic because it belongs to someone else's. Notably common during the 1960s, it is becoming less so in the 1980s. But it may prompt a final word of warning.

The Gita is 'about' *dharma*, which the West has generally understood chiefly in its aspect of 'duty'. And in III:35 there is the injunction: 'One's own duty, though defective, is better than another's duty well performed. Death in (performing) one's own duty is preferable; the (performance of the) duty of others is dangerous' (Telang's translation, SBE VIII:56). Virtually the same categorical statement is found in XVIII:47. The meaning in the Gita's own context is that one cannot change caste (*varṇa*) at will, thereby securing a different duty (*dharma*) to perform. However badly one may perform the duty one has been allotted, even a thoroughly incompetent performance is preferable to the meticulous carrying out of the rules of another *dharma* than one's own. Might one be permitted to extend this principle beyond its original bounds, and suggest that one of the West's problems has been that it has been far too ready to follow what it has supposed Hindu *dharma* to consist of?

---

[17] Ibid., loc.cit.

And that it has done so largely due to its own failure to grasp the nature of the *dharma* which has come to it along its own chain of tradition? *The Imitation of Sree Krishna* was written for Hindus, after all! As Jung insisted in the 1920s, unassimilated impulses from the East can cause havoc in the mind of the West, since they have a significance far beyond that of immediate impressions.

In another sense, though, the West's images of the Gita, once they have passed out of the realms of straight history and inter-religious polemics, have had less to do with duty than with the longing for an unattainable transcendent. The greater the distance to the workaday world of the modern West, the brighter the image has been – almost after the manner of *la princesse lointaine* of the Troubadours. At least the images have been wide, bright and colourful. If some have borne little enough resemblance to anything capable of being recognised by Hindu India, then that is perhaps not too surprising, all things considered. At least the presence in print of the Gita has assisted in keeping the West in touch with Hindu India, real or imagined. And because of that presence, in an important sense Hinduism itself has been recreated on the Gita's foundations. It has been claimed that 'Hinduism' was created in Chicago in 1893 by Swami Vivekānanda. Might the paradox be expanded still further? Might it not also be claimed that, whatever the impression the Gita has made on the mind of the West over the past two centuries, it was on the appearance of Charles Wilkins' Gita translation in 1785 that 'Hinduism', all unawares, took its first step toward its present identity?

Glossary

Sanskrit and other Indian words in this book have been spelt as they appear in the various sources. Elsewhere a few diacritical marks have been used. The most usual are:

ā = long 'a' as in 'car'
ś or ṣ = 'sh' as in 'fish'
ṁ or ṃ = nasal 'ng'

In the earlier English-language descriptions of India and Hinduism words were spelt phonetically as they were heard by the English ear; thus: Hindoo (Hindu), Geeta (Gita), etc. In Bengal, for the same reason, 'a' tended to become 'u', as in 'Shastrus', 'suttee' and the name Keshub Chunder Sen (Keshab Chandra Sen).

adharma absence or negation of *dharma*: lawlessness, irreligion
adhyāya 'section', 'book' or 'chapter' of the Gita
ahiṁsā not doing harm: 'non-violence'
Anugītā episode of the *Mahābhārata*, partly a recapitulation of the Gita
ātatāyin man of violence
ātman soul, spirit, essential reality
avatāra descent (of a god): incarnation
Bhāgavata Purāṇa chief source for the stories of the birth and youth of Krishna
bhakti loving devotion
chela disciple of a *guru*
dharma law, custom, religion
gītā song
guṇa attribute of matter in *Sāṁkhya* theory
guru teacher

hiṁsā violence

Hindutva Hindu-ness; Hindu identity

Holī spring festival in honour of Krishna

jñāna knowledge leading to release from rebirth

kāma desire for that belonging to the world of the senses

karma works, deeds

karmayoga the discipline of works, the faithful performance of duty

karmayogin one who follows the path of duty

Kauravas sons of Kuru – the 'evil' side in the battle of the Gita

Krishna-bhakti devotion to Krishna

kṣatriya/kshatriya 'warrior': the second of the four 'original' social classes

lingam stylized phallic symbol of the god Śiva/Shiva

Mahābhārata the great Epic within which the Gita is placed

mahātma literally 'great soul': person of outstanding spiritual attainment

manas mind, will

Mānavadharmaśāstra 'The Laws of Manu', the oldest code of Hindu law

mantra sacred, supernaturally powerful utterance

mleccha foreigner

nāmarūpa 'name-form', i.e. that which belongs to the world of the senses

nirvāṇa literally 'blowing out', i.e. of desires. In Buddhism, the goal to which spiritual discipline leads, but also found in the Gita

nishkāma karma desireless action, selfless endeavour: the performance of one's duty without desire for the fruits

Pāṇḍavas sons of Pāṇḍu – the 'good' side in the battle of the Gita. Arjuna was one, and Krishna his charioteer

purāṇa treatise concerning the mythology and worship of Hindu deities

rajas 'passion': one of the three *guṇas* (attributes of matter) of *Sāṁkhya* theory

Rig Veda collection of 1028 liturgical texts (hymns), the oldest of Hindu scriptures

sādhana spiritual discipline

śakti/shakti 'emanation' of the supreme, usually depicted in female form as a goddess

Sāṁkhya one of the 'six schools' of classical Hindu philosophy; the theoretical foundation of Yoga

Sanātana dharma 'the eternal law/religion': synonym for the Western term 'Hinduism'

Sanatsujātīya episode of the *Mahābhārata* in dialogue form *śāstra* Hindu scripture, of any kind

sat being, truth, reality

satī/suttee the immolation of a Hindu widow on her husband's funeral pyre

sattva/sattwa 'goodness, light': one of the three *guṇas* (attributes of matter) in *Sāṃkhya* theory

satyāgraha 'truth-force': the fundamental concept of Gandhian philosophy, often regarded as synonym for 'non-violence'

smārta orthodox Hindu

smṛti 'that which is transmitted by tradition': comprehensive term for all Hindu scriptures other than the Veda

swāmī fully initiated teaching member of a Hindu religious order

śruti 'revelation': term applied to the Vedic scriptures as distinct from later religious writings

tamas 'darkness, heaviness, inertia': one of the three *guṇas* (attributes of matter) in *Sāṃkhya* theory

tantra esoteric writing in dialogue form, in which sexual symbolism plays an important part

Tripiṭaka 'three baskets': the fundamental scriptures of the Therevāda Buddhist tradition

Upaniṣads/Upanishads speculative writings expounding the innermost meaning of the *Veda*

varṇa literally 'colour': the symbolical colours by which the four original castes (classes) were identified; hence 'caste' in a general sense

varṇāśramadharma the law (rule) of class (*varṇa*) and the stages of life (*āśrama*): comprehensive term providing a Hindu equivalent of the English word 'Hinduism'

Vaiṣṇava devoted to, or belonging to, Viṣṇu (Vishnu)

Veda 'knowledge': collective term for the most authoritative stratum of Hindu scripture

Vedānta 'the end, or fulfilment, of the Veda': the most widely acknowledged of the 'six schools' of Hindu philosophy, which has also taken on modern forms

Viṣṇu (Vishnu) Purāṇa treatise in which the birth and youth of Krishna are described, though more compact than the *Bhāgavata Purāṇa*

Vishva Hindu Parishad modern Hindu umbrella organization to coordinate Hindu life and work in all parts of the world

Yoga discipline, physical and mental. One of the 'six schools' of Hindu philosophy. Also has a more general meaning as any discipline involving the control of the body

yogin one who follows the discipline of *Yoga*

Bibliography

The best bibliographical work of reference is KAPOOR, J.C., *Bhagavad-Gītā: An International Bibliography of 1785-1979 Imprints* (New York and London: Garland Publishing, Inc., 1983), with almost 3000 entries.

Books and articles chiefly consulted in the preparation of this book:

ANDREWS, C.F.	*The Renaissance in India*. London 1912
—	*Mahatma Gandhi's Ideas*. London 1929
ARNOLD, E.	*The Song Celestial*. 5th ed. London 1891
BAZAZ, P.N.	*The Role of Bhagavad Gita in Indian History*. New Delhi 1975
BEARCE, G.D.	*British Attitudes towards India 1784-1858*. Oxford 1961
BESANT, A.	*Hints on the Study of the Bhagavad-Gîtâ*. Benares and London 1906
BHAKTIVEDANTA, Swami A.C.	*The Bhagavad Gita As It Is*. New York 1968
BHAVE, V.	*Talks on the Gita*. London 1960
CALDWELL, R.	*Bishop Caldwell on Krishna and the Bhagavad-Gita*. Madras 1894
CASHMAN, R.I.	*The Myth of the Lokamanya*. Berkeley 1975
CAVE, S.	*Hinduism or Christianity?* London 1939
CHAUDHURI, N.	*Scholar Extraordinary: The Life of …*

	Friedrich Max Müller. London 1974
CHIROL, V.	*Indian Unrest.* London 1910
CHRISTY, A.	*The Orient in American Transcendentalism.* New York 1932
COUSIN, V.	*Cours de l'histoire de la philosophie.* 2nd ed. Paris 1841
COWEN, M.	*Humanist without Portfolio.* New York 1963
DAICHES, D.	*Literary Essays.* 2nd ed. Edinburgh & London 1966
DAVIES, A.M.	*Strange Destiny: A Biography of Warren Hastings.* New York 1935
DEUSSEN, P.	*Der Gesang des Heiligen.* Leipzig 1911
EDGERTON, F.	Review of OTTO, R., *The Original Gita,* in *Review of Religion* IV/4 (May 1940), pp. 447-50
EEK, S.	*Damodar and the Pioneers of the Theosophical Movement.* Adyar 1965
ELIADE, M.	*No Souvenirs.* Eng. trans. London 1978
EMERSON, R.W.	*The Letters of Ralph Waldo Emerson,* edited by Ralph L. Rusk. New York 1939
—	*The Journals and Miscellaneous Notebooks of Ralph Waldo Emerson,* edited by Merton M. Sealts, Jr. Vol. 5, 1831-1838. Cambridge, Mass. 1965
FARQUHAR, J.N.	(*pseud.* Neil Alexander) *Gita and Gospel.* Calcutta 1903
— (under own name)	*Permanent Lessons of the Gita.* Madras 1903
—	*The Age and Origin of the Gita.* Madras 1904
—	*An Outline of the Religious Literature of India.* Oxford 1920
GANDHI, M.K.	*Young India 1924-1926.* Madras 1927
—	*Hindu Dharma.* Ahmedabad 1950
—	*The Story of my Experiments with Truth.* Ahmedabad 1969

GARBE, R.	'Bhagavad-Gītā', in HASTINGS, J. (ed.), *Encyclopaedia of Religion and Ethics* II (Edinburgh 1909), pp. 535-8
—	*Indien und das Christentum.* Tübingen 1914
GARRETT, J. (ed.)	*The Bhagavat-Geeta, or Dialogues of Krishna and Arjoon.* Bangalore 1849
GAYET, C.	*The Intellectual Development of Henry David Thoreau.* Uppsala 1981
GEDEN, A.S.	*Studies in the Religion of the East.* London 1913
GHOSH, A.	*Bande Mataram: Early Political Writings I*
—	*Karmayogin: Early Political Writings II*
	(Sri Aurobindo Birth Centenary Library I-II). Pondicherry 1972
GLASENAPP, H. von	*Das Indienbild deutscher Denker.* Stuttgart 1960
GREENBERGER, A.J.	*The British Image of India.* London 1969
GRIERSON, G.A.	'Hinduism and early Christianity', in *The East and the West* 4/14 (April 1906), pp. 135-57
—	'Bhakti-Marga', in HASTINGS, J. (ed.), *Encyclopaedia of Religion and Ethics* II (Edinburgh 1909), pp. 538-51
HAUER, J.W.	*Eine indo-arische Metaphysik des Kampfes und der Tat.* Stuttgart 1934
HAYM, K.	*Wilhelm von Humboldt.* repr. Osnabrück 1965
HILL, W.D.P.	*The Bhagavadgītā.* 2nd ed. Oxford 1953
HOLTZMANN, A.	*Das Mahābhārata und seine Theile.* repr. Osnabrück 1971
HOPKINS, E.W.	*The Religions of India.* New York 1898
—	*India Old and New.* New York 1901
HOWELLS, G.	'The Bhagavad-Gita and the

Christian Gospel', in (Baptist) *Missionary Herald* (1906), pp. 14f., 55f., 75f., 111f., 139f., 181f., 218f., 247ff., 282ff.

HUBERT, P.   *Histoire de la Bhagavad-Gîtâ: ses diverses éditions de 1785 à nos jours.* Paris 1949

JONES, J.P.   *India's Problem: Krishna or Christ.* New York 1903

JUDGE, W.Q.   *Notes on the Bhagavad-Gita.* Los Angeles 1918

KHAIR, G.S.   *Quest for the Original Gita.* Bombay 1969

LAMOTTE, E.   *Notes sur la Bhagavadgītā.* Paris 1929

LARSON, G.J.   'The Bhagavad-Gītā as cross-cultural process', in *Journal of the American Academy of Religion* XVIII/14 (December 1975), pp. 651-69

LLOYD, M.   'Sir Charles Wilkins, 1749-1836', in *India Office Library and Records: Report ... 1978* (London 1979), pp. 9-39

LORINSER, F.   *Die Bhagavad-Gita: Uebersetzt und erläutert.* Breslau 1869

McLANE, J. (ed.)   *The Political Awakening in India.* Englewood Cliffs 1970

MACNICOL, N.   *Indian Theism.* Oxford 1915

MALHOTRA, S.L.   *The Role of the Bhagavadgītā in Indian Politics.* Chandigarh 1962

MARSHALL, P.J.   *The British Discovery of Hinduism in the Eighteenth Century.* Cambridge 1970

MATTHIESSEN, F.O.   *American Renaissance: Art and Expression in the Age of Emerson and Whitman.* New York 1940

MAURICE, F.D.   *The Religions of the World.* 5th ed. London 1877

MEEBOLD, A.   *Indien.* München 1907

MODDIE, A.D.   *The Brahmanical Culture and Modernity.* New York 1968

MONIER-WILLIAMS, M.   *Indian Wisdom.* London 1875

—	*Hinduism.* London 1878
MORGAN, K.W. (ed.)	*The Religion of the Hindus.* New York 1953
MÜLLER, F.M.	*Natural Religion.* London 1889
—	*Physical Religion.* London 1891
—	*India: What Can It Teach Us?* 2nd ed. London 1892
—	*Last Essays: Second Series: Essays on the Science of Religion.* London 1901
NATARAJA GURU	*The Bhagavad Gita: A Sublime Hymn of Dialectics ...* London 1961
NEHRU, J.	*The Discovery of India.* Bombay 1961
NIGAM, R.L.	'Science and Indian Culture', in SHAH, A.B. and RAO, C.R.M., *Tradition and Modernity in India.* Bombay 1961
OTTO, R.	*The Original Gita.* Eng. trans. London 1939
PAL, B.C.	*The Spirit of Indian Nationalism.* London 1910
—	*Indian Nationalism: Its Principles and Personalities.* Madras 1918
—	*Memories of my Life and Times.* Calcutta 1932
PARRINDER, E.G.	*The Significance of the Bhagavad-Gītā for Christian Theology.* London 1968
—	*Avatar and Incarnation.* London 1970
PRATT, J.B.	*India and its Faiths: A Traveller's Record.* London 1916
RIEPE, D.	*The Philosophy of India and its Impact on American Thought.* Springfield 1970
ROY, R.M.	*A Second Conference between and advocate for, and an opponent of, the practice of burning widows alive.* Calcutta 1820
ROY, S.C.	*The Bhagavad-Gītā and Modern Scholarship.* London 1941
SAID, E.W.	*Orientalism.* London 1978
SHARMA, A.	'The Gita, Suttee and Rammohun

	Roy', *Indian Social and Economic History Review* XX/3 (1983), pp. 341-7
SHARPE, E.J.	*J.N. Farquhar: a Memoir.* Calcutta 1962
—	*Not to Destroy but to Fulfil.* Uppsala 1965
—	*Comparative Religion: a History.* London 1975
—	'Avatāra and Śakti: traditional symbols in the Hindu Renaissance', in BIEZAIS, H. (ed.), *New Religions.* Uppsala 1975, pp. 55-69
SINGH, K.	*Prophet of Indian Nationalism: A Study of the Political Thought of Sri Aurobindo Ghosh, 1863-1910.* Bombay 1970
SMITH, W.C.	'The study of religion and the study of the Bible', in OXTOBY, W.G. (ed.), *Religious Diversity* (New York 1976), pp. 41-56
THOMPSON, E.W.	*The Word of the Cross to Hindus.* London 1933
THOREAU, H.D.	*A Week on the Concord and Merriman Rivers.* London 1906
—	*Walden.* New York 1964
TÖRNGREN, A.	*Opium för folket: till kritiken av religionshistorien.* Lund 1969
VAUGHAN, R.A.	*Hours with the Mystics: A Contribution to the History of Religious Opinion.* 6th ed. London 1893
VIVEKANANDA, Swami	*Thoughts on the Gita.* Calcutta 1974
WALTERS, D.	*The Path: Autobiography of a Western Yogi.* Nevada City 1977
WELBON, G.R.	*The Buddhist Nirvāṇa and its Western Interpreters.* Chicago 1968
WILKINS, C.	*The Bhagavat-Gēētā.* Reprint New York 1959
WRIGHT, B.	*Interpreter of Buddhism to the West: Sir Edwin Arnold.* New York 1957
ZAEHNER, R.C.	*The Bhagavad-Gītā.* London 1973

Index